About the Author

Dustin Romney earned his MBA from Arizona State University. He is the Coalitions Director for the state of Arizona with the Convention of States Project. He was a high school teacher for 6 years, teaching Spanish, Business, Leadership and Technology classes. *Rule of Law* is Romney's first book and is the culmination of nearly 6 years of research. He blogs at foundersliberty.com. He lives in Arizona with his Wife Kate and children Kase and McKinsey. He is active in his local church and enjoys camping, fishing, and defending liberty.

RULE OF LAW

WHY AND HOW WE MUST AMEND
THE CONSTITUTION

DUSTIN D. ROMNEY

Printed by CreateSpace, an Amazon.com Company

Printed in the United States of America

First Edition, 2014

ISBN-13: 978-1499159783
ISBN-10: 1499159781

Library of Congress Control Number: 2014908095

Available on Kindle

Orders by U.S. trade bookstores and wholesalers. Please contact the author at ddromney@gmail.com

Cover design by the author

Acknowledgements

I wish to thank Melanie Hoopes, Ira Lundell, Ashley Gurney, Gregory Watson, and my wife Kate for their feedback, council and assistance with editing.

To my children Kase and McKinsey

May their generation benefit from these ideas

CONTENTS

FOREWARD

It is rare that an author comes along with such a clear and coherent message for restoring America to the great nation that it once was. Not only does Dustin Romney point out where the United States has gone so badly astray, but he actually offers detailed solutions to correct the past missteps – something that so many authors, who lament the downfall of our glorious country, glaringly fail to do.

Reading *Rule of Law* was extremely refreshing. Richly researched, this watershed work points out where the United States Congress, the United States Supreme Court, and the President of the United States, have willfully chosen to ignore the provisions of the Federal Constitution – and the dire results of their having done so. Each and every day, average Americans – while they may not fully realize it – are directly and indirectly harmed by a Federal government that started going rogue in the early 20th Century.

So lucid is Romney's writing style – and so persuasive his assertions – that he changed my own opinion as to the wisdom of adding a Balanced Budget Amendment to the Federal Constitution. For years, I walked around believing that a Balanced Budget Amendment would be immensely beneficial in reigning in a Federal government that has deemed fit to spend like a drunken sailor. Romney, however, urges an alternative amendment, one that would cap Federal spending and limit taxation, and thereby avoid the unintended negative consequences that a Balanced Budget Amendment could, and doubtless would, bring about. Romney is not alone. As recently as 2011, state lawmakers in Louisiana and North Dakota adopted concurrent resolutions – and sent them to Capitol Hill for verbatim entry in the *Congressional Record* – seeking just such a national constitutional amendment, pursuant to the mechanisms of the Constitution's Article V. My favorite quote from *Rule of Law*: "Decades of inaction should tell us that Constitutional amendments which limit the capacity of Congress to tax and spend are the most plausible way to impose discipline on the federal budget."

Rule of Law is well worth your reading time and I heartily recommend it. Our America has been on the wrong track for far too long. But we still have a narrow window of opportunity to correct its maladjusted compass. We must not idly and supinely allow our magnificent United States to simply morph into one great, big, nationwide version of Detroit.

– Gregory D. Watson, National Coordinator of the movement to ratify the 27th Amendment to the United States Constitution

INTRODUCTION

While watching a football game one night, the announcer was discussing a controversial call for a rule which was particularly difficult to consistently enforce. One thing the announcer said struck me: "enforce the rule as is, or change it." There is an inherent understanding in all of us that rules should be enforced, and if they are unenforceable or otherwise unsound, they should be changed. That serves as a solid definition of the rule of law, and it captures a central premise of this book. The rules of government are spelled out in the Constitution. Yet we have strayed so far from it that much of it is now unenforceable. How did we get here? How does this affect our political processes? What can we do to fix it? These are some of the questions addressed in this book.

The rule of law is extremely important for the preservation of liberty and the maintenance of order. For the most part, the United States ensures the rule of law fairly well when it comes to protecting victims from crime, punishing criminals and protecting property rights. But there is another side to the rule of law which applies to politicians and bureaucrats. It is the idea that they should be subject to the rule of law just as forcibly as the rest of us. Rule of law is a self-explanatory phrase. It means that the law rules, not people. People are fallible, corruptible, biased and should always be held in suspicion when in power. The law is unbending, unbiased, and immovable. The rule of law means that politicians and bureaucrats, endowed with authority, are accountable to something higher than themselves. I am not talking about voters. I mean they are accountable to the law first and foremost. When politicians take their oath of office, they do not swear to please the voters, they swear to protect and defend the law - the supreme law of the land - the Constitution. Adherence to the Constitution is the most important manifestation of the rule of law.

The so-called elites in this country have successfully convinced the public that the Constitution is too complex for the average citizen to understand. They have made themselves to appear like scientists who assure us that their calculations are over our head and that we should trust their conclusions. But unlike science, the law is not capable of linear progression. There is nothing new to discover. Democracies and Republics have been around for thousands of years. The legal arguments had among the Greeks and Romans were fundamentally the same as the ones we have today. That is why most legal principles are expressed in Latin. Government policy may be rebranded or repackaged, but it only slides back and forth across the scale between liberty and tyranny.

The long, sad history of mankind is primarily a tale of the struggle of people to restrain governments and the natural tendency of humans to lust for power. Well-versed in this history, and having been victims themselves of abusive power, the Founders of America created the capstone on the Age of Enlightenment: the Constitution. That document gave rise to history's most successful attempt at liberty and limited government.

It behooves every responsible citizen to become acquainted with the law; not the mind-numbing heap of nonsense contained in endless statutes, but the natural and Constitutional law which are the only legitimate sources of government power. When we understand the true nature of the law, its identity as a set of rules based on eternal and easily discernable principles, we understand that an inquiry into its past is not a call for a return to a bygone era. It is a necessary part of the endless struggle to protect natural rights, which requires constitutionally limited government. In this book we make just such an inquiry to show, without a doubt, that our government has abandoned the Constitution and replaced it with an over-taxing, over-regulating entitlement state which has jeopardized our liberties and way of life. The enlightened citizen may be fully aware of this, but he will require a broad tool kit to influence those who are not. When it is understood that an abandoned Constitution is at the heart of our problems, it will become clear that an amended and revitalized Constitution is the key to returning America closer to the liberty side of the scale.

CHAPTER ONE

START FROM THE BEGINNING

"History is a guide to navigation in perilous times. History is who we are and why we are the way we are."

"A nation that forgets its past can function no better than an individual with amnesia."[1]

- David McCullough (Author of "1776")

Many people tend to think of history as a useless knowledge of the obsolete and abstruse. On the contrary, history is a useful tool for retracing steps to see how we arrived where we are. That knowledge is crucial to help set a course for the future. It is even more crucial when a person is lost. The first thing a lost person should do is try to get back to the place where they started. So it is with societies. Our government is totally lost, wandering in a treacherous forest of politics and corruption. Like a lost person, we must retrace our steps and attempt to get back to the origin; not so we can stay there, but so that we can chart a better course for the future. Therefore, the first task in making the case for amending the Constitution will be to retrace our steps and show the extent to which we have departed from its original precepts. Only then can we best know why and how to amend the Constitution so that it can endure as the great compact of a free and prosperous society for generations to come.

While there are many parts of the Constitution, and many ways in which it has been mangled, our focus will be on a particular section that has been a great source of controversy, and has given the government, more so than any other provision, powers which were not intended for it to have. After the Preamble, the Constitution begins in Article 1 by laying out the structure of Congress. The reader is encouraged to read Article 1 to better understand this and the following chapter. In Section 8 of Article 1, the powers of Congress are listed. That section begins:

> The Congress shall have the power to lay and collect taxes, duties, imposts and excises, to pay the debts and provide for the common defense and general welfare of the United States; but all duties, imposts and excises shall be uniform throughout the United States:[2]

This clause has been the source of the greatest and most persistent confusion regarding federal power. It will occupy the majority of our discussion of the Constitution. Following this clause is a list of seventeen additional powers which Congress may exercise; establishing post roads, raising and supporting an army and navy, establishing rules for bankruptcy etc. In the beginning, it was widely accepted that Congress could not do anything outside the powers listed in Section 8 and in a few other parts of the Constitution. That has all changed.

Unfortunately, in today's environment it is taken for granted that Congress can legislate in virtually any manner it sees fit. Nothing could be more radically hostile to the intention of the Constitution, or to the principles of good government. This Constitutional amnesia, particularly concerning the General Welfare Clause, is the root cause of the most serious problems our government faces today.

[3]From 1781 to 1787, the United States were held together by a legal compact called the Articles of Confederation. Each State was intensely independent and wielded much more power than the Confederation Congress, which was created by the Articles. As a result, the central government was weak. It had accumulated a large amount of debt while fighting the Revolutionary War and struggled to make payments because the States were not required by law to fund Congress. Thus, in 1787 a convention was called, as often happened during that period, to consider amendments to the Articles of Confederation. The States, except Rhode Island, sent 55 delegates to the convention in

Philadelphia. But instead of amending the articles, the delegates created a new Constitution altogether - the one we still use today.

The challenge for the delegates in drafting a new Constitution was to create a central government that was strong enough to be effective, but not so strong that it would tend to tyranny and eventually overpower the States. The delegates knew that if they gave the Federal Government too much power, the States would not ratify the Constitution and the plan of union would have been frustrated. But they also understood the value of having State governments handle most domestic affairs because they would be closer to the people and would help to serve as a check on centralized power; something they all feared with few exceptions. After months of secret debates and deliberations, the convention agreed to send their newly created Constitution to the States for ratification. Given the enormous complexity of the task and various competing interests, this accomplishment was a miraculous achievement.

However, many were bitterly opposed to the new Constitution and a nation-wide debate began as to whether the States should ratify it. Until they did so, the Constitution would not be in effect. Those opposed to the Constitution, led by Virginia elites George Mason and Richard Henry Lee among others, came to be known as the Anti-Federalists. They feared that the Constitution gave the new government too much power, or, at best, it did not define clearly enough what powers were reserved for the States and which were reserved for the Federal Government. Richard Henry Lee put forth one complaint in particular that has come to be perhaps the most prophetic of any of the Anti-Federalists' objections. He feared that the General Welfare Clause of Section 8 would eventually be interpreted by Congress to mean that it could legislate with impunity as long as it was deemed to be for the "general welfare" of the country.[4] Citing this, as well as other reasons, the Anti-Federalists insisted that the Constitution be amended to guarantee that the government would remain within clear boundaries. Namely, they wanted a bill of rights to ensure that Americans would have certain freedoms the government could not touch.[5] In other words, they wanted the rule of law to ensure that Americans' liberty would be protected from government intrusion.

The other side of the ratification debate was led by James Madison and Alexander Hamilton. Eventually these two would become political foes but in 1787 they teamed up to defend the new Constitution. Their effort resulted in, perhaps, the supreme authority of Constitutional interpretation: The Federalist Papers. Originally, this work was written as a series of newspaper articles in Hamilton's home state of New York to help combat the influence of Governor George Clinton who was an Anti-Federalist. The writings give us a methodical and detailed review of nearly every provision contained in the Constitution, along with a response to anti-federalist critiques. Writing in Federalist #41 James Madison gave us the federalist response to Lee's complaint that the General Welfare Clause would be abused.

> It has been urged and echoed that the power... amounts to an unlimited commission to exercise every power which may be alleged to be necessary for the common defense or general welfare. No stronger proof could be given of the distress under which these writers labor for objections, than to their stooping to such a misconstruction.

> Had no other enumeration or definition of the powers of the Congress been found in the Constitution than the general expressions just cited, [Madison had just explained each of the powers given to congress in Section 8] the authors of the objection might have had some color for it; though it would have been difficult to find a reason for so awkward a form of describing an authority to legislate in all possible cases. A power to destroy the freedom of the press, the trial by jury, or even to regulate the course of descents, or the forms of conveyances must be very singularly expressed by the terms "to raise money for the general welfare."

> But what color can the objection have, when a specification of the objects alluded to by these general terms immediately follows and is not even separated by a longer pause than a semicolon? If the different parts of the same instrument ought to be so expounded as to give meaning to every part which will bear it, shall one part of the same sentence be excluded all together from a share in the meaning; and shall the more doubtful and indefinite terms be retained in their full extent, and the clear and precise expressions be denied any signification whatsoever? For what purpose could the enumeration of particular powers be inserted, if these and all others were meant to be included in the preceding general power? Nothing is more natural nor common than first to use a general phrase, and then to explain and qualify it by a recital of

particulars. But the idea of an enumeration of particulars which neither explain nor qualify the general meaning, and can have no other effect than to confound and mislead, is an absurdity...[6]

In other words, why put a list of Congress's specific powers, as the Constitution does in Article 1 Section 8, if the General Welfare Clause meant that Congress could do whatever it wanted in the name of the general welfare? If Congress can act however it wants in the name of the general welfare, then there would be no need to enumerate its specific powers. The General Welfare Clause may be partially thought of as an introduction and an explanation for why Congress had each of those powers, i.e. to promote the general welfare. Thus, the General Welfare Clause was not to be interpreted as a distinct grant of broad power to the Federal Government.

Using this and many other arguments, the Federalists maintained that a bill of rights was totally unnecessary because the new government would only have those powers enumerated in the Constitution. Therefore, there was no need to specify what the government could not do. Writing in Federalist 84 Alexander Hamilton asked: "...why declare that things shall not be done which there is no power to do?"[7] On the other hand, Madison reasoned that a bill of rights probably could not hurt, and if passing one gained more support for the Constitution then it would be all the better. In the end, of course, the Constitution was amended in 1791, after it was ratified, with the first ten amendments or the Bill of Rights.

The 9th and 10th Amendments are keys to understanding the founder's beliefs about the doctrine of limited powers. More than being skeptical of the need for a bill of rights, some Federalists thought that it would actually be dangerous. They reasoned that if the Constitution specified certain rights for citizens then an imaginative future Congress might construe that any rights not listed could be denied. The 9th Amendment addressed that concern by clarifying that although the Bill of Rights lists which rights cannot be infringed, it does not follow that Congress can infringe on any rights not listed. This can only refer to our natural rights, which precede and supersede government. On the other side of this argument's coin is the 10th Amendment. It says that any power not delegated to the Federal Government is reserved for the States; further clarifying that the new government could only exercise those powers granted to it. The 9th and 10th Amendments thus clarify that we were to have unlimited rights under a government of limited powers. These Amendments were intentionally redundant safeguards to ensure that Congress would be limited to those powers enumerated in Section 8. The Anti-Federalists, at least to some extent, had been appeased.

The idea that the Federal Government could only do what the Constitution specifically authorized it to do was so widely understood that the passage of the Bill of Rights was not regarded by most as a significant event at the time. When Thomas Jefferson, then the Secretary of State, sent a letter to notify the States of its passage, He mentioned it only after writing about an act concerning fisheries and an act to establish the Post Office; Jefferson's letter gave the Bill of Rights barely more attention than a footnote.[8] The first ten Amendments were viewed by many as being totally unnecessary and redundant because they understood that the new government could only legislate in those matters listed in the Constitution. Further bolstering this point is the ratification debates in the States. If the State's ratifying conventions had any notion that Congress was empowered to legislate in any way necessary for the general welfare, they never would have ratified the Constitution. Ever jealous of their powers, the idea that the States would delegate a general and unlimited legislative authority to a new central government is repugnant to any fair construction of the historical record.

In spite of this, controversy immediately began about what exactly the Constitution authorized. Alexander Hamilton, who had sided with Madison in favor of the new Constitution, began promoting a different view of the General Welfare Clause than what was offered in the Federalist Papers and in the State's ratifying conventions. It is important here to explore in depth Hamilton's positions because his view later became the rationale for government's eventual usurpation of powers.

From the beginning of the Constitutional convention, Hamilton had been a proponent of a strong central government. In fact, one of his few contributions at the convention was a lengthy speech about the virtues of the British form of government, then a constitutional monarchy, and the need to have an aristocracy with lifetime appointments running the government.[9] Hamilton made one of at least five proposals that would have granted broad powers to Congress. He wanted the legislature to have power to pass "all laws whatsoever" with only a few exceptions. All of these proposals were unequivocally rejected by the convention.[10] In fact, the day after Hamilton's speech, his proposals were virtually ignored because they were so different from the general tone of the convention.[11]

So it is clear that Hamilton had always wanted much more power for the Federal Government than what the framers were willing to concede, and certainly what the Constitution eventually authorized. In fact, Hamilton admitted that his views were out of touch with his colleagues.[12] Hamilton only went along with the Constitution for pragmatic reasons. He knew that any measure which granted expansive powers to the Federal Government would never be ratified. Instead, his strategy was to bend the language of the Constitution to meet the vision he had for the new government. Nearly as soon as the Constitution was ratified, he began advocating for a much broader interpretation of the General Welfare Clause, the very thing that Anti-Federalists had feared. He did this knowing full-well that the convention never intended for broad powers to be given to Congress.

James Madison, on the other hand, remained a proponent of what most of the Constitution's signatories had understood about the true meaning of the General Welfare Clause; namely, that it granted no power to Congress beyond those listed immediately after it. Madison believed strongly enough in this interpretation that in 1794 he opposed a $15,000 bill for relief of French refugees, asserting that the Constitution did not grant "a right to Congress of expending, on objects of benevolence, the money of their constituents."[13] The bill did not pass.

Thus, Madison and Hamilton became political enemies, with Hamilton advocating for an interpretation of the Constitution that allowed Congress to do nearly anything it thought necessary, and Madison advocating for a government strictly prohibited from exercising any power not delegated to it by the Constitution. This division of philosophy eventually gave rise to the first political parties in the United States with the Federalist Party adopting the Hamilton view and the Republican Party (not the one of today) taking the Madison view. The struggle between these two philosophies largely defined the political landscape in the early years of the country.

In some ways, it may seem that Hamilton's views prevailed at first, as with the passage of legislation authorizing the first central bank. The debate surrounding the Bank Bill was illustrative of the differing views on Constitutional interpretation. After receiving papers from Secretary of State Thomas Jefferson and Attorney General Edmund Randolph, both strenuously objecting to the central bank on Constitutional grounds, George Washington asked Treasury Secretary Alexander Hamilton to submit his opinion in writing. In response, Hamilton produced his famous work "Report on Manufacturers," in which he argued that the term "general welfare" was meant to give Congress the authority to legislate over "a vast variety of particulars which are susceptible neither of specification nor of definition."[14] Arguing against the bill in the House of Representatives, James Madison maintained that the term "general welfare" was "explained by the particular enumerations subjoined."[15] Unfortunately, Washington, a first-hand victim of Congress's inadequate finances as the leader of the Army, succumbed to the pressure and signed the Bank Bill into law. It must be noted, however, that Washington believed he was acting out of necessity for the nation's dire financial situation after the Revolutionary War. It is unclear whether he truly believed in the constitutionality of the central bank. He also believed that the bank would only be temporary under an initial charter of 20 years and fully assumed it would not be renewed.[16]

Succeeding Washington to the Presidency was John Adams, who tended to accept a broader interpretation of the Constitution. It was Adams who signed into law the infamous and blatantly unconstitutional Alien and Sedition Acts, which, among other things, jailed people for being critical of the President. As President, Adams was essentially the leader of the Federalist Party which generally favored a more energetic central government.

In other ways, however, Madison's views seem to have prevailed. Apparently, most of Congress took the Madison view of the Constitution when, in 1796, they overwhelmingly defeated a bill for relief of residents in Savannah, Georgia, where a fire had destroyed a part of the city.[17] To relieve a city from damage could be easily construed as acting in the general welfare of the country, yet Congress did not assume an authority to act.

In spite of the apparent controversy, it is inaccurate to say that one philosophy or the other triumphed. Strong opinions do not change facts. There is only one philosophy which lined up with the truth. Hamilton, an advocate of big government from the beginning, was bending the Constitution's words to fit what he wanted it to be. Madison, on the other hand, was representing the view of the majority of the Constitution's signatories and the state conventions that ratified it. Speaking in Congress in 1793 Madison said:

I, sir, have always conceived—I believe those who proposed the Constitution conceived, and it is still more fully known, and more material to observe that those who ratified the Constitution conceived—that this is not an indefinite

Government, deriving its powers from the general terms [general welfare] prefixed to the specified powers, but a limited Government, tied down to the specified powers which explain and define the general terms.[18]

The political struggle of the 1790's culminated with the rancorous election of 1800, highlighted by the presidential race between John Adams and his own vice-president Thomas Jefferson. The debate centered largely on what should be the proper role of government under the Constitution. In a letter to Elbridge Gerry, Jefferson essentially laid out what could have been considered the Republican platform:

I do... with sincere zeal wish an inviolable preservation of our present federal Constitution according to the true sense in which it was adopted by the States, that in which it was advocated by its friends and not that which its enemies apprehended...

I am for preserving to the States the powers not yielded by them to the Union, and to the legislature of the Union its Constitutional share in the division of powers; and I am not for transferring all the powers of the States to the general government...[19]

Throughout the 1790's opposition to Hamilton and the Federalists had been mounting. When Thomas Jefferson won the presidency, it was largely seen as a repudiation of the Hamiltonian philosophy.[20] Then Jefferson won a second term and was followed by James Madison, who also won two terms as President. During this time the original intent of the Constitution as a charter of enumerated powers was firmly clarified. In 1817 Jefferson wrote to Albert Gallatin, a former senator and treasury secretary who opposed Hamilton's philosophy. In his letter, Jefferson reflected on an internal improvements bill that had recently been vetoed by James Madison. Internal improvements, the building of canals, roads and bridges etc., were where much of the early debate over the General Welfare Clause took place in the early 19th century. It wasn't long after the country's founding before congressmen began fighting for canals and roads in their home districts and States, what we call today "pork barrel" spending.

The act was founded, avowedly, on the principle that the phrase in the Constitution which authorizes Congress "to lay taxes, to pay the debts and provide for the general welfare," was an extension of the powers specifically enumerated to whatever would promote the general welfare; and this, you know, was the federal doctrine. Whereas, our tenet ever was, and, indeed, it is almost the only landmark which now divides the Federalists from the Republicans, that Congress had not unlimited powers to provide for the general welfare, but were restrained to those specifically enumerated; and that, as it was never meant that they should provide for that welfare but by the exercise of the enumerated powers, so it could not have been meant they should raise money for purposes which the enumeration did not place under their action; consequently, that the specification of powers is a limitation of the purposes for which they may raise money. I think the passage and rejection of this bill a fortunate incident. Every State will certainly concede the power; and this will be a national confirmation of the grounds of appeal to them, *and will settle forever the meaning of this phrase*, which, by a mere grammatical quibble, has countenanced the General Government in a claim of universal power.[21] (emphasis added)

In Jefferson's mind the meaning of the General Welfare Clause had been settled. We had a government which was limited to the powers specifically enumerated in the Constitution and a separate power to act for the general welfare was not among them. Jefferson must have been pleased when James Monroe, a long-time friend and ally of Madison, succeeded him to the presidency. Jefferson must have been much less pleased, however, when the pendulum began swinging back toward the Hamilton philosophy. Monroe, apparently, had a change of heart while in office and though he vetoed an internal improvements bill for other reasons, he came to accept the Hamilton doctrine.[22]

This trend continued under Monroe's successor John Quincy Adams, who approved more funding for internal improvements than the previous five presidents combined.[23] It should be noted that Congress, while inconsistent, did reject some of Adam's big government proposals, such as the establishment of a national university. During this time - the late 1820's and early 1830's - a renewed and vigorous debate resumed about the proper role of government and the General Welfare Clause, precipitated by President Adams' surge in spending on internal improvements.

It should not surprise us that these early debates over Constitutional government took place. Many big-government apologists like to claim that this proves there was uncertainty surrounding the meaning of the General Welfare Clause which, at some point, would have to be clarified by the Supreme Court. But these early controversies, rather than proving uncertainty as to what the General Welfare Clause meant, only proved that the tendency to tyranny is ever-present.

Consider, for example, John Adams signing of the Alien and Sedition Acts. How could a man who spoke so passionately about liberty and who was a first-hand participant in the formation of the Declaration of Independence and the Constitution, have possibly justified signing laws so blatantly offensive to Constitutional principles? The answer is found in human nature. Adams had power, and those who have power, even the best of them, nearly always want more. People in power nearly always look for ways to expand their influence. This is not necessarily bad in and of itself. Every politician thinks they do good through the policies they promote. But whether or not a policy is good is a separate issue from whether or not the policy is Constitutional.

Many feel they are simply being pragmatic, as Hamilton believed when he complained in his Report on Manufacturers that a strict reading of the Constitution would leave "numerous exigencies incident to the affairs of a Nation... without a provision."[24] This argument may have been correct but it would not change what the Constitution says or what its authors intended. Nonetheless, a simple reading of the General Welfare Clause was just too tempting for many statesmen to overlook as a possible means to usurp an unwarranted power to control the affairs of the nation. And, of course, politics always takes its toll on the rule of law. It should not surprise us in the least that many congressmen have been willing to set aside Constitutional concerns in the name of "progress" or the "public welfare," so as to show their constituents that they are doing something "useful." Besides, who could oppose something as benign as building a road or canal? Nevertheless, many statesmen were keenly aware of the dangers in setting aside Constitutional restraints, and political divides intensified around familiar themes, namely, the role of Congress in promoting economic activity.

Perhaps in response to the political environment at the time, a Supreme Court Justice named Joseph Story published his "Commentaries on the Constitution of the United States" in 1833. Story was a believer in the Hamiltonian philosophy, and, as we shall see, his writings contributed much to the misrepresentation of the General Welfare Clause. His extensive work on the Constitution gives us the best defense of Hamilton's philosophy. As such, we will use it to enter the debate and thoroughly demonstrate the inadequacy of this philosophy as an accurate reading of the Constitution.

I should give you a fair warning that the first dozen pages of the next chapter read much like a law review article. I include it because it is absolutely crucial to make the case as thoroughly as possible; but if you are not interested in the nitty-gritty details of Constitutional interpretation, you can spare yourself and skip ahead to page 26 ...unless you need a sleep-aid.

CHAPTER TWO

THE TRUE MEANING

There are three possible views of the General Welfare Clause. They are referred to as (1) the strong Hamilton view, (2) the weak Hamilton view and (3) the Madison view. The strong Hamilton view asserts that the General Welfare Clause is an independent grant of power for Congress to legislate in any way it sees fit for the general welfare of the Union. The strong Hamilton view can be discarded easily. The text of Section 8 clearly makes the clause part of the power to tax, rather than separating it as an independent power. Each power granted in Section 8 begins with a new paragraph. But the general welfare phrase appears in the same sentence as the power to lay and collect taxes. We can, therefore, conclude that the phrase "provide for the common defense and general welfare" is not a separate grant of power. Story agrees that the strong Hamilton view is wrong because "The Constitution was, from its very origin, contemplated to be the frame of a national government, of special and enumerated powers, and not of general and unlimited powers."[1]

The weak Hamilton view is where things get shady. The weak Hamilton view and the Madison view both share the understanding that the General Welfare Clause is a limit on Congress's power to tax, i.e.

Congress can only lay taxes to pay the debts and provide for the common defense and general welfare, as opposed to taxing for whatever reason they want. The weak Hamilton view differs from the Madison view in how the terms "common defense and general welfare" relate to the subsequently enumerated powers. The Madison view asserts that this phrase is shorthand for the other powers. In other words, Congress can only tax and provide for the common defense and general welfare by applying one or more of the other specified powers. The weak Hamilton view asserts that the phrase "common defense and general welfare" is not tied to the enumerated powers and, thus, stands alone as a grant of power. According to this view, Congress is allowed to spend money in aid of the general welfare independent of the other powers given. It asserts that the power to tax is also the power to spend. Thus Congress can spend in aid of the general welfare. This is the view advocated by Story and, at times, by Hamilton himself.

If you are having a difficult time distinguishing between the strong and weak Hamilton views, it is because *there is no distinction*. Therein lies the fatal flaw of the Story/Hamilton philosophy. This was the contention of those who advocated for the Madison view. Once it is asserted that Congress can spend in aid of the general welfare, independent of the enumerated powers, those powers at once become meaningless. The reason is that Congress, and no one else, is to determine what is in the general welfare of the country. That being the case, Congress may deem any legislation it passes to be necessary for the general welfare and, thus, within its Constitutional authority. Story and his disciples are placed in the impossible position of trying to explain how the Constitution grants a power to spend in aid of the general welfare, while also creating a government "of special and enumerated powers, and not of general and unlimited powers." Story's attempt to do just that is as follows:

> A power to lay taxes for the common defense and general welfare of the United States is not in common sense a general power. It is limited to those objects. It cannot constitutionally transcend them. If the defense proposed by a tax be not the common defense of the United States, if the welfare be not general, but special, or local, as contradistinguished from national, it is not within the scope of the Constitution. If the tax be not proposed for the common defense, or general welfare, but for other objects, wholly extraneous, (as for instance, for propagating Mahometanism among the Turks, or giving aids

and subsidies to a foreign nation...) it would be wholly indefensible upon Constitutional principles.[2]

Story's error in the first sentence is so obvious that it almost needs no attention. A power to lay taxes for the *general* welfare *is* clearly a *general* power. Does the word 'general' mean something different when coupled with the word power than what it means when coupled with the word welfare? If 'general' in the term 'general welfare' is meant to convey the welfare of the nation as a whole then the power to promote it must also be general. How then can it be asserted that it is not a general power? The word 'general,' with no other clarification given in the Constitution, can only mean what Congress wants it to mean if we are to accept the Hamilton/Story philosophy.

Story attempts to limit the spending power by asserting that Congress cannot spend on local, special or extraneous interests such as foreign aid. But when Congress spends money, it eventually goes to some organization or group which could be called local or special. How are we to clearly distinguish between spending on general and local/special projects? Again, only Congress can say, since they have the power. In addition, experience has shown us the futility of Story's imagined limitations. No act of Congress has ever been struck down by applying these supposed limits of the General Welfare Clause. Congress spends billions on local and special interests such as parks, bridges, hiking trails and a host of other projects. We are also equally aware of Congress's profligate spending on foreign aid. We have already seen how Congress has justified spending for these objects. Schools, for example, are clearly local interests, but because Congress gives money to *all* the States for their operation, it is contended that spending on education is for the general welfare. In a similar manner, foreign aid is considered beneficial to the "common defense" because the countries who receive the aid are less likely to attack us (or so the argument goes). So, not only are the limitations which Story presents painfully weak in the first place, but our experience has shown that Congress has already laid waste to them.

There is no middle ground. Either the General Welfare Clause grants Congress the authority to pass specific legislation in aid of the general welfare *in addition* to the enumerated powers, or it does not. If it does, then the only limit on Congress's power is its discretion and the explicit limitations in the Bill of Rights. Such a philosophy creates a Constitution completely at odds with what the convention intended. Indeed, Story drives a stake through the heart of his own argument by insisting that Congress should be given "wide discretion" in determining the means of applying its powers.[3] It is no wonder then that Story's analysis is full of a maddening twist of contradictions, as he makes a futile attempt to somehow limit and qualify a power, which, on its face, has no limits other than what Congress itself may impose. In one instance he says that the General Welfare Clause "contains no grant of any power whatsoever,"[4] yet, in another he says "It is, on its face, a distinct, substantive, and independent power."[5]

Let's go back to the Convention and examine why the phrase was put in place to begin with. Was it put in place to grant a substantive power to Congress, or for some other reason? The first draft of the Constitution did not contain the phrase in question. The first clause of Section 8 (which was then article 7) read simply "The Congress shall have power to lay and collect taxes, duties imposts and excises." Some in the Convention worried that this power was too dangerous to be left to Congress with no qualification. If the power were left as it was then Congress might choose to tax citizens or companies it did not like for whatever reason. To quell these fears, the phrase "to pay the debts and provide for the common defense and general welfare" was put in place as a limit on the power to tax by specifying that it could only be used for those purposes. Story himself confirms this historical reading:

> [The General Welfare Clause] was first brought forward in connection with the power to lay taxes; that it was originally adopted, as a qualification or limitation of the objects of that power; and that it was not discussed as an independent power, or as a general phrase pointing to or connected with, the subsequent enumerated powers.[6]

Story even asserts that this view "has been the generally received sense of the nation, and seems supported by reasoning at once solid and impregnable."[7]

Can it be that the phrase was intended to limit the taxing power while at the same time granting a broad power to Congress to spend in aid of the general welfare? This is highly unlikely but even if we concede that it does, we are forced to examine the question of what is appropriate for the general welfare. Is it up to Congress to decide or are they bound to aid the general welfare only by applying the other enumerated powers?

We have already seen that if it is left to Congress's discretion, then the enumerated powers become senseless, as Congress could choose to exercise those, as well as any others they deem necessary, for the general welfare. We, therefore, are obliged to show the connection between the General Welfare Clause and the enumerated powers that follow it. This is not done easily because as Story tells us, such a connection was not discussed by the framers, at least in the surviving records. However, a reading of Clause 1 of Section 8 in its entirety may reveal that a connection does exist. Even without an explanation from an author, it may be possible to ascertain an intention from the text itself. Recall that it reads "The Congress shall have power to lay and collect taxes, duties, imposts and excises, [1] to pay the debts and [2] provide for the common defense and [3] general welfare of the United States." These are the only three reasons for which Congress can lay taxes. If it can be shown that the first two, to pay the debts and provide for the common defense, have a connection with the other enumerations, then it is only sensible that the term "general welfare" in the same sentence also holds a connection with them. Let's examine each one in turn.

First, "to pay the debts" may be said to be connected to the enumerated power: "to borrow money on the credit of the United States." In other words, the first instance in which Congress can lay taxes is to pay the debts incurred from the enumerated power of borrowing money. This shows that the convention did not intend to grant a broad power by mere implication. If we assume that the power to "pay the debts" implies a power to borrow, then why would the subsequent enumeration, "to borrow money," have been given? The answer can only be that no power is given by the phrase "to pay the debts," but rather it is merely a general phrase pointing to the other enumerations which may require the borrowing of money. That being the case, it is only sensible to assume that the "general welfare" phrase also does not imply any powers beyond the enumerations. In fact, the specific power to "pay the debts" was a left-over phrase from a previous effort to give Congress the power to pay down the revolutionary war debts contracted before the Constitution was ratified.[8] However, that was specifically provided for in Article 6. The status of the "pay the debts" phrase as a vestige of a separate issue lends further support to the idea that the entire sentence was not considered separately as an independent grant of broad powers, but was merely a qualification on the power to tax.

The next qualification on the taxing power is that it may be for the common defense. Again we ask, is this a separate and distinct power to provide for the common defense? If so, why do we find the following enumerations related to defense?

> To define and punish piracies and felonies committed on the high seas, and offenses against the law of nations;
> To declare war, grant letters of marque and reprisal, and make rules concerning captures on land and water;
> To raise and support armies...
> To provide and maintain a navy;
> To make rules for the government and regulation of the land and naval forces;
> To provide for calling forth the militia to execute the laws of the union, suppress insurrections and repel invasions;

Are these not intended to provide for the common defense? Why would the convention take the trouble to include these specific and carefully contemplated powers if Congress could do these, and all others necessary for defense, by the mere inclusion of the phrase in Clause 1 to provide for the common defense? The obvious purpose of these enumerations is to clarify the means which Congress can use to provide for the common defense. This clearly shows the connection between them and the general power given in Clause 1 of Section 8.

In an identical manner, the Constitution enumerates various powers for Congress which are clearly intended to provide for the general welfare, i.e. regulate interstate commerce, establish laws for bankruptcy, coin money and regulate the value thereof etc. All these are the limits of the power to provide for the general welfare. The connection therefore is obvious: the enumerated powers are designed to achieve the more general purposes of common defense and general welfare.

Story argues that those enumerated powers are not comprehensive enough to include all powers which might be conducive to the common defense and general welfare. He feared, for example, that economic forces and external convulsions, then unknown, may conspire to ruin the country if Congress were not empowered to act. This was the general reasoning of all those who advocated for a broader interpretation of the Constitution. Even if this argument were valid, it is irrelevant. The discussion is not about the wisdom or extent of the powers given but rather about whether Congress is limited to them. Should Congress or the States deem that other powers may be necessary for the common defense and general welfare that are not included in the enumerations then an amendment to the Constitution must be added before Congress may act.

Let us examine here some other proofs of the connection between the enumerated powers and the general terms affixed to the taxing power. Story's position is this; the power to tax, given in Clause 1 of Section 8 also implies the power to spend. The power to tax is in the same clause as the power to *"provide* for the common defense and general welfare." Therefore, according to him, the power to tax is synonymous with the power to spend in aid of the common defense and general welfare. In order to *provide* something Congress must spend money. This is how Story asserts an independent power to spend in aid of the common defense and general welfare in addition to the other enumerations.

For a moment, let us concede that this is true, and the convention intended to imply a spending power along with the taxing power. If the power to tax is also the power to spend, then can we assume that Congress has the power to spend money on the subsequent enumerations? The answer is obviously yes, and therein lies the connection. Remember that Story believes the taxing and spending powers to be unrelated to the enumerated powers. However, the spending power, if we presume it is given in the tax clause, must be applicable to the other enumerations. The power to tax is given first in Section 8 because all other powers, presumably, require funds to be executed. How can Congress establish post offices and post roads without appropriating money for that purpose? If Story chooses to weld together the General Welfare Clause with the power to tax by asserting a power to spend for the general welfare, then, by extension, the General Welfare Clause is connected with the other enumerated powers because they also require money to be appropriated. Where else could the money come from to execute those powers which are intended to provide for the common defense and general welfare if not from taxes?

Think about it by considering one particular enumeration: the power to coin money. Is the power to coin money conducive to the general welfare? Yes. Is money required to build the mint that will coin the money? Yes. Where will that money come from? Congress's authority to lay and collect taxes, duties, imposts and excises. The intimate connection between the power of taxation and the subsequent enumerations is therefore obvious. If we link the General Welfare Clause with the powers of taxation and spending, then it does not diminish in the least the clause's connection with the enumerations, for they are all, presumably, for the common defense and general welfare, and will require revenues from taxation. Thus, even if we assume that a spending power is given along with the power to tax, such a spending power *is limited* by the enumerations which were clearly intended to qualify the general powers "to provide for the common defense and general welfare." The connection remains as strong, with or without a presumed power to spend in aid of the general welfare, because what is in the general welfare is defined by the enumerations and is not left to the discretion of Congress.

In reality, however, no general spending power should be implied by the power to tax. Clause 1 of Section 8 was only meant to deal with the power of taxation. As evidence for this, let's rehearse what we stated about Congress's power to borrow money. Since the specific power was given to pay the debts, might it be safely implied that Congress would therefore have the power to incur debt by borrowing money? Such an implication may seem obvious until we read a few lines down where the power to borrow money is given in a separate clause. In the same manner, Story assumes that the power to spend is implied by the power to tax. It might be argued with equal efficacy to say that the power to tax is also the power to spend, as to say the power to pay debts is the power to borrow. If so, why is Congress expressly given the power "to borrow money on credit of the United States" in the enumerations? The answer is because the convention did not intend to imply any general power to spend or borrow in Clause 1 of Section 8. Thus, we may safely assume that no spending power at all is granted in the power to tax. The spending power is actually granted in each of the enumerations, and more specifically, in the power "to make all laws which shall be necessary and proper for carrying into execution" the enumerated powers. How else could Congress raise armies without the appropriation of money? But again, whether or not we concede a power to spend in Clause 1, the connection with, and therefore the limitation of, the power to provide for the common defense and general welfare and the enumerations has been clearly shown.

Story's position is contradictory because it is nearly impossible to distinguish from the strong Hamilton view, which Story enthusiastically rejects. It is utterly senseless to rail against the strong Hamilton view, which asserts a substantive and independent power in the General Welfare Clause, while at the same time asserting, that because the clause is attached to another substantive and independent power, the taxing power, it must therefore *also be substantive and independent.* Whether by extension or direct assertion, the result is the same: an independent power to legislate for the general welfare. William Drayton, a South Carolina Congressman in 1828, made a similar point on the floor of the House when he asked:

> Can it be conceived that the great and wise men who devised our Constitution; whose minds were specially tuned to the nature and operation of the powers contained in it... should have failed so egregiously as to permit that to be done, indirectly, which could not be done directly — as to grant a power which rendered restriction upon power practically unavailing?[9]

In other words, why would the convention have permitted an *indirect* grant of broad legislative power when they specifically rejected a *direct* grant of broad legislative power? Suppose, for a moment, that the convention had written the text of clause 1 to read as follows, rather than making it all into one continuous sentence:

> The Congress shall have power to lay and collect taxes, duties, imposts and excises;
> To pay the debts and provide for the common defense and general welfare of the United States...

If this were the structure of the first clause, it would lend considerable weight to the strong Hamilton position because to provide for the common defense and general welfare are given as separate and distinct powers. Each power given to Congress in Section 8 was given as a separate clause on a new line separated by a semicolon. In point of fact, a similar construction was proposed in early drafts of the Constitution and it was unequivocally rejected.[10] But would there be any less of a limitation on this power if structured in the manner above than what Story asserts for it in the weak Hamilton position? Clearly not, because the language is the same. Congress would still be limited to legislation that aids the general, as opposed to the local, welfare; but because the convention did not structure the clause in this way, we have more evidence that they did not intend for it to grant any specific power, but only meant it to be a qualification on the power to tax. If this is wrong, then we have entered a bizarro world where there is no distinction between two positions that have the same effect. Story made a valiant attempt to create such a world, but sophistry is no match for the plain truth.

Either Congress is limited to the powers enumerated, or it is not. Either Congress can spend in aid of the general welfare beyond the subsequent enumerations, or it cannot. If it can, then a Constitution emerges that is completely alien to what the Founders intended. As Madison put it

> it exceeds the possibility of belief, that the known advocates in the convention for a jealous grant, and cautious definition of federal powers, should have silently permitted the introduction of words or phrases, in a sense rendering fruitless the restrictions and definitions elaborated by them.[11]

Let us look at yet another flaw in Story's analysis. He accuses Madison of wanting to erase the General Welfare Clause altogether by asserting that his view:

> ...is neither more nor less, than an attempt to obliterate from the Constitution the whole clause "to pay the debts, and provide for the common defense and general welfare of the United States" as entirely senseless, or inexpressive of any intention whatsoever. Strike them out, and the Constitution is exactly what the argument contends for. It is, therefore, an argument that the words ought not to be in the Constitution; because if they are, and have any meaning, they enlarge it beyond the scope of certain other enumerated powers... Being in the Constitution, they are to be deemed... an empty sound and vain phraseology, a fingerboard pointing to other powers... If words are inserted, we are bound to presume that they have some definite object, and intent...[12]

Story here offers another contradiction. *Madison asserted, and Story agreed, that the words do have an important meaning and function.* As has been shown, they were intended to be a limit on the power to tax. If it were left alone as it were in the original draft, then the taxing power could have been used by Congress in an arbitrary way against any group which might draw the ire of the government. Story even repeats his belief that the language in question was inserted to limit the power to tax by saying "that it is the truest, safest and the most authoritative construction of the Constitution."[13] It is perfectly practicable to deem these words as having an express purpose without construing them to mean that they grant a near universal power to Congress.

What is more egregious about this argument from Story is the blatant hypocrisy it contains. Story's view of the General Welfare Clause would *obliterate nearly all of section 8 as entirely "senseless."* If we struck out the enumerations, the Constitution would be exactly what Story argues for. Why would the enumerations be included if Congress had a general power to legislate for the common defense and general welfare? He does a woefully inadequate job of demonstrating how the enumerated powers would have any meaning while Congress could exercise them, as well as any other power conducive to the general welfare. Story is correct. "If words are inserted, we are bound to presume that they have some definite object and intent." Only the Madison view gives meaning to the entirety of section 8 by construing the General Welfare Clause as a limit on the power to tax, and by asserting that Congress is limited to only those powers which were carefully listed.

The truth is that the convention did not explore the issue of the General Welfare Clause with nearly the depth that we are now. This is because the terms were simply overlooked as being a possible source of mischief (at least until Anti-Federalists pointed it out after the convention sent the Constitution to the States). As Jefferson said in his letter to Albert Gallatin, it was a "grammatical quibble." Whoever insisted that the clause be included clearly did so with the intent to limit Congress's power to tax. But they apparently did not consider the full ramifications of the phraseology. James Madison indicated as much when he explained why a more clearly worded reference to the enumerated powers, and thus a clarification of its meaning, was not inserted. He wrote:

> although it might have easily been done, and experience shows it might be well, if it had been done, yet the omission is accounted for by an inattention to the phraseology; …it was taken for granted, that the terms were harmless…[14]

The Anti-Federalists, wisely, did foresee that the terms were not harmless. They were able to predict that men like John Quincy Adams and Joseph Story would eventually misconstrue their meaning. This was partly the reason they insisted for, and achieved, ratification of the tenth amendment which reads: "The powers not delegated to the United States by the Constitution, nor prohibited by it to the States, are reserved for the States respectively, or to the people."[15] What powers could possibly be reserved to the States if *all* powers to provide for the general welfare were delegated to Congress? To reserve something means that no one else can claim it.

The records are actually scant as to how the development of the General Welfare Clause developed during the convention. We know little more aside from the fact that the language was inserted after complaints of an unlimited power of taxation. Most of the debate on Clause 1 of Section 8 centered on the power to tax, more specifically on internal versus external taxes. The delegates simply did not discuss a power to spend in aid of the general welfare. Even the State ratifying conventions are mostly void of discussion about the general welfare phraseology. All of this is certainly proof that the Founders did not view the General Welfare Clause to mean anything beyond a limit on the power to tax, and that it did not grant any substantive power whatsoever. If the intention were otherwise, it unquestionably would have received far more deliberation during the debates.

Before we move on, it may be instructive to point out that for the first 44 years of the Constitution's use we had only two one-term presidents; John Adams and his son John Quincy Adams. These two presidents were the only executives during this time period who consistently took a broader view of Congress's role under the Constitution.[16] And both of them were defeated by Presidents who strictly applied the limited powers doctrine of the Constitution; Jefferson over the first Adams and Andrew Jackson over the second. In both cases government was expanding its role into unconstitutional territory, and in both cases their philosophy was rejected. In the case of John Quincy Adams, an argument could be soundly made that his policies were never sought for in the first place. He was the only President to be elected without a majority of the popular or electoral votes, winning a four-way race that was eventually decided by the House of Representatives. This does not imply that the electoral history of this period proves the correct Constitutional interpretation. Elections do not dictate what the Constitution says. It is, however an additional, albeit small, proof of the Constitutional interpretation for which I am contending; that the general sense of the nation during our first decades seemed to be in harmony with it.

As noted, Andrew Jackson defeated John Quincy Adams in 1828 largely on a platform criticizing Adam's big-government programs, which, some have referred to as a mini New Deal. While Jackson has been cited as the first President to significantly expand presidential powers, he was a strong proponent of limited government and believed that Congress was limited to the enumerations in Section 8. He was very critical of Adam's nationalist agenda and fought against internal improvements. In his 1834 state of the union address, Jackson made his views clear:

> To suppose that, because our Government has been instituted for the benefit of the people, it must therefore have the power to do whatever may seem to conduce to the public good, is an error, into which even honest minds are too apt to fall. In yielding themselves to this fallacy, they overlook the great considerations in which the federal Constitution was founded. They forget that, in consequence of the conceded diversities in the interest and condition of the different States, it was foreseen, at the period of its adoption, that although a particular measure of the Government might be beneficial and proper in one State, it might be the reverse in another— that it was for this reason the States would not consent to make a grant to the Federal Government of the general and usual powers of Government, but of such only as were specifically enumerated...[17]

Jackson is perhaps most famous for his determined and successful fight to abolish the central bank, the signature achievement of Hamilton's big-government agenda. Jackson believed strongly, not only that the bank was unconstitutional, but that it was a center for corruption and a dangerous instrument for perpetuating debt.

After Jackson, the country was guided by eight one-term Presidents who, for the most part, believed in the Madison interpretation of the Constitution. Many scholars have overlooked these Presidents as weak and mostly inconsequential. But the measure of presidential quality lies not with ambition or force of will, but rather in an ability to enforce the Constitution and preserve liberty, which usually means playing a more passive role in the operation of government. Unfortunately, most scholars prefer the Presidents that looked for ways around the Constitution while trying to impose their vision on the country. Presidents Van Buren, Tyler, Polk, Pierce and Buchanan understood that their job was very limited. All of them fought against activist government, namely internal improvements of various kinds, which they believed were unconstitutional.

The proponents of federal funding for internal improvements constantly shifted their ground when looking for Constitutional authority for their plans. They never agreed among themselves whether the authority for these projects came from the Commerce Clause or the General Welfare Clause. They even tried on occasion to call upon the Necessary and Proper Clause when seeking authority for internal improvements. If the meaning of the General Welfare Clause clearly authorized broad legislative power, then there would have been no need to shift positions. This further indicates the mistaken notion that any clause, but particularly the general welfare, granted broad and substantive powers to Congress; something these Presidents understood well.

In 1847 President James K. Polk vetoed a bill to improve harbors and rivers saying "No express grant of this power is found in the Constitution." He went on to say:

> ...the investigation of this subject has impressed me more strongly than ever with the solemn conviction that the usefulness and permanency of this government, and the happiness of the millions over whom it spreads its protection, will be best promoted by carefully abstaining from the exercise of all powers not clearly granted by the Constitution.[18]

James Polk was even gracious and honorable enough to fulfill his promise to voluntarily limit himself to one term. While this is not directly relatable to the General Welfare Clause, it is a clear indication of his understanding of the role of a President. He did not believe he was the father-figure of the country, tasked with cajoling Congress to implement a vast national agenda. Rather, he believed he was a public servant, tasked with playing a ministerial role, checking the power of Congress should they pass unconstitutional laws and focusing on foreign policy. He served his four years and honorably followed through with his self-imposed term limit.

In 1854, President Franklin Peirce, a successful lawyer, vetoed a bill to grant land for insane asylums. In his veto message he gave us one of the most eloquent and powerful legal arguments against big-government entitlement policies which operate under the false authority to provide for the general welfare.

> The question presented, therefore clearly is upon the Constitutionality and propriety of the Federal Government

assuming to enter into a novel and vast field of legislation, namely – that of providing for the care and support of all those, among the people of the United States, who by any form of calamity become fit objects of public philanthropy. I readily, and, I trust, feelingly acknowledge the duty incumbent on us all, as men and citizens, and as among the highest and holiest of our duties, to provide for those who, in the mysterious order of Providence, are subject to want, and to disease of body or mind; but I cannot find any authority in the Constitution for making the Federal Government the great almoner of public charity throughout the United States. To do so would, in my judgment, be contrary to the letter and spirit of the Constitution, and subversive of the whole theory upon which the union of these States is founded. I shall not discuss at length the question of power sometimes claimed for the General Government under the clause of the eighth section of the Constitution, which gives Congress the power 'to lay and collect taxes, duties, imposts, and excises, to pay debts and provide for the common defense and general welfare of the United States,' *because if it has not already been settled upon sound reason and authority it never will be.* I take the received and just construction of that article, as if written to lay and collect taxes, duties, imposts, and excises in order to pay the debts and in order to provide for the common defense and general welfare. It is not a substantive general power to provide for the welfare of the United States, but is a limitation on the grant of power to raise money by taxes, duties, and imposts. If it were otherwise, all the rest of the Constitution, consisting of carefully enumerated and cautiously guarded grants of specific powers, would have been useless, if not delusive.[19] (emphasis added)

President Peirce's successor James Buchanan vetoed a bill which would have donated land for agricultural colleges. In his veto message he directly cited Article 1, Section 8 and gave us this instructive warning:

Should Congress exercise such a power, this would be to break down the barriers which have been so carefully constructed in the Constitution to separate the Federal from State authority. We should then not only "lay and collect taxes, duties, imposts, and excises" for Federal purposes, but for every State purpose which Congress might deem expedient or useful. This would be an actual consolidation of the Federal and State Governments so far as the great taxing and money power is concerned, and constitute a sort of partnership between the two in the Treasury of the United States, equally ruinous to both.[20]

Buchanan's warning is reminiscent of Anti-Federalists' assertions that such a consolidation of government was inevitable under the Constitution.

Following this series of presidents is, perhaps, most American's favorite chief executive: Abraham Lincoln. As far as limited government goes, Lincoln was certainly no role model. The civil war vastly expanded the Federal Government's power and Lincoln conducted it with little regard for civil liberties. In any event, little can be gleaned about the General Welfare Clause from Lincoln's presidency, as this time period was dominated by war rather than domestic issues concerning the general welfare. Inter arma silent leges: in times of war, law is silent. Lincoln did, however, sign essentially the same bill which his predecessor had vetoed, granting federal funds for agricultural colleges.[21] But with the Civil War raging and southern representatives in Congress, who opposed the bill, out of the way, Lincoln signed it after an amendment was added requiring the newly created colleges to teach military tactics. Because Lincoln was engulfed with the war, it is difficult to know what his real views on the bill were with regard to the General Welfare Clause. We do know that Lincoln often spoke eloquently about the need for Constitutional discipline. What is most likely is that Lincoln saw an urgent need for trained military leaders, and signed the bill primarily for that purpose.

Between Lincoln and the turn of the twentieth century, we see another long series of Presidents considered by most scholars to be weak and/or inconsequential. But in terms of adherence to the Constitution and rule of law, this time period was similar to the era before Lincoln. A few Presidents are worthy of particular note. Among them are Rutherford B. Hayes, Chester Arthur and Grover Cleveland. For example, in 1887, Cleveland, well-known for his honesty, vetoed a bill which appropriated $10,000 for seeds for Texas farmers suffering through a drought. He wrote:

I can find no warrant for such an appropriation in the Constitution... Federal aid in such cases encourages the expectation of paternal care on the part of the government and weakens the sturdiness of our national character.[22]

For the first 150 years of the Constitution's use, including the years before Jefferson's presidency, no law was passed by Congress, signed by the President and sustained by the Supreme Court under the supposed authority of the General Welfare Clause. When laws were passed under that imagined authority they were mostly inconsequential enough to not warrant any legal challenge. In spite of the sporadic appearances of Hamilton's philosophy, this set an unmistakable understanding that our government is limited to specified powers, rather than an unlimited government authorized to act as it sees fit for the general welfare.

No doubt there were many constitutionally dubious things done by the Federal Government during this time period. Many members of Congress fought for legislation outside the Constitution's enumerated powers throughout the 19th century. The proponents of Hamilton's view, most notably John Quincy Adams and Justice Joseph Story, remained vigilant. It is also true that some Presidents, including Jefferson and Madison, contradicted their own rhetoric about the Constitution during their presidencies when they faced difficult scenarios.[23] But most of us have faced situations where the pressure to be "pragmatic" has overwhelmed allegiance to principle. And we must not forget the ever powerful influence of politics. Politicians find the urge to make themselves seem important too great to allow the law to prevent them from acting, particularly when ambiguity surrounding the law can be easily conjured - and especially in times of perceived emergency. This has always, and will always be so.

However, these isolated cases deserve no reference as evidence that an expansive Federal Government is sanctioned by the Constitution, as some progressives have asserted. What was politically or pragmatically convenient does not change the text and intent of our supreme law. Again we turn to Congressman William Drayton to emphasize this point. He said:

> A few instances where, perhaps, Constitutional objections were not thought of, or, if suggested, under the influence of excited generosity and sensibility, were faintly pressed, cannot seriously be insisted upon as precedents entitled to any consideration. ...I could mention laws passed by Congress, after the most deliberate consideration, which, I am sure, a great majority of this House believes to be unconstitutional. If we were now discussing the questions involved in these laws, we should not

respect them as precedents, but feel ourselves at much at liberty to depart from them as if they had never existed.[24]

No significant court challenge ever surfaced against the types of laws Drayton was referring to. This is because they were mostly harmless. No one could bring a suit against the government claiming they had been harmed by the building of a canal or the grant of a small amount of relief to suffering groups, which happened from time to time. But it is unquestionable that the majority of Congresses and Presidents during this time period mostly stayed within the bounds set by the Constitution as envisioned by the Founders, giving little respect to the General Welfare Clause as a grant of any substantive power.

In the 1907 case of *Kansas v. Colorado* the Supreme Court affirmed the long-established precedent;

> By reason of the fact that there is no general grant of legislative power it has become an accepted Constitutional rule that this is a government of enumerated powers... [The 10th] Amendment, which was seemingly adopted with prescience of just such contention as the present, disclosed the widespread fear that the national government might, under the pressure of a supposed general welfare, attempt to exercise powers which had not been granted. With equal determination the framers intended that no such assumption should ever find justification in the organic act, and that if, in the future, further powers seemed necessary, they should be granted by the people in the manner they had provided for amending that act.[25]

One more proof will be given of the limited nature of the Federal Government as established before, during, and after the 19th century. In 1920, the 18th Amendment took effect, prohibiting the sale, manufacture, and distribution of alcohol. If Congress believed itself endowed with an independent power to aid the general welfare, then why did it pass a Constitutional amendment authorizing the imposition of laws clearly meant to achieve that purpose? It would have been far easier for Congress to prohibit alcohol, without a Constitutional amendment, by claiming it would be for the general welfare of the country; and it is apparent just how persuasive those claims might have been.

The evidence given up to this point clearly shows that there was a generally established understanding among our country's early leaders that the General Welfare Clause conveyed no broad grant of power to Congress. But even if you take away every quote, reference, and argument I have given thus far, we need look no further than the text of the Constitution itself to settle the issue. Does it make sense that a group of men who had just fought a revolution to throw off an oppressive, overreaching government would then grant near unlimited power to their own newly created government? Read Section 8 of Article 1 again and ask yourself which interpretation makes more sense to you. Does it make sense that the General Welfare Clause allows Congress to do whatever it wants in the name of the general welfare, even though a specific list of powers follows immediately after it? Any fair-minded person must acknowledge that any such interpretation is inconsistent with the text of the document and the context of the time in which it was written. You may argue that the Constitution is flawed and does not allow for legislation that may be needed. I would disagree, but at least, that is an honest argument. It is far better than offending the rule of law by suggesting that the Constitution conveys powers to Congress which are nowhere to be found in that document. Unfortunately, a new era of politicians and lawyers arose in the twentieth century that did just that.

CHAPTER THREE

USURPATION

In the early 20th century, spurred by a variety of cultural and economic changes, pressure began to mount for increasing the role of the Federal Government in social and economic policy. Theodore Roosevelt and Woodrow Wilson were two Presidents who made great strides in expanding government's power. But it was during the 1930's when the most sweeping assaults on constitutionally restrained government were launched. Herbert Hoover, in an effort to thwart a crashing economy, intervened in ways previously untried, doubling federal spending during his one term, increasing taxes, raising tariffs and convincing businesses to not lower wages.[1] These policies, and, perhaps also an inept Federal Reserve, sank the country into depression. This opened the way for the man who would enshrine big-government in Washington.

Franklin Delano Roosevelt inherited a disastrous economy with poverty and unemployment rising rapidly. His response, collectively referred to as the New Deal, was to dramatically increase the role of the Federal Government in alleviating poverty, increasing employment, and regulating the economy. In his first term, many of his proposals were ruled unconstitutional by the Supreme Court, as it generally held to the traditional understanding of Congress's constitutionally limited powers.

One of the most significant of these cases was a lawsuit involving the Railroad Retirement Act, passed by congress in 1934. Essentially, this was a social security system for railroad workers. Younger workers, and the railroad companies, would be forced to contribute to retirement benefits for older workers. This law was struck down by the Supreme Court in 1935 as unconstitutional. Proponents of the law argued that it was "necessary and proper" for Congress to do in order to regulate interstate commerce, a power granted in Section 8 of the Constitution. But in a 5-4 decision, the Court disagreed, reaffirming its responsibility to uphold Constitutional limits on Congress. Justice Owen Roberts delivered the majority opinion:

Our duty... is fairly to construe the powers of Congress, and to ascertain whether or not the enactment falls within them, uninfluenced by predilection for or against the policy disclosed in the legislation. The fact that the compulsory scheme is novel is, of course, no evidence of unconstitutionality. Even should we consider the act unwise and prejudicial to both public and private interest, if it be fairly within delegated power, our obligation is to sustain it. On the other hand, though we should think the measure embodies a valuable social plan and be in entire sympathy with its purpose and intended results, if the provisions go beyond the boundaries of Constitutional power we must so declare...[2]

Having pointed out the proper role of the Court, Roberts proclaimed the act to be outside the powers of Congress.

There is no warrant for taking the property or money of one and transferring it to another without compensation, whether the object of the transfer be to build up the equipment of the transferee or to pension its employees... The act is not in purpose or effect a regulation of interstate commerce within the meaning of the Constitution...[3]

Undaunted, and unable to use the Commerce Clause, the Roosevelt administration and Congress kept enacting unprecedented laws. In order to take effect however, they needed to find ways to get them through the Supreme Court. In 1936, the case of United States v Butler was brought before the Court. This case involved a challenge to the Agricultural Adjustment Act (AAA), which, taxed food processors and gave the proceeds to farmers in a scheme to control agricultural production. The government asserted that it had power to enact the legislation in aid of the general welfare as supposedly authorized in Section 8, Clause 1 of the Constitution.

The Court, in its meandering opinion, spoke briefly about the controversy over the General Welfare Clause since the founding. They concluded that the reading advocated for by Joseph Story was the correct one. However, true to the contradictory spirit inherent in Story's argument, the Court refused to answer the question as to whether AAA was within the scope of the General Welfare Clause. The Court tried, as Story did his Commentaries, to explain and defend an inexplicable and indefensible position: that the General Welfare Clause is independent of the enumerated powers, but that Congress is still somehow limited. Once again, Justice Roberts delivered the opinion for the majority. In one instance we find him saying: "The view that the clause grants power to provide for the general welfare, independently of the taxing power, has never been authoritatively accepted."[4] Then this:

> The necessary implication from the terms of the grant is that the public funds may be appropriated 'to provide for the general welfare of the United States.' ...the power of Congress to authorize expenditure of public moneys for public purposes *is not limited by the direct grants of legislative power found in the Constitution.* ...we naturally require a showing that by no reasonable possibility can the challenged legislation fall within the wide range of discretion permitted to the Congress. How great is the extent of that range when the subject is the promotion of the general welfare of the United States we hardly need remark.[5]

Yet in the same opinion, the Court strangely concluded:

> We are not now required to ascertain the scope of the phrase "general welfare of the United States," or to determine whether an appropriation in aid of agriculture falls within it.[6]

Instead, the Court chose another route to strike down the law:

> The act invades the reserved rights of the States. It is a statutory plan to regulate and control agricultural production, a matter

beyond the powers delegated to the Federal Government. ...From the accepted doctrine that the United States is a government of delegated powers, it follows that those not expressly granted, or reasonably to be implied from such as are conferred, are reserved to the States or to the people. To forestall any suggestion to the contrary, the Tenth Amendment was adopted. The same proposition, otherwise stated, is that powers not granted are prohibited. None to regulate agricultural production is given, and therefore legislation by Congress for that purpose is forbidden.[7]

What if Congress wants to regulate agricultural production for the general welfare? Would that not fall within the "wide range of discretion permitted to the Congress?" This was precisely the government's contention in this case. Why or how the Court chose not to address that contention, *while at the same time declaring it to be valid*, is a riddle. But we will not rehearse these types of contradictions as we have already done so in the previous chapter. Let them stand as they are for their own condemnation. Suffice it to say, the Court struck down the law and the New Deal continued to be stalled.

Roosevelt was fed up. It is difficult to overstate the anger and animosity the administration felt against the Court. For nearly the entirety of his first term, FDR and his "brain trust" were scheming for ways around the Court to get the New Deal into action. They gave serious consideration to promoting Constitutional amendments and even to flatly ignoring the Court's rulings, but ultimately decided on a direct assault on the judiciary.[8] In 1937, FDR introduced the Judicial Procedures Reform Bill, more commonly referred to as his court-packing plan. This legislation would have allowed the President to appoint more justices to the Supreme Court by replacing any judge over the age of 70, increasing the number on the bench to as many as 15, and thereby allowing him to put in place judges who would fall in line with his New Deal policies. (Several of the Justices who opposed his policies were over 70.) In a speech given shortly after introducing his plan, FDR displayed his frustration with the Court and attempted to make his case by saying:

...I described the American form of Government as a three horse team provided by the Constitution to the American people so that their field might be plowed. The three horses are, of course, the three branches of government - the

Congress, the Executive and the Courts. Two of the horses are pulling in unison today; the third [the Courts] is not... It is the American people themselves who expect the third horse to pull in unison with the other two.[9]

Anyone who has passed a ninth grade social studies class knows that the three branches of our government, Congress, The President and The Supreme Court, are not anything like a team of horses that should all be moving in lock step; to say nothing of the fact that economic progress comes from private initiative, not bureaucratic agencies. Each branch of the government is separated by its own unique powers. The Founders made it this way so that no single branch of government would gain too much power, and so that each could be a check on the other if an overreach was attempted. In reality, the Supreme Court was doing exactly what it was designed to do, as Justice Roberts explained in the Railroad Retirement case: reign in the powers of Congress when they attempt to enact legislation not authorized by the Constitution. But later in the same speech FDR went even further:

Having in mind that in succeeding generations many other problems then undreamed of would become national problems, they [the Founders] gave to the Congress the ample broad powers "to levy taxes ... and provide for the common defense and general welfare of the United States.[10]

The Founders granted no such power but they did have in mind that many problems would arise in the future which they could not anticipate. That is why they wrote Article V of the Constitution, the process by which it could be amended to afford government the means to meet unforeseen needs. However, this process was ignored by Roosevelt and Congress because it was too inconvenient.

Eventually President Roosevelt's plan to pack the Court was defeated and he suffered politically for it. But his ultimate goal of a more cooperative Supreme Court was achieved nonetheless. In 1937, several other cases came before the Supreme Court. Among them were *Steward Machine Company v Davis* and *Helvering v Davis*. Both of these were challenges to different provisions in the Social Security Act of 1935, the law which established the national retirement and disability plan we all know today.

In the *Steward* case, the pay roll tax provision of the law was being challenged. In a 5-4 decision, the tax was upheld as Constitutional.

How could that be? In *Butler*, the Court went to great lengths, citing numerous Supreme Court rulings, to show that:

> A tax, in the general understanding of the term, and as used in the Constitution, signifies an exaction for the support of the government. The word has never been thought to connote the expropriation of money from one group for the benefit of another.[11]

How then could the Court sanction the Social Security Act, which was clearly a scheme to transfer money from one group (workers) to another (retirees)? The government was able to get around this by structuring the Social Security Act so that its taxes would not be earmarked in any way, but would be sent directly to the treasury to be used at the discretion of Congress. Thus, tax receipts from Social Security can legally be used for any purpose Congress wishes. However, regardless of Congress's lawyerly tactic to make payroll tax receipts general revenue, the Court knew full-well what the intention behind those taxes was. As the Court said in *Butler*: "It is an established principle that the attainment of a prohibited end may not be accomplished under the pretext of the exertion of powers which are granted."[12] In other words, because the Court understood that the Social Security scheme was intended to take money from one group to give to another, they were fully obligated to strike down the tax as unconstitutional, as the very same Court established that redistributive taxes were not valid.

The more pertinent of the two cases involving Social Security is the *Helvering* case because it dealt directly with the General Welfare Clause. Part of this case was a challenge to the old age benefits portion of the law. A central question before the Court was whether Congress had the authority to give retirement benefits as part of the Social Security scheme. In a 7-2 decision, the Constitutionality of the act was upheld on the grounds that Congress could act in the general welfare of the country in any way it saw fit, regardless of enumerated powers. Although the Court's broad interpretation of the General Welfare Clause had already been indicated in *Butler*, this was the first time in the country's history that a law was upheld using that clause. Justice Benjamin Cardozo, with little discussion, simply declared:

> Congress may spend money in aid of the 'general welfare'... There have been great Statesmen in our history who have stood

for other views. We will not resurrect the contest. It is now settled by decision. The conception of the spending power advocated by Hamilton and strongly reinforced by Story has prevailed over that of Madison, which has not been lacking in adherents.[13]

Cardozo went on to make the same vain attempt that Story had made to limit the powers of Congress. This was necessary to give the perception that the Court's ruling was consistent with the Constitutional principle of limited powers:

> The line must still be drawn between one welfare and another, between particular and general. Where this shall be placed cannot be known through a formula in advance of the event. There is a middle ground or certainly a penumbra in which discretion is at large. The discretion, however, is not confided to the courts. *The discretion belongs to Congress,* unless the choice is clearly wrong, a display of arbitrary power, not an exercise of judgment. (emphasis added)

Consider the profound implication of these words. What is "clearly wrong" or "arbitrary power" is nearly impossible to uniformly define as Cardozo himself says that the formula cannot be known in advance of the event. But having a formula in advance of the event is a defining characteristic of the rule of law, and stands in stark contrast to arbitrary rule. That is why a formula *was* provided in the Constitution: the enumeration of powers. Only a strict reading of those powers avoids the necessary and menacing implication of the Story/Hamilton view, which is that Congress assumes the arbitrary power alluded to by Cardozo: "the discretion belongs to Congress". Therefore, the Court left us with the very thing it was claiming should not exist: an arbitrary formula which some future Court would eventually have to pull out of its hat if they ever decided to judge that Congress went too far in promoting the general welfare. That has not happened once in the 77 years since the ruling.[14]

How is anyone to distinguish arbitrary power from "an exercise of judgment"? Can anyone ever say that *any* legislation passed by Congress is *not* an "exercise of judgment"? Thus, reading between the lines reveals a rather plain admission that the Court had just instituted a new and arbitrary form of government without changing a single word of the Constitution. If discretion is left to Congress to legislate for the general welfare, then it cannot possibly be limited to the bounds originally intended by the Constitution. The limits attempted here by Cardozo, that Congress cannot do something "clearly wrong" or display "arbitrary power", were merely lip service to the long-standing concept of enumerated powers. The Court was essentially inviting Congress to begin experimenting to their heart's content, and to embark on a quest to see just how far they could take this power, which, they were all-to-willing to accept. Just as we predicted in the previous chapter, once it is accepted that the General Welfare Clause is a separate grant of power, one searches in vain for the limits on Congress's ability to legislate.

The Court clearly erred, and removed the bounds which had carefully been placed on Congress and wisely protected for 150 years. Is it clearly wrong for Congress to dictate the amount of wheat a farmer can grow and sell? Is it clearly wrong for Congress to tell me what I can and can't put into my own body? Is it clearly wrong for Congress to force me into a retirement plan of which I want no part. Is it clearly wrong for Congress to force me to buy health insurance and to dictate what insurance companies must sell? To me, and millions of other Americans, these things *are clearly wrong*, but that means nothing because the discretion, and therefore, the power, intended to be vested in the States or the people, now lies with Congress.

The incredible legal upheaval that had taken place with these rulings cannot be overstated. One author who thoroughly studied this revolution of Court opinion said:

> These rulings marked a historic change in Constitutional doctrine. The Court was now stating that local and national governments had a whole range of powers that this same tribunal had been saying for the past two years these governments did not have. ...If the Social Security opinions are contrasted to the *Rail Pension* ruling and to *Butler* ...it is clear that the Court, and specifically Mr. Justice Roberts, had shifted ground.[15]

Not only did Robert's inexplicable shift undo Constitutional restraints, but a short time afterward, Justice Van Devanter, one of the jurists who consistently opposed the New Deal, announced his retirement. It was a fitting symbol of surrender to the big-government forces clamoring for unconstitutional action. Over the next three years, Roosevelt appointed a total of five new justices to the Court, packing it more effectively than even his court-packing plan would have allowed. In 1940, Wendell

Willkie, FDR's opponent in his unprecedented campaign for a third term wrote:

> When a series of reinterpretations overturning well-argued precedents are made in a brief time by a newly appointed group of judges, all tending to indicate the same basic disagreement with the established conception of government, the thoughtful observer can only conclude that something revolutionary is going on. And that is what has happened here.
>
> During the past three years the American people have had a series of Majority opinions from the Supreme Court that substantially change their form of government. On almost every occasion on which the court has been called upon to decide, it has wiped out state and local lines, and has relentlessly extended Federal authority to every farm, every hamlet, every business firm and manufacturing plant in the country.[16]

So profound was this shift in Constitutional interpretation that many leading lawyers found that the entire "doctrine of stare decisis went into the discard."[17] In other words, previous court precedent no longer carried any weight because the precedent had been completely overturned by the Court's reversal.[18] Attorney General Homer Cummings, who authored the court-packing bill, observed that "the Constitution [in] 1937 does not mean the same thing that it meant [in] 1936."[19] Another observer said it was "the Greatest Constitutional somersault in History," and that "[Justice] Owen Roberts, one single human being, had amended the Constitution of the United States..."[20]

What changed? Why did the Court find in *Butler* that controlling agricultural production was not warranted under the General Welfare Clause, but in *Helvering*, providing old age benefits was? Such a reversal is a prime example of "arbitrary rule". Why did the Court reverse its finding in the Railroad Retirement decision, which barred the practice of "taking the property or money of one and transferring it to another without compensation?"[21]

When you pair these decisions with the New Deal Court's other reversals, such as their 180 degree about face on minimum wage laws[22], we are left with a puzzling picture that has generated much speculation. What explains the Court's reversal? Were they cowering in the face of Roosevelt's court-packing plan? Did they have a revelation? Were they overcome with guilt that they might be preventing aid to a suffering nation? We may never know and I will not attempt to dissect the mind of the Court. I will however, offer the following: It is with a sense of irony that I add Alexander Hamilton's words as a means to shed some light on why the Court may have reversed course. He said:

> it would require an uncommon portion of fortitude in the judges to do their duty as faithful guardians of the Constitution, where legislative invasions of it had been instigated by the major voice of the community.[23]

Here was the Supreme Court using Hamilton's arguments to uphold an unconstitutional law because, perhaps, they simply did not have the fortitude which Hamilton himself prophesied would be necessary to protect the Constitution. For several years, FDR and the majority in Congress had been clamoring for more forceful government action to combat the devastating depression, only to be repeatedly rebuffed by the Courts. The result was that enormous public pressure was put on the Court to fall in line. It may be satisfactory to conclude that the Court simply did not have the "uncommon portion of fortitude" required to do the right thing and uphold the long established understanding of the General Welfare Clause and the Constitution's limits on Congress.

From 1789 to 1937, in spite of the many attempts from Hamilton and others after him, the Federal Government stayed mostly within the confines of enumerated powers. Now those enumerations were rendered virtually meaningless by the Supreme Court's decision in *Helvering*, using Hamilton's long-rejected arguments. While it was Theodore Roosevelt and Woodrow Wilson that began chipping away at the Constitution's limits on government, the Supreme Court's ruling in *Helvering v Davis* was the principle bombshell to the Constitution's dam against the relentless waters of government overreach. More than any other single ruling from the Court, it has been the source of government's biggest and most fiscally dysfunctional programs. But before we get into that, let's reflect a little more on the ruling itself.

Why should the Supreme Court give more weight to the opinions of Hamilton and Story as opposed to Madison, Jefferson and many others? They could have just as easily ruled the other way by saying that "the conception of the spending power advocated by Madison and strongly reinforced by Jefferson has prevailed." It almost seems as though a coin toss could have decided the issue. Cardozo's opinion is strikingly void of legal reasoning with regard to the General Welfare Clause. His decision to "not resurrect the contest" was tantamount to intellectual cowardice. A judge has a duty to explain the legal justification for decisions rendered. Instead, the Court dedicated most of its opinion to citing statistics, provided by none other than the defendants (the government) in the case, to show an urgent need for national action. That shows a complete abandonment of judicial restraint and a step into the realm of judicial activism. It is not the Court's job to ascertain the necessity or urgency of a law based on economic conditions, but to declare whether or not Congress has the power to enact it. As the same Court declared when striking down the similar Railroad Retirement Act only a few years earlier, their duty was "fairly to construe the powers of Congress ...uninfluenced by predilection for or against the policy disclosed in the legislation."[24] Cardozo's attempt to show the need for the legislation betrayed his clear predilection for it.

The reality is that the conception of the spending power advocated by the majority of those at the Constitutional convention, and those who ratified it, should have prevailed. The Courts have a duty, in difficult cases, to rely on long-established precedent. As has been explained, no law was passed by Congress, signed by the President and upheld by the Courts under the General Welfare Clause for 150 years. If Congress did indeed have the power to act in the general welfare, irrespective of enumerated powers, then why had that never occurred to the Federal Government prior to 1937? Surely there was an ample supply of emergencies and national crisis that could have supplied the justification.

The numerous interpretations and opinions cited in the previous chapters, including Court opinions, repeatedly reinforcing the concept that no broad power was intended for Congress, should have served as a guide for the Court. Hamilton's and Story's interpretations were not legal precedent, yet the Court cited them as support for their decision as though they were entitled to such weight. Furthermore, those opinions had been rejected numerous times, beginning at the Constitutional convention itself and continuing through numerous administrations and courts well into the 20th century. It is true that some laws were passed which some members of Congress justified with the General Welfare Clause, but that doctrine never gained traction as an authoritative interpretation. Further, none of those acts were on the scale, or were of the coercive nature of the Social Security Act. Here was a national retirement plan, which forced virtually every working American to take part and was perpetuated indefinitely into the future.

Clearly, justification for a program such as that could not be found in a precedent of building canals and donating land for agricultural colleges, which, at any rate, were strictly unconstitutional.

In his dissenting opinion in the *Steward Machine Company* case, Justice McReynolds condemned the Social Security Act as violating the carefully-guarded line of separation between State and Federal sovereignty:

> The doctrine thus announced and often repeated, *I had supposed was firmly established.* Apparently the States remained really free to exercise governmental powers, not delegated or prohibited, without interference by the Federal Government through threats of punitive measures or offers of seductive favors. Unfortunately, the decision just announced opens the way for practical annihilation of this theory; and no cloud of words or ostentatious parade of irrelevant statistics should be permitted to obscure that fact.[25]

Perhaps the most damning indictments of the Court's decisions in *Helvering* and *Steward* are the words of FDR himself and his advisors. It is evident from some of their statements that they knew perfectly well that most of the New Deal was unconstitutional. In a letter to the chairman of the House Ways and Means Committee, Roosevelt pleaded with Congressman Samuel Hill to pass a bill for relief of the coal industry. In that letter he finished by saying "I hope your committee will not permit doubts as to Constitutionality, however reasonable, to block the suggested legislation."[26] While unrelated to the Social Security Act, these words demonstrate Roosevelt's attitude toward the Constitution while President. He essentially asked Congressman Hill to ignore his oath to uphold the Constitution and leave it to the Courts to decide. Homer Cummings admitted in his journal that a key piece of New Deal legislation, the National Labor Relations Act, was "of rather doubtful Constitutionality".[27] Years after the New Deal, one of its chief architects, Rexford G. Tugwell, would finally own up to what few progressives have been willing to admit: that virtually the entire New Deal was unconstitutional. Here is a sampling of how he described the dismantling of our founding document during the New Deal era.

> Eventually the Congress approved immense programs of public works, established a regulatory system for industries affected with a public interest, and set up a welfare system intended to

be a universal protection from want. The President, with a duty to execute the laws, began to initiate them and, when he could, coerced a hesitant Congress to pass them... *So it was that all three branches escaped the confines of the Constitution even if liberally interpreted.* The Federal Government, as a whole, escaped as well from the constriction of specified powers. The basic law [The Constitution], first made for the people, and ratified by them, was rewritten again and again by extension, by interpretation, and, in emergency, by simply ignoring its limitations... The Constitution, referred to so fondly by earnest patriots, no longer really existed ... Obviously the framers had not intended their Constitution to be thus elasticized.[28] (emphasis added)

Tugwell also admitted that arguments in favor of the New Deal's programs "...were tortured interpretations of a document [The Constitution] that was meant to prevent them."[29] Tugwell believed the Constitution to be completely inadequate for the twentieth century. He therefore came to the conclusion that either the Constitution should be amended, or we needed a new one altogether. Whether or not you agree with that conclusion, it must be respected as an honest argument, unlike the tangled cloud of words used by the Court to give the New Deal the false veneer of constitutionality.

The New Deal was a clear violation of the rule of law; the concept that the law rules, not the judgment of man. That means that even if the judgment of political and judicial leaders believes a policy is rightly needed, they must not be allowed to pass it until the law allows it. The reason lady justice is depicted with a blindfold is to convey the principle that justice can only be properly administered while those who are tasked to dispense it display no bias or sympathy for litigants beyond each party's strict legal reasoning. William Howard Taft, during his tenure as a Supreme Court justice after serving as President, put it this way:

It is the high duty and function of this court in cases regularly brought to its bar to decline to recognize or enforce seeming laws of Congress, dealing with subjects not entrusted to Congress, but left or committed by the supreme law of the land to the control of the States. *We cannot avoid the duty, even though it require us to refuse to give effect to legislation designed to promote the highest good.* The good sought in unconstitutional legislation is an insidious feature, because it leads citizens and legislators of good purpose to promote it, without thought of the serious breach it will make in the ark of our covenant, or the harm which will come from breaking down recognized standards. In the maintenance of local self-government, on the one hand, and the national power, on the other, our country has been able to endure and prosper for near a century and a half.[30] (emphasis added)

Regardless of the perceived good of the Social Security Act, or any other New Deal legislation, there is no Constitutional provision which authorizes Congress to enact it. Therefore, the Court should have done their duty and struck down the law. To ignore that duty was to jeopardize the carefully established line between State and Federal power. Worse, Congress was now free to embark on a limitless field of legislation which would not only subdue the States, but would subject its citizens to a centralized power intent on multiplying laws and vastly expanding the national debt.

CHAPTER FOUR

---

2 + 2 = WHATEVER IS NEEDED

There are two more Supreme Court cases which rise to a similar level of offensiveness to the Constitution as *Helvering,* and also represent a seismic shift in favor of government power. The first is the 1942 case of *Wickard v Filburn.* In spite of the enormous implications of *Helvering,* there was still one more major hurdle for Congress to overcome before it could claim near absolute power: reshaping the Commerce Clause. Confident that the Court was now on their side, Congress began dusting off the pre-*Helvering* legislation which the Dr. Jekyll version of the Court had struck down. In 1938, the President signed the Agricultural Adjustment Act, the reincarnation of the scheme by the same name intended to control crop production.

Part of AAA regulated the amount of a crop a farmer could grow. A farmer named Roscoe Filburn challenged the constitutionality of the act because it fined him for growing too much wheat. The wheat which he grew in excess of his government-assigned limit was used only for his consumption and only a small portion was sold within the State. Therefore, he argued, Congress had no authority to regulate these activities under the operative clause: "Congress shall have power to... regulate commerce... among the several States" as given in the

Constitution. The government's argument was a stretch that Gumby himself could not have completed. It contended that because Filburn was using his own wheat, he did not have to buy it on the open market; and because he did not have to buy it, his actions *may have affected* commerce, therefore, Filburn's actions were within the scope of Congress's regulatory power.[1]

While the Court had expanded the Commerce Clause somewhat in the decades leading up to the New Deal, the issues being decided in *Wickard* had consequences of federal control which were undreamed of by the Founders. By the time the case was decided, Roosevelt had appointed a total of seven justices to the Supreme Court. It could not be hoped that these judges would give any respect to the Court's previous findings in the original Agricultural Adjustment Act, let alone the original understanding of the Commerce Clause.

The Commerce Clause was put in place because it was understood at the convention that uniformity in the nation's commerce might be frustrated by various States enacting punitive regulations against each other. It was intended mostly to be a check on the States, to keep them from disputing with one another over commercial interests.[2] The Founders made no contemplation of allowing the central government to control the local production and consumption of goods, or to declare itself manager of the national economy. Furthermore, at the time of the convention, farming and manufacturing were not considered commerce and were well-understood to be beyond the authority of Congress to regulate. As proof of this, we turn to the words of none other than Joseph Story, who condemned the doctrine, used in *Wickard*, that because something *might affect* a power which Congress has, then they might regulate that also. In his Commentaries he wrote:

> Can a power, granted for one purpose, be transferred to another? If it can, where is the limitation in the Constitution? Are not commerce and manufacturers as distinct as commerce and agriculture? If they are, how can a power to regulate one arise from the power to regulate the other? It is true, that commerce and manufacturers are, or may be, intimately connected with each other. But this is not the point in controversy. It is, whether congress have a right to regulate that, which is not committed to them, simply because there is, or may be, an intimate connection between the powers. If this were admitted, the enumeration of powers of congress would be wholly unnecessary and nugatory. Agriculture, colonies,

capital, machinery, the wages of labor, the profits of stock, the rents of land, the punctual performance of contracts, and the diffusion of knowledge would all be within the scope of the power; for all of them bear an intimate relation with commerce. The result would be, that the powers of congress would embrace the widest extent of legislative functions, to the utter demolition of all Constitutional boundaries between the state and national governments.[3]

It appears the Court wasn't willing to call on Story for their decision in *Wickard* as they did in *Helvering*. Consider the implication of Story's words. He rattles off a list of items presumed not to be within the scope of congressional power, yet, today those items are regulated by Congress without a second thought. It is clear that manufacturing and farming were at least two activities that were not intended to be regulated by Congress. Further, even if they could be regulated, the activity would have to be commercial, and would have to cross State lines for it to fall within congressional power. But Filburn's growing of wheat for his own consumption was not commercial activity at all. Constitutional lawyers William Mellor and Robert A. Levy explained the implications this way:

The power to regulate *all* commerce is broader, of course, than the power to regulate only interstate commerce. And the power to regulate all intrastate activities *substantially affecting* interstate commerce is broader still. Perhaps most important, allowing the government to regulate *noncommercial* activity that does not itself substantially affect interstate commerce but that, taken in the aggregate with other similar activities, *may* substantially affect interstate commerce is a power so broad that it admits almost no limitation.[4]

If Congress can regulate a man's growth and personal consumption of wheat, then federal regulation can reach a vast array of other activities that cannot possibly be construed as "commerce ...among the several States." Unfortunately, albeit, not surprisingly, FDR's Court ruled against Filburn, and thereby transformed the Commerce Clause into a power many times broader than what the Framers intended. Now Congress had two means by which it could pass nearly any legislation under the sun. If, by some remote chance, Congress could not pass a law under the guise of the general welfare, then they could likely find a way to argue that, even if the law dealt with a noncommercial activity, it *may* have some effect on commerce, and, therefore, it would fall under the scope of Congress's authority. Try to think of as many activities as you can that could not be construed to have some effect on commerce and you might count them on one hand.

The Court's departure from the text and intent of the Constitution was nearly complete. Practically the only thing left for the Court to do was to enforce those parts of the Constitution meant to prohibit Congress from doing certain things, such as are contained in the Bill of Rights. This is partly the reason the Bill of Rights has become more important over time. As government's powers advanced, the people retreated to the safe havens found in the first ten amendments, which if you recall, were originally not considered extremely important to most. Thus, what was once "a sea of liberty with islands of government power" has become "a sea of government power with islands of liberty."[5]

The second case to review is much more recent and the dust is still settling. The implications behind the Court's ruling are profound and may lead to an even greater expansion of government control. *National Federation of Independent Businesses (NFIB) v Sebelius* was the Supreme Court case that decided the constitutionality of the misnamed Patient Protection and Affordable Care Act (ACA). As we all know, this law requires every American to buy health insurance if they can afford it, according to the government's definition of affordability. This is the so-called individual mandate or minimum coverage provision. This provision of the law was the primary target in the lawsuit brought by the Federation and 26 States. As most are aware, the Court upheld the constitutionality of the law in a 5-4 decision.

Chief Justice John Roberts delivered the opinion for the majority. The first thing Justice Roberts had to do was address the Tax Anti-Injunction Act. This law requires that if someone is going to sue the government over a tax, they must first pay it, and then sue for a refund. Since the individual mandate portion of ACA wouldn't go into effect until 2014, nobody could sue over the law because no one had yet paid the tax for not buying insurance. Not to worry, said Roberts, Congress designated the payment for not buying insurance as a "penalty" not a "tax". The Court, therefore, could still review the case; so far, so good. Next, Justice Roberts addressed Congress's authority under the Commerce Clause. The question was whether the individual mandate was a legitimate function of Congress's authority to regulate commerce. The Court held that there is a distinction between regulating commerce and bringing commerce into existence. Congress can *regulate* commerce but they can't compel it. Therefore, Congress cannot force people to buy insurance under the Commerce Clause; again, so far, so good.

Justice Roberts then turned to the other clause in the Constitution which the Court had broadly interpreted; Congress's taxing authority. Did Congress have the authority to issue a penalty to someone for not buying insurance by virtue of their taxing powers? That may be arguable *if the penalty were a tax*. But Congress did not write the law to make it a tax. They consistently and purposefully call it a "penalty" in the language of ACA. That didn't stop Justice Roberts from renaming it as a tax; even though he went along with the penalty designation when considering the Anti-Injunction Act! Roberts Said: "...Congress did not intend the payment to be treated as a "tax" for purposes of the Anti-Injunction Act." But then he said that "the shared responsibility payment may for Constitutional purposes be considered a tax."[6]

Roberts had no problem construing the payment as a penalty in one instance, and then construing it as a tax in another. The health care law repeatedly refers to the payment as a penalty. Congress even tried to pass the bill as a tax, but it failed and was only successful after the language was changed to make it a penalty. Thus, there could be no mistaking what the minimum-coverage provision was. Yet Justice Roberts found a way to make the law what he thought it had to be in order for it to pass Constitutional muster. Though the absurdity of this legal sophistry stands on its own, we turn to the dissenters in the case to describe it:

> The provision challenged under the Constitution is either a penalty or else a tax... we know of no case, and the Government cites none, in which the imposition was, for Constitutional purposes, both... The issue is not whether Congress had the *power* to frame the minimum-coverage provision as a tax, but whether it *did* so. Our cases establish a clear line between a tax and a penalty: "'[A] tax is an enforced contribution to provide for the support of government; a penalty is an exaction imposed by statute as punishment for an unlawful act.'" *United States* v. *Reorganized CF&I Fabricators of Utah, Inc.*, 518 U. S. 213, 224 (1996) (quoting *United States* v. *La Franca*, 282 U. S. 568, 572 (1931)). We have never held that *any* exaction imposed for violation of the law is an exercise of Congress's taxing power— even when the statute *calls* it a tax, much less when (as here) the statute repeatedly calls it a penalty. ...to say that the

Individual Mandate merely imposes a tax is not to interpret the statute but to rewrite it... The rhetorical device that tries to cloak this argument in superficial plausibility is the same device employed in arguing that for Constitutional purposes the minimum-coverage provision is a tax: confusing the question of what Congress *did* with the question of what Congress *could have done...* What the Government would have us believe in these cases is that the very same textual indications that show this is *not* a tax under the Anti-Injunction Act show that it *is* a tax under the Constitution. That carries verbal wizardry too far, deep into the forbidden land of the sophists.[7]

Thus, the law should have been struck down as being beyond Congress's power, as they have no Constitutional authority to impose a penalty for not buying insurance, or for not doing anything else for that matter. Even if we go along with Robert's inexcusable contempt for reality and agree that it is a tax, we are forced to answer whether Congress's authority to tax has any limits. After all, if they can tax you for not buying insurance then what else can they tax you for not doing?

Roberts, recognizing this, made a fruitless attempt to allay these fears. Instead, he only tightened the knot in which he had tied himself:

Congress's ability to use its taxing power to influence conduct is not without limits. A few of our cases policed these limits aggressively, invalidating punitive exactions obviously designed to regulate behavior otherwise regarded at the time as beyond federal authority. See, *e.g.*, *United States* v. *Butler*, 297 U. S. 1 (1936); *Drexel Furniture*, 259 U. S. 20. More often and more recently we have declined to closely examine the regulatory motive or effect of revenue-raising measures. We have nonetheless maintained that "'there comes a time in the extension of the penalizing features of the so-called tax when it loses its character as such and becomes a mere penalty with the characteristics of regulation and punishment.'"[8]

Does not the individual mandate in ACA have the characteristics of regulation and punishment? If it doesn't then no one could determine what tax *would* be designated as losing its character as a tax so that it becomes "regulation and punishment." Recall that in the Butler case, which Roberts himself cites, the Court found that a tax had always been interpreted as an "exaction for the support of government." The penalty in ACA is clearly not intended for the support of government but for the regulation and punishment of behavior. The Roberts Court didn't see it that way and it is therefore, unlikely that a future Court will see any other tax which Congress wishes to impose as having the characteristics of "regulation and punishment" which would render it invalid. That exposes all of us to an unlimited scope of regulation to an extent that not only includes our current behaviors but also behavior which Congress might wish to compel us to engage in.

While Congress has, for a long time, exercised a power to influence behavior by offering tax *incentives*, it has never used tax *punishments* to induce behavior of which it approves. Now, the Roberts Court authorized Congress to do just that. Congress can, in effect, force people to do whatever they want as long as it falls within the narrow limitation of not violating another provision in the Constitution and, if it is attached to a tax. If you own land, Congress can force you to grow corn and sell it to ethanol producers by taxing you if you choose not to. Congress can force you to buy a fuel-efficient car and tax you if you choose not to. Congress can tax you if you choose not to put solar panels on your roof. Congress can tax you if you choose not to: fill in the blank with your preferred government nightmare.

Not only did the *Helvering* decision authorize Congress to spend money in aid of the general welfare, independent of enumerated powers, but now, under the *NFIB* decision, they can compel *you* to spend in aid of the general welfare. This opens up a whole new Pandora's Box of government control. If the growth of government after the *Helvering* decision is any indication of what happens when the Court abdicates in a case of this magnitude, we are surely in for another unprecedented increase in government activism.

One of the main reasons I chose to talk about this case is that it proves the futility of attaching any limits to the General Welfare Clause once it is detached from the enumerated powers. Can there be any doubt now that Congress's authority to tax and spend under Article 1 of Section 8 carries none of the limitations which were asserted by Story and New Deal Court? In spite of Justice Cardozo's lip service to limitations in his opinion in *Helvering*, not one act of Congress has been struck down under the supposed limits of the General Welfare Clause. This in spite of the fact that Congress has clearly violated some of the specific limitations spelled out by Joseph Story; foreign aid and numerous local projects to name a few. Further, it is now asserted that Congress can use the General Welfare Clause to compel citizens to do things which they think are necessary for the welfare of the country.

Thus, what was not possible to achieve under the Commerce Clause was achieved nonetheless through the General Welfare Clause.

In the *NFIB* case, Roberts may have a point in one respect. Part of his argument was that if Congress can use tax *incentives* to influence behavior, then why can't they use tax *penalties* for the same purpose? The answer is that, when we construe the General Welfare Clause as it was intended, Congress does not have the authority to offer tax incentives. Congress has the power to lay and collect taxes. For what purpose? "To pay the debts and provide for the common defense and general welfare." What does that mean? It means to do only those things specifically enumerated, which does not include a power to influence American's behavior through a complex system of tax credits and deductions. Roberts only has a point if we agree with the *Helvering* decision; that Congress can decide what is in the general welfare. Thus, the Court's decision in *NFIB* was merely a formality in recognizing power that Congress had already been given by the New Deal Court. This vindicated Madison's argument (though the argument is already vindicated by its merits) that if Congress could legislate for the general welfare beyond the enumerated powers, then the only limits they would have would be the negatives contained in the Constitution, i.e. the Bill of Rights, or anything that was not politically expedient.

NFIB gives us a perfect example of why the convention placed limits on Congress's authority to tax. That power was to be reserved for specific purposes; raising money to carry out the enumerated powers. It was not intended to be a cattle prod to get people to do Congress's bidding. It is unfortunate that the arguments made on both sides in this case did not explore specifically the general welfare phraseology – the very clause intended to prevent Congress from using the taxing authority in this manner. It is therefore obvious from *NFIB* that the General Welfare Clause has lost its meaning as a limit on the taxing power, which, even the original proponents of an independent power to legislate for the general welfare recognized was its true purpose.

In the movie "A Man For All Seasons" Sir Thomas More, a 16th century lawyer, asked "If the earth is flat can the king's command make it round, and if it is round can the king's command make it flat?" We should ask a similar question today: "Can the Supreme Court's decree make the Constitution say something it does not?" The answer is that the Supreme Court, nor the most expedient national needs, nor the angels in Heaven, can do such a thing. It is true the Supreme Court is tasked with interpreting the Constitution, but this does not give them license to rewrite it. The next logical question then becomes what to do about it. That will occupy the bulk of the remainder of this book, but first we must explore the consequences of our departure from the Constitution.

CHAPTER FIVE

LEVIATHAN

Not surprisingly, government has grown rapidly since the 1930's. From 1790 to 1930, federal expenditures, other than during the Civil War and World War 1, never rose above 6% of the Country's total income.[1] It now stands at about 22% and has averaged roughly 18% of GDP since World War II, a 200% increase since the time of the Supreme Court's ruling in *Helvering v. Davis*.[2] The vast majority of this increase in spending can be accounted for by the reinterpretation of the General Welfare and Commerce Clauses. The broadness of those clauses gave Congress the presumed power to legislate in matters that were intended to be reserved to the States. Clearly, the Court's abandonment of the rule of law has allowed for a massive government to spiral out of control. The reader is likely already aware of the enormous size and scope of the Federal Government. However, it will be instructive to take a few pages to rehearse the most damaging results of the New Deal Court's decisions. In this chapter we briefly examine some of the low-lights and the attendant consequences of government's growth.

Legal Complexity and Regulations

Since 1937, the number of Federal laws has exploded. The Constitution mentions only three federal crimes: treason, piracy and counterfeiting. By the early twentieth century, Federal crimes numbered in the dozens. As it took a while for tradition to give way after the New Deal, a spike in federal crimes didn't take off until the 1970's. In the early 80's, there was a big push to get Congress to reform the Federal criminal code. As part of that effort, a two-year project was undertaken by the Justice Department to try and determine just how many federal crimes there actually were. The project ended with a compilation of approximately 3,000 criminal offenses found in the more than 27,000 pages of the United States Code.[3] The judicial interpretations of that code, which are necessary for their understanding, are found in more than *2800 volumes consisting of more than four million pages of text*.[4] The man who headed the project, Ronald Gainer said: "you will have died and been resurrected three times before you could determine how many federal crimes there are."[5] Remember, this was more than 30 years ago. More recent studies estimate that there are currently more than 4,000 Federal criminal offenses,[6] ranging from the illegal use of Girl Scout badges to the criminalization of marijuana use. These laws do not even include regulatory provisions as set out by various executive branch agencies. When these are added to the list, estimates range *from 10,000 to 300,000 additional regulations which may be criminally enforced*.[7] Furthermore, these reports are from the 90's and do not include the explosion of regulation over the last decade, led by ACA and the Dodd-Frank financial reforms, which are still being written. The Federal Register, which contains all Federal regulations, is now over 80,000 pages long.

These staggering statistics are troubling to say the least. This trend has led, and will continue to lead, to the degradation of the rule of law. The laws of society are important because they communicate our values. Laws are the manifestation of what most of society already believes to be wrongful behavior. They should be obeyed because the behavior a particular law is meant to prevent is wrong, in and of itself; but what happens when laws are passed which are intended to prevent behavior which is not inherently wrong, such as growing too much wheat? The result is a degradation of respect for the law. When society is inundated with numerous and tedious laws, it eventually becomes easier for citizens to break the law than to follow it. When this happens, respect for the law diminishes and corruption will follow close behind.

I have witnessed this first hand, having lived in Mexico and seeing my family do business there. Mexico is notorious for its corruption. Is it because Mexicans are simply corrupt people? Of course not. It is because their government's onerous laws make it more sensible to be corrupt. In many cases, when you try to follow the law in Mexico, you're a sucker. For example, my father owns a piece of farm land on which he was trying to secure permits for several wells. He likely could have easily bribed an official and secured the permits; but because he attempted to get the permits legally, he was bogged down in a tedious legal process tainted by political pressure from competitors – even though my father's land is technically in a zone that is outside the jurisdiction of the bureaucracy in question. Years later, the issue is still unresolved. This type of uncertainty, resulting from complicated and unpredictable legal processes, can be a huge drag on business and often leads to corruption. Such is the plight of societies with a weak rule of law because of how burdensome and tedious their laws are. Wide-spread corruption is not the result of culture. It is more often the result of bad government policies. To be sure, it is more than just the number of laws that affects the quality of institutions. But the more laws there are the more difficult and burdensome it becomes to enforce them.

This is where we are headed in the United States if we continue to pile on more laws and regulations. Humans are mostly rational. If the more rational choice is to break the law because it would be easier than to follow it, disrespect for the law will develop and this will lead to an environment conducive to corruption. A perfect example of how this may begin to develop more fully in the United States is the Affordable Care Act. The law, according to one group, has already imposed 111 million hours of paperwork *before* it has been fully implemented.[8] (Imagine the advancements that might be made in medical research with 111 million hours of work.) We are all too aware of the enormous burden this law will become for businesses, families and tax payers. And we still don't know many of the law's provisions, which are still to be determined by the Secretary of Health and Human Services. This law, if not repealed, could trigger the beginning of a widespread movement of civil disobedience because complying with it is simply too difficult. If and when that happens, the government will have three choices: (1) Employ drastic and costly measures to enforce the law which will lead to outright tyranny, (2) Give in to civil disobedience and pave the way for wide-spread corruption or (3) Repeal the law.

Another troubling consequence of the explosion of Federal criminal law is the number of innocent people who are in jeopardy of prosecution. James Baker, the co-author of one of the studies cited previously stated: "There is no one in the United States over the age of 18 who cannot be indicted for some federal crime."[9] With more than 300,000 offenses, chances are you have broken a Federal law. This opens the door to the possibility of random prosecutions and government oppression, as the Feds now likely have some legal excuse to come after you should they choose to. That may sound quite dramatic to some, but our current legal system is a hidden tumor of tyranny, which, if left untreated, may eventually metastasize into our worst fears. The most familiar example for many people is the IRS. The federal tax code, more than 70,000 pages long, surely contains something you have violated. And if the IRS audits you, the burden of proof lies with you to show you have done nothing wrong; guilty until proven innocent.

In many cases, people are not even aware that they are breaking the law but may still be prosecuted. In recent years, it has been shown that Congress and the Courts are increasingly ignoring a critical protection for citizens when it comes to the legal code: mens rea.[10] This basically means that in order to be criminally liable, the accused must have intentionally or knowingly violated the law or intended to do harm. Just a small sampling of legislation shows that from 2005-06 over 220 non-violent criminal offenses were passed by Congress which lacked adequate mens rea requirements.[11] Of course, Congress is only acting out of necessity in order to enforce the law. No one can seriously be expected to be up-to-date on federal rules and regulations. But if anyone can claim ignorance then the laws have little bite. This illustrates the point that the only way government can enforce tedious laws is to become increasingly tyrannical and disrespectful of natural rights. That is why the law should be designed to prevent only behavior that is inherently wrong, and it should remain simple, limited and discernable.

What does it say about the rule of law when nearly every citizen is technically a criminal, whether they know it or not? With so many tedious laws covering so many subjects, we effectively live in a society governed by *people* with a vast amount of discretion, as opposed to being governed by simple *laws,* narrowly designed to restrain government and punish people with criminal intent. This is the exact opposite of the founder's intentions in drafting the Constitution. The vast accumulation of laws originally intended to protect citizens are now akin to a sword hanging over them. Only politics and the last bastions of liberty contained in the Constitution's Bill of Rights are staying the sword, though even these have come under assault lately through complex laws such as the Patriot Act.

You may feel secure, for now, in the belief that the Federal Government has no need to come after you and you may be right. But what happens when a "national emergency" occurs? Remember that it was the Great Depression which served as the impetus for government to usurp power regardless of the plain language of the Constitution. How much more will government assert itself in an emergency when those Constitutional restraints have already been removed and when any one of thousands of statutes might be called on to complete the government's purpose? At the time of this writing, we are witnessing the government of Cyprus seize private bank accounts in an attempt to thwart financial collapse. Would our government do that? I do not intend to be a doomsday prophesier. I simply believe, as our Founders did, that governments are not to be trusted with vast amounts of power. The long, sad history of mankind is littered with the ruins of civilizations ravaged by tyrants and oppressive governments. We would be wise to believe that these things could happen to us if we do not more carefully guard our liberties. With each new law that is passed, those liberties are put in a more precarious position.

Of course, there are much more practical consequences of a large and complex legal system, not least of which is the drag on economic growth. For example, we have recently seen the development of a multi-billion dollar industry in health related software applications. However, many potentially life-saving apps are in limbo because of uncertain rules from the Food and Drug Administration. Not only does this negatively affect job creation, but it also prevents good products from getting to market in a timely manner. Complex FDA rules cost drug companies billions of dollars and years of research to bring a life-saving medicine to market. Then, of course, once the drug is on the market, it is prohibitively expensive for many patients because of the enormous cost to develop it. The government responds by raising taxes and/or increasing debt to pay for another entitlement to help people afford prescription drugs. We could go on all day with examples of how this pattern has been repeated by government: complex rules cause market distortions; market distortions cause prices to rise; rising prices prompts government to raise taxes/debt in order to help people afford the rising prices which they caused; and to boot, the politicians blame the free market. The worst part of this pattern is that the problem of rising costs is never solved; it is only exacerbated by subsidies and entitlements which enable, and often cause, prices to continue rising. In a few cases, government's market distortions are so extreme that they cause huge bubbles which, when broken, lead to economic disaster such as in 2008.[12]

This is what happens when a law-making authority has such broad powers that it must delegate its rule-making authority to armies of agencies with nothing better to do than to justify their own existence by making more rules. Had the Courts enforced the originally intended Constitutional limits on Congress, we would likely have much simpler and more effective laws and regulations. This, in turn, means we would have a more efficiently functioning free market with less boom and bust, lower prices, higher quality across industries, and higher employment.

The table below offers some evidence for these claims. Each year, the Heritage Foundation and The Wall Street Journal put together an index of economic freedom of countries throughout the world using measures such as the regulatory burden and the strength of the rule of law. The United States is ranked 10th on that list. This table shows the average economic growth rate and unemployment rate for the 9 countries ahead of us and behind us in economic freedom.

More Freedom Means More Growth and Employment

	Avg. Growth Rate	Avg. Unemployment Rate
Top 9 Countries	3.3%	5.6%
United States	1.7%	7.8%
Countries 11-19	2.6%	7.6%

Author's calculations based on 2013 data from the Index of Economic Freedom, www.heritage.org/index/ranking

Clearly, countries with fewer regulations and smaller/simpler governments tend to have more growth and employment than countries with more regulations and bigger/more complex governments. While the averages are better in both groups than in the U.S., it is clear which direction is best for economic prosperity and job creation. Simpler rules create more certainty and put a smaller burden on businesses which leads to more opportunity and growth. Instead, we are passing laws like ACA and Dodd-Frank, which are leading the recent increase in the regulatory burden on businesses in the United States. A recent Federal Reserve report has confirmed that regulations such as ACA are the reason for many employers' planned layoffs and reluctance to hire new staff.[13] One recent report attempted to calculate the cost of all federal regulations and found that it was about $1.8 trillion, roughly 12% of GDP.[14] While we can't get rid of all regulations, that represents a staggering amount of wealth that could certainly be put to much better use in the private sector, not just in terms of the dollar amount, but in terms of the increased productive capacity of entrepreneurs operating more freely.

Government Spending

The dangers just outlined of an arbitrary and widely oppressive legal system are only surpassed by another major consequence of our departure from the Constitution: out-of-control government spending. As cited at the beginning of this chapter, government spending has exploded since the 1930's as a direct result of the Supreme Court's refusal to apply traditionally held Constitutional limits on Congress. For emphasis, let's look at some figures. In 2013, the Federal Government spent $3.6 trillion.[15] That's about $40,000 for each family of three in the country. It is more than double what we were spending in the year 2000.

Federal Outlays Since 1900

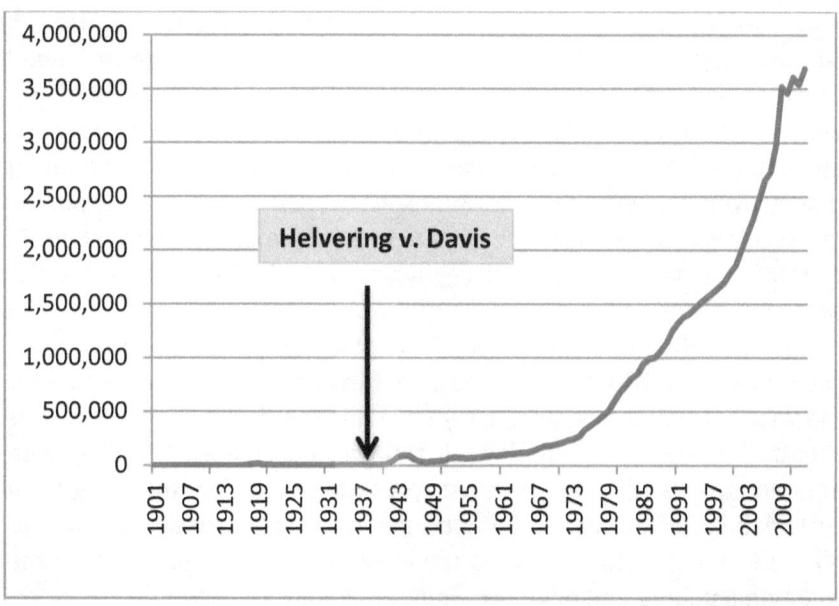

Source: whitehouse.gov chart of total federal outlays

Unlike the onerous laws and regulations previously discussed, most of this spending is driven by programs intended to help people. The largest share of Federal spending, 46%, goes to Social Security, Medicare and Medicaid. 19% is spent on defense, 6% on interest payments for our debts. The other 31% is filled with an extraordinary array of wasteful, inefficient and downright angering programs.[16] Let's briefly examine each of these areas of spending.

Entitlements

Social Security, Medicare and Medicaid, collectively referred to as entitlements, are a ticking time bomb which will bring this country to its knees unless drastically reformed. These programs are the main target of this book's central premise. Remember that it was Social Security that was being challenged in *Helvering v Davis*. The Court's ruling on the Constitutionality of this program opened the door to a vast array of other unconstitutional programs. But most damaging to the long-term health of the country was that Social Security established the precedent for Medicare and Medicaid to pass in the 1960's. These three programs combined are responsible for an unfathomable amount of debt. Unfortunately, politicians get to play by a different set of rules so they don't have to call it debt. Our "official" debt is over $17 trillion but if government had to abide by the same generally accepted accounting principles (GAAP), which, if violated by private business would result in jail time, the Federal Government's debt would include the unfunded liabilities of Social Security, Medicare and Medicaid. Estimates of this debt range from $45 trillion to over $100 trillion.[17] If these programs are left unreformed, we will have to come up with that amount of money over the next few generations *in addition* to currently projected tax receipts. If we don't come up with the money, drastic cuts in benefits will have to take place, which would likely accelerate the breakdown of the rule of law.

If we confiscated the wealth of every millionaire in the country we could not pay off that debt. Thus, whatever sanctity you may feel for the value of these programs, they have left the country in a disastrous situation unless extremely difficult reforms are enacted. Dealing with entitlements is the single most pressing issue for the long-term sustainability of our economy and indeed, our country as we know it. All this is directly attributable to the government's abandonment of the traditional understanding of the General Welfare Clause.

Interest on Debt

The government's $17 trillion plus debt carries with it at least two enormous burdens. First, paying the interest on that debt is very expensive; currently 6% of total expenditures, or roughly $230 billion a year. This is sometimes referred to as "dead weight spending" because it is money that provides no actual benefit to anyone other than the country's creditors (which include some of those countries whom we consider to be potential threats to our national security). Most good companies know to keep their debt low because these debt service payments eat into profits and inhibit expansion. If current trends continue, interest payments on the debt could become the single largest expense item in the federal budget by 2050.[18] This would be a calamitous occurrence and would leave us with that much fewer resources to defend the country and deal with other essential government functions. Of course, these debt payments depend greatly on interest rates. While future interest rates are impossible to predict, there is little reason to believe that buyers of U.S. government debt will not demand higher interest rates given the country's expanding debt relative to our national income; the key factor that any creditor looks at. If interest on our debt rises, then debt service payments could grow much quicker than under current projections. If caught off guard in this manner, we may go the way of the unwise companies who accumulated too much debt leading up to the financial crisis.

The second reason this high level of debt is a concern is its drag on the economy. When investors buy government debt, they, and the economy, are incurring an opportunity cost to private investment. For example, rather than giving money to the Feds in order to finance the DEA's drug eradication projects in Latin America, an investor could give money to an entrepreneur who is trying to bring a new medical device to market (assuming, of course, the FDA approves it). Government certainly has many worthy purposes, but to incur debt and consume private investment in order to finance its not-so-worthy projects is to waste money and is nothing shy of tyranny, to say nothing of the tendency of debt to stagnate growth, as many studies have shown.[19]

Defense

Defense spending currently consumes 17% of federal expenditures. Congress is authorized in the Constitution to provide for the common defense through certain other enumerated powers such as to raise and support armies and to declare war. However, as with spending on the general welfare, Congress has gone well beyond those enumerations to a point where much of what is classified as "defense" spending does nothing to "provide for the common defense... of the United States". Benjamin Friedman and Christopher Preble of the Cato Institute summed it up nicely:

> These days, policymakers want the U.S. military to contain China; transform failed States into stable democracies; chase terrorists; train various foreign militaries to chase terrorists; protect sea lanes; keep oil cheap; democratize the Middle East; protect European, Asian, and Middle Eastern States from aggression; spread good will through humanitarian missions; respond to natural disasters at home and abroad; secure cyberspace, and much more. For the supporters of such missions, the military forces and budget needed to pursue these goals can never be enough. But the relationship between all these objectives and the proper mission of the Department of Defense to protect Americans is tenuous.[20]

The unfortunate result of this is that we are left with billions of dollars in spending that does little or nothing to improve national security. For example, the U.S. currently maintains a military presence in such advanced countries as Britain, Germany, Australia and Japan; countries perfectly capable of defending themselves with their own citizen's tax money. Spending our money to put troops in countries around the world bears little relation to providing for the "common defense ...of the United States." Worse, any mention of cuts to defense spending is quickly met with political gamesmanship, usually driven by politician's efforts to protect military contractors in their districts as much as it is driven by a hawkish zeal to protect Americans. Too many Republicans have a blind eye to out-of-control, wasteful government when it comes to the Department of Defense.

The remaining 31% of federal expenditures covers a staggering number of programs, most of which are beyond the Constitutional scope of government. Here is a small sampling of the most blatantly unconstitutional.

Subsidies

This is perhaps the ugliest of federal spending because of its inherent corruption, promotion of cronyism, contempt for equality, and complete overall ineffectiveness. A power for Congress to give money to particular businesses or industries cannot be gleaned from anywhere in the Constitution, even using the liberal interpretations of Joseph Story and the New Deal Court. The latest count of Federal subsidy programs at the time of this writing was 2,215.[21] These programs include everything from payments to colleges who graduate more minorities in agriculture to the development of Indian arts and crafts. An entire library could be written on the madness contained in these programs. Here is a look at just a few.

Government is notoriously inept at forming a rational strategy of economic policy. Subsidies tend to be Frankenstein-like appendages to an irrational body of strategies that make no sense when taken together. For example, you may be aware that government, for years, has taxed the tobacco industry and spent money on ad campaigns in an attempt to reduce smoking and tobacco use. Yet, a federal subsidy exists for tobacco producers!

Producers may benefit from subsidies, but only at the expense of the consumer and taxpayer. In the case of food, prices are driven up by agriculture subsidies only to prompt government to turn around and subsidize poor people to be able to afford the food which government makes more expensive. Agriculture subsidies have been around since the Great Depression but at best, they are outdated and ineffective at producing any net benefit for the economy.

For example, sugar subsidies and other regulations have caused U.S. sugar prices to be as much as 78% higher than the world average.[22] Of course, this makes domestic sugar producers happy, but it also causes consumers and producers of food and candy to pay more. A 2006 report from the Department of Commerce showed that for every sugar farming job saved as a result of high prices, *nearly three* food manufacturing jobs are lost in the U.S.[23] Kraft and Hershey are just a few of the businesses who have moved some of their operations to Canada where sugar prices are half as high as in the United States.[24] But aside from big business, many small businesses, such as bakeries, get a bad deal from sugar subsidies. This underscores the propensity of government regulations to end up doing more harm than good. Of course, this situation is repeated again and again for the numerous other industries which Congress subsidizes.

Subsidies to businesses cost taxpayers nearly $100 billion a year.[25] Payments and guarantees to companies like Solyndra distort markets, waste money and create unfair advantages for politically connected firms. A brewery in Michigan recently received $220,000 from the Department of Housing and Urban Development to expand its operations.[26] Why should the government take the tax receipts from other breweries and give it to their competitors? Such unfair practices are inherent in nearly all subsidy programs and are grossly offensive to the bedrock concept that all should receive equal treatment under the law.

Of course, there are many programs that might sound more worthy to most people, such as grants to protect children from substance abuse. But the worthiness of a project should not be the only litmus test for whether or not it should be funded by the Federal Government. The Constitution was crafted to limit the scope of federal programs. If federal money should be spent on any project that has a worthy goal then where is the end of federal spending? Apparently, according to Congress and the Courts, there is none, at least none other than what is politically unwise.

As a result, there also seems to be no end to the line of groups showing up in Washington with their hands out seeking funding for their "worthy" causes. This creates an army of lobbyists which in turn creates a breeding ground for corruption and improper relationships between politicians and the moneyed class who can afford the lobbyists.

Education

In 1943, the United States Constitution Sesquicentennial Commission under the direction of the President, Franklin Roosevelt, published *The History of the Formation of the Union under the Constitution*. In a section entitled "Questions and Answers Pertaining to the Constitution" we find the following:

Q. Where, in the Constitution, is there mention of education?

A. There is none; education is a matter reserved for the States.

Joseph Story also saw no justification for using the General Welfare Clause to allow Congress to legislate and spend money on education. He said:

...The power to regulate manufacturers is no more confided to congress than the power to interfere with the systems of education, the poor laws, or the road laws of the States.[27]

Why Justice Story couldn't see that Congress would eventually construe his interpretation of the General Welfare Clause to justify education spending and, thus, move beyond the Constitution's limits is hard to know. That is precisely what happened after a long and gradual process of increasing federal involvement in education. In 1979, a formal department was created. With increased federal funding has come increased centralization and stagnated student achievement. Over the last 30 years, Federal spending on K-12 education per pupil has risen over 350% with no change in standardized test scores.[28]

If we are to term these increased expenditures "investments," as progressives would have us do, then it is time to sell. Education was no less important in 1787 than it is in 2014. Yet, the Constitution left education in the hands of the States because the Framers understood that more centralization had a greater potential to produce negative outcomes, as it would likely lead to less responsiveness and more waste. This is precisely what has happened to education in America as outdated, one-size-fits-all methodologies are crammed down the throats of parents and students.

As a former teacher, I speak from experience on this issue. President Bush's No Child Left Behind Act put public school administrators in a trance over standardized tests, leaving them handicapped at responding to individual student and parent needs. President Obama's "race to the top" and Common Core programs double down on the growing trend of centralization. The inevitable result of centralized control over education is more waste, less flexibility, and an increasing reliance on standardized tests.

Educational success should not depend on a child's ability to be proficient on math and science tests. Educational success should be measured by work-force and entrepreneurial success – which means educators should focus on developing the individual talents and skills of each child, in addition to responding to the requirements of employers rather than politicians. Employers increasingly complain about the lack of qualified candidates to fill jobs in an era when education funding has grown enormously. Adjustments to employer's needs are much more likely to materialize in a market-based or, at a minimum, less centralized, education system controlled by State and local communities.

<u>Welfare</u>

In his January 8, 1964 state of the union address, President Lyndon B. Johnson famously declared war on poverty. From that year to 2012, Federal and State governments spent roughly $15 trillion dollars fighting poverty.[29] Yes, trillion with a T lest you mistake this for a misprint. The Federal Government now operates more than 120 separate programs intended to fight poverty. One might think that after all of this there wouldn't be a single poor person left in the country. In fact, the amount of money we spend right now on poverty is equal to about $60,000 per poor family of three![30] That's more money than I make as a teacher for my family of three. How is it that the equivalent of a respectable salary can be spent for each poor family, yet poverty remains?

Instead of improving, the poverty rate in America has hovered between 10% and 16% since the 60's and was even falling rapidly *before* the government began redistributing large amounts of wealth.[31] This year, the 50th anniversary of the "war on poverty" is a good time to reflect on how poorly our government-centered strategies are failing. Our strategy in the war on poverty is severely flawed. It is based on redistribution of wealth administered by a large, inefficient and often redundant bureaucratic blob. A strategy based on government redistribution is destined to fail as decades of evidence clearly indicate. Our strategy should be to promote the bedrock principles of work, strong families and self-reliance, which mostly fall outside the purview of government whether Federal or State. Unfortunately, our current programs too often encourage the opposite: unemployment, the break-up of families and dependence on government.

Once again, the Founders were well-aware of poverty in 1787. In fact, it was likely a bigger issue then as no one at that time had ever heard the term "middle class." Yet again, they left these policies to the States and to private charity. I repeat the quote from Justice Story that the "poor laws" are "not confided to congress". The advantage of leaving anti-poverty measures to the States and private citizens is that private charity will much more carefully and efficiently spend the money where it is needed the most, without creating as much dependency; while strategies employed in States with lower levels of poverty will be emulated by others. In addition, States cannot accumulate the same power as the Federal Government because they must compete with each other. They also cannot accumulate as much debt as the Federal Government. Therefore, anti-poverty programs will likely be more efficient when administered by the States.

Benjamin Franklin was rumored to have said: "When the people find they can vote themselves money that will herald the end of the Republic."[32] When politicians engage in a contest to see who can be the most generous without legal or practical limits, there will be no end to spending on "anti-poverty" programs regardless of whether those programs actually reduce poverty. The result will be enormous debts and higher taxes to pay for the programs. A public safety net, while a good and worthy thing, is not among the powers vested in the Federal Government by the Constitution. Besides that, it will likely be more effective at targeting the truly needy and minimizing dependence when administered by States and private charity.

Foreign Aid

When Joseph Story made his case for a separate power for Congress to spend in aid of the general welfare, he explicitly cited foreign aid as a limitation on that power as it did not promote the general welfare of the United States. The New Deal Court echoed that limitation. Yet, as my arguments and history have shown, any attempt to limit the General Welfare Clause is futile once the power is given. All Congress need do is claim that foreign aid actually *does* promote the common defense and general welfare because it improves national security by creating less poverty in other countries, and therefore, less radical dictators and more stability …or something.

Spending on foreign aid is very small compared to the overall budget, but it is the ultimate slap in the face to U.S. taxpayers, especially at a time when politicians are crying poor when it comes to things like education and infrastructure. Perhaps the most infuriating illustrations of foreign aid are when we give money to middle-eastern countries who hate us. Pakistan, who receives about $1.5 billion a year in non-military aid, famously upset the U.S. when they imprisoned the doctor who helped us find Osama Bin Laden.[33] It is all but obvious that Pakistan harbored Bin Laden in the compound where he was killed by U.S. special-forces. Think on this the next time you hear politicians tell you we need to raise taxes in order to fix a bridge or hire a teacher.

Pork Barrel Projects

Like foreign aid, this ugly type of Federal spending was also cited by Story as a limitation on Congress's power to spend in aid of the general welfare because they serve local, not general welfare. These little budget gems usually come in the form of earmarks; awkward appendages to pieces of legislation that have nothing to do with the intent of the original bill. In many cases these goodies are used as tools of official bribery to get reluctant congressmen to vote for legislation in exchange for a chunk of money they can take back to their State or district. In other cases, they get slipped in because a representative might know that the sponsor of a bill isn't willing to risk its passage by fighting over a "mere" few million dollars or so. A disgraceful example is the emergency relief Congress appropriated for Hurricane Sandy. The "emergency" funds included $118 million for Amtrak upgrades and $2 billion for federal highways across the country, among other corrupt little nuggets.[34]

The overall spending on earmarks is small relative to the budget and this has led some to pay less attention to these smaller items. But to ignore this spending as inconsequential would be to ignore principle and the law. That very attitude has created an out-of-control government. Several billion dollars might be a *relatively* small amount but it is an *absolutely* huge amount of money – especially to the thousands of small businesses across the country who have to pay it while they struggle to meet payrolls and support their families. Any degree of respect for other people's money seems to have been lost on most politicians. Given the political difficulty of cutting any spending, every dime of taxpayer money should be scrutinized and put on the table. Whether it adds up to $10 billion or $100 billion, it is a significant amount to the people who paid it.

The Federal Government is clearly operating a myriad of programs which are unconstitutional, even if we liberally interpret it according to Story's conception of the General Welfare Clause. Foreign aid, local projects, education, the "poor laws" (welfare of various kinds), and the regulation of manufacturing and agriculture were all listed by him as being outside the scope of Federal power. Yet even though his arguments were used to reinvent the General Welfare Clause, Congress has claimed a near-universal power to legislate in areas intended to be reserved for the States.

While most of this chapter focused on spending, another consequence of Congress's usurpation of powers is the erosion of our liberty. Over 150 years ago the great French scholar Alexis de Tocqueville visited America to learn about our new society. Speaking of what he believed would eventually happen to democracies in the future he wrote an excellent summary of this chapter:

Above this race of men stands an immense and tutelary power, which takes upon itself alone to secure their gratifications and to watch over their fate. That power is absolute, minute, regular, provident, and mild. It would be like the authority of a parent if, like that authority, its object was to prepare men for manhood; but it seeks, on the contrary, to keep them in perpetual childhood: it is well content that the people should rejoice, provided they think of nothing but rejoicing. For their happiness such a government willingly labors, but it chooses to be the sole agent and the only arbiter of that happiness; it provides for their security, foresees and supplies their necessities, facilitates their pleasures, manages their principal concerns, directs their industry, regulates the descent of property, and subdivides their inheritances: what remains, but to spare them all the care of thinking and all the trouble of living?

Thus it every day renders the exercise of the free agency of man less useful and less frequent; it circumscribes the will within a narrower range and gradually robs a man of all the uses of himself. The principle of equality has prepared men for these things; it has predisposed men to endure them and often to look on them as benefits.

After having thus successively taken each member of the community in its powerful grasp and fashioned him at will, the supreme power then extends its arm over the whole community. It covers the surface of society with a network of small complicated rules, minute and uniform, through which the most original minds and the most energetic characters cannot penetrate, to rise above the crowd. The will of man is not shattered, but softened, bent, and guided; men are seldom forced by it to act, but they are constantly restrained from acting. Such a power does not destroy, but it prevents existence; it does not tyrannize, but it compresses, enervates, extinguishes, and stupefies a people, till each nation is reduced to nothing better than a flock of timid and industrious animals, of which the government is the shepherd.[35]

Tocqueville's words are an incredibly accurate picture of our society today. While we are not openly tyrannized, we are subtly restrained from acting by a variety of boards, bureaus and rules. We have laws that control the right and use of property; what we can build and where, what type of building, how high, what color, what type of signs, laws that control our health care; what has to be included in our insurance plans; laws that license occupations; laws that force us to contribute to retirement; laws that dictate our schooling, provide us with unemployment insurance, flood insurance, food and housing; laws that restrict what we can put into our bodies; government commercials that tell us to cook our food properly, eat right, exercise, save money, but induce us to get a loan with artificially low interest rates; laws that regulate cleaning products, toys, food, travel and a thousand other things. "[W]hat remains, but to spare us all the care of thinking and all the trouble of living?" Our freedoms have been diminished. We are restrained from acting. We have been compressed, enervated and stupefied.

The Founding Fathers had a profound understanding of the importance of the rule of law and a government limited by Constitutional bounds. Britain had a Constitution but it did not follow it. This was one of the primary complaints of the rebels who broke off to form a new nation. Thomas Jefferson outlined in the Declaration of Independence the "long train of abuses and usurpations" of the king. To usurp means to seize powers which the law has not sanctioned. Among those usurpations listed in the Declaration were the king's efforts "to subject us to a jurisdiction foreign to our Constitution" and "For suspending our own legislature, and declaring themselves invested with power to legislate for us in all cases whatsoever."

The rule of law begins with the understanding that government is limited to a specific set of powers. The Founders knew all too well the danger of arbitrary government and they designed their own Constitution to be a bulwark against it. Unfortunately, like our Founders, we are also subject to a government that claims near universal power to "legislate for us in all cases whatsoever." That power, unjustly sanctioned by the Court for Congress to exercise, is manifest in the vast expanse of federal programs just summarized. The abandonment of the rule of law; the Constitutional restrictions on what the Federal Government can do, has led us to a government with few limits. To put it in a more revealing way, we have become the very thing our Founders rebelled against in the first place: an overextended quasi-empire with too many military entanglements around the world, too many taxes, too many regulations, and too much debt, all managed by a corrupt central bureaucracy far removed from its people.

CHAPTER SIX

RULE OF LAW

"If the people come to believe that the government is no longer constrained by the laws then they will conclude that neither are they."[1]

- Michael Cannon

It is easy to see why citizens are not justified in taking the law into their own hands to mete out justice. We don't believe in vigilantism. But the rule of law applies equally to government. Why should government be justified in taking the law into its own hands by violating the Constitution to bring about what it perceives as justice? Neither we nor the government should replace the law with our own judgment, no matter how just we believe the end to be; the law rules. It is true that there are narrow cases in which government officials or individuals may be justified in violating the law in a time of extreme emergency or unique circumstance. But what we are mainly concerned with is the government's systematic and fundamental disregard for Constitutional law. When government goes down that path, the effects, while more subtly developed over time, will eventually be no less chaotic than the effects of citizen vigilantism. That chaos is best exemplified by the monstrous and complex legal system created by the Federal

Government since the 1930s. For a nation to survive long it must adhere to its core principles. For us, those principles are embodied in the Declaration of Independence and the Constitution. When those principles are abandoned we leave ourselves without guidance on major issues. The only thing left to take their place is an ugly and unstable political process.

Many deride those of us who have a healthy respect for core Constitutional principles for lacking pragmatism. This could sum up nearly every argument made in favor of forceful government action. The constant claim is that unless government acts, justice, equality and progress, as they see it, cannot be fully realized. We usually get a patronizing figurative pat on the head for being principled, but, they say, we cannot let principle get in the way of progress.

Upon deeper reflection, and a discussion of historical fact and empirical evidence, the self-defeating nature of this philosophy becomes evident. Principles are principles precisely because they have pragmatic applications. Decisions are hard when we are tempted by short-term benefits and quick fixes. That is why principles and values are so important. They give us perspective and call our attention to the long-term consequences of abandoning them. What makes principles useful is that they keep us on track by setting the boundaries over which we commit not to step. When government adheres to core Constitutional principles it provides for a healthy and liberated society. The philosophy of pragmatism in favor of government action preaches the exact opposite: that somehow those principles bind us down and impede "progress." But we know that successful nations (and organizations and individuals) depend on the discipline necessary to resist short-term gains and adhere to core values. In the end, we discover that there is no conflict between principles and pragmatism. *Being principled is pragmatic.* If you don't believe that, then go back and reread Chapter Five. The magnitude of the New Deal Court's radical departure from the core values of our founding is matched only by the consequences of it, namely, a crushing amount of debt, unfunded liabilities, and a leviathan government ever more menacing to liberty and equality.

Of course, statists would argue that it is that leviathan which has promoted our core values notwithstanding Constitutional restraints. But one of the core founding values is the rule of law itself. In matters of public policy, it is extremely important to understand the difference between the law and various outcomes in society which may be perceived as consistent with core values such as poverty reduction, maximizing employment and improving education. There are many instances where we may be tempted to believe that the law may be incompatible with a desired outcome. In those cases, it is the duty of elected officials and appointed judges to follow the law, even if it means forfeiting a perceived benefit such as higher employment, or, to alter it through the proper procedures. This is where the rubber meets the road as it concerns the rule of law. It is easy to follow the law when it protects us. It is hard when it is perceived that it hurts us. But if we arbitrarily set the law aside simply because we believe it will cause harm or prevent "progress," then we may as well abandon the rule of law altogether and proclaim a social democracy in which politicians can do whatever they want, checked only by the political process. In fact, we are dangerously close to just such a system.

We believe in the rule of law because we take the long view which warns that if legal barriers are broken, government inevitably becomes destructive to the ends it was created to protect: life, liberty and property. We do not believe it justifiable to replace the law with the judgment of man or woman because that person whom we currently favor may become someone whom we do not favor, empowered to abuse us without restriction. With this understanding in mind, let's address the several specific arguments made in favor of the Federal Government's many unconstitutional programs. This chapter will show that not only is the rule of law necessary as a protection of rights, but it is essential to provide the conditions which allow progress, i.e. eliminating poverty, increasing employment etc. to flourish.

Economics is a good place to start. It is not difficult to show that government actions often distort and worsen market outcomes as opposed to making them better; strengthening the case for government to be restrained by law. The Federal Government has taken it upon itself to subsidize and regulate housing, healthcare, and education among many other things. The claim is that these things would be out of reach or unsafe for many people if it weren't for government interventions.

Let's look at just the housing industry to examine this claim. Through a complex mosaic that includes tax credits, subsidies, government sponsored entities (GSE), and loose-money policies, the Federal Government has sought to extend home ownership to more Americans. Whether or not these policies have achieved the goal of increased home ownership is a simple matter of looking at the numbers. From 1960 to 2000, the mortgage interest tax deduction, often defended as an absolute necessity for the middle class and poor, widely fluctuated, yet, the home ownership rate remained essentially constant at a little over 60%.[2] As for the involvement of GSEs Fannie Mae and Freddie Mac, their share of the mortgage market went from less than 5% in 1960 to over 50% in 2000.[3] Again, ownership rates remained constant.   Contrast that with the period which saw the greatest expansion of home ownership in the country's history. From 1940 to 1960, the home ownership rate grew from 43% to 62%, with little involvement from the Federal Government.[4] That demonstrates well the creative power of the free market.

Compare that period with an episode in which the government *was* successful at increasing home ownership: 1995-2005. During this period, the rate went from 64% to 69%.[5] That increase was partially due to the Federal Reserve's policy of unusually low interest rates from 2002-04. Of course, at the time, many applauded the growth in home ownership, and it is irrefutable that it was government's stated goal to expand it. Yet, somehow, government tries to wash its hands of any culpability in the housing bubble and subsequent burst which caused a near-collapse of the financial system. Predictably, the free market and deregulation became the scapegoats. While big banks did take on too much risk, they never would have done so if the Federal Reserve had not created money out of thin air for them to lend; or if it had not guaranteed to bail out the banks if the loans went bad. So, either the government's attempts to increase home ownership were unsuccessful, in which case they wasted our money, or they were successful, in which case they greatly contributed to the financial crisis that left millions unemployed and out of home ownership. Either way, there is no case for federal involvement in housing markets; or health care, agriculture, education, automobiles, manufacturing, energy, or transportation.

The laws of supply and demand are as irrefutable as gravity. The equilibrium price in a free market accurately reflects the maximum price consumers are willing to pay while making it profitable enough for suppliers to produce. If the price is relatively high, then suppliers will naturally gravitate to that industry and the price will fall, increasing accessibility for many more people. This concept is applicable to any industry.   If the price is relatively low, then, of course, no one complains. Well-intentioned people may not like what a given price is because not everyone can afford it. But getting angry at equilibrium prices because not everyone can afford them is every bit as senseless as getting angry at gravity because people fall and get hurt; and it is equally futile to legislate against either.

Every case in which we see government try to fight against the price system, we see artificially high prices and/or malinvestment which inevitably lead to painful adjustments at some point. Therefore, one of the primary functions of the rule of law is to guard against government's harmful interventions in the price system. It is a common fallacy that the Constitution is an outdated relic that cannot meet the needs of our complex economy. In fact, the Founders were well-versed in free market economics, and they were very much aware of the negative effects of the truly outdated relic of interventionist policies, which are as old as government itself. The framers were heavily influenced by Adam Smith's "The Wealth of Nations," and they fully intended to put its principles into practice by limiting the Federal Government's ability to distort markets. No amount of economic "complexity," so long as it is derived from developments in a free market, alters the price system to a point where government must intervene.

Another argument made by apologists for usurpation is that it was necessary for the Federal Government to "take action" in order to bring about desired social changes. Without those changes we might still be living in a segregated society with more poverty and injustice. Consider, for example, civil rights laws. Remember again that the legal issues, Congress's Constitutional authority to pass the laws, are different from the intended outcome of the laws themselves.

When the Civil Rights Act of 1964 was passed, the Court had already decimated the meaning of the Commerce Clause. There is simply no authority given to Congress to pass laws which dictate to private local businesses the practices they must follow, regardless of how worthy we may deem those practices to be. But had Congress not usurped the power, say the progressives, we never would have been able to extend civil rights to all. Of course, if there was ever a valid reason for forceful action from the Federal Government, it was certainly to ensure civil rights. But there are several other ways government could have extended equality, which, would have been more consistent with the rule of law and may have been even more effective in some ways. For example, in Article IV of the Constitution, all citizens are guaranteed the same privileges and immunities in all States. This could have been used as the authority for Congress to pass a civil rights bill, without asserting a broad power over commerce, which could have eradicated the discriminatory practices of businesses and States abridging the privileges and immunities of minorities. No doubt such an interpretation would have been inconsistent with the clause's original intention, as the framers did not contemplate a method for mitigating the unequal treatment of minorities. However, such an interpretation would have been consistent with the text, and certainly the spirit, of the Constitution.   Unfortunately, this clause has received little attention throughout our history.

We should not overlook the power and effectiveness of boycotts, strikes and other peaceful citizen protests to bring about desired social changes. Peaceful citizen movements are capable of changing social norms without government legislation.   Short of government enforcement, a boycott is perhaps the quickest way to get a business to change its practices. Those who would refuse to give service to minorities naturally punish themselves by reducing their customer base. Given the momentum of the movement for equality, it is unlikely that any significant number of businesses would have held out very long against competitors who were willing to serve all on equal terms. It is unfortunate that passing a law is often seen as the culmination and end goal of a movement, rather than the much more effective and lasting goal of changing hearts and minds through the private exchange of ideas. While these methods may not be as forceful as we might like, they have several advantages over government usurpation.

First, they are one of the principle embodiments of self-government, a core value of American civics. As citizens come to rely on themselves to bring about the changes they want to see, they are more likely to inform themselves and participate, rather than sit back and let government "handle it."

Another key advantage to relying on organic movements, as opposed to government force, is that people will retain more freedom. There will never be a time when we will like every decision made by the people around us. But that does not justify us in using the force of government to bend people to our way of thinking. We should have tolerance and patience even for the people that don't have tolerance and patience. People acting independently from government through protest and voluntary exchange are a far more effective means of bringing about desired social change *in the long run*. It is far better to have private businesses accountable to customers than to bureaucrats. Free markets are a catalyst for bringing people together in ways that overcome social and cultural differences.[6] Good can triumph without government's laws, and social change can come about without the Federal Government overstepping its Constitutional bounds. That does not mean that laws cannot bring about good. But if the law is incompatible with policy goals, it must be changed in proper order so that we can better protect the integrity of social institutions.

Of course, the thesis of this book could not fail to remind us of the option of a Constitutional amendment, which would have been preferable although, admittedly, difficult. Large majorities in both parties voted for the Civil Rights Act, indicating that a Constitutional amendment might have been possible. The advantages of passing an amendment are that it would have been consistent with the rule of law and it would have kept Congress from asserting even more power over private businesses. There is no question that the equal treatment of all, regardless of race, is a core value which would have fit perfectly into a Constitutional amendment. There is much more that could be added to a discussion about passing amendments but that will be saved for later chapters.

Sometimes forceful, even improper action is necessary to promote a higher good; and it seems to be an inherent part of the American conscience to admire those who "damn the torpedoes." Equality certainly carries with it the distinguishing fact that it is a core government responsibility to promote it. But this should not diminish the voices warning against a government with too much power. It was never contended that government could not do any good with expansive powers; it was only asserted that it was dangerous in the long run and that the bad would tend to outweigh the good.

Setting aside the uniqueness of civil rights, the arguments made above could be much more forcefully applied to most other federal laws which are claimed to be essential for social justice, including unemployment insurance and Social Security among many others. In addition, and unlike civil rights where the States were the primary abusers, it is imperative to add that the States have broad powers under our federalist system to legislate on behalf of their citizens.

The concept of federalism, deeply woven into the fabric of the Constitution, was an essential means of dispersing power and ensuring light-handed government. There is no reason to suppose that the States are incompetent in passing appropriate legislation where needed according to the will of their respective voters. The States, as sovereign entities endowed with all powers not delegated to the Union, are perfectly capable of meeting the needs of their respective populations should their legislatures deem it necessary and practicable. It is simply untrue that the States could not meet the needs of the nation. A historical review of some statistics makes this clear. More than half the States had enacted old-age pension plans by the time Social Security was passed[7], and twenty-eight States had passed unemployment benefits by the time the feds got around to it in 1937.[8] There is little reason to doubt that most other States would not have followed eventually; but even if they never did, those legislatures would have answered to the voters that put them there.

Some progressives have argued that the Federal Government has to take over many programs in order to meet "excessive demand" in times of crises because of its ability to take on more debt than the States, and to ensure that every State plays along. Setting aside the fact that government *always* increases benefits regardless of economic conditions, this argument has it exactly backwards. It is true that some States balked at providing some programs because of a fear that they might have to raise taxes too high, but this is precisely what keeps governments disciplined and makes for programs that are more sustainable. If the level of taxes or public benefits is unsatisfactory to the voters in a State, they can make a change at the polls or leave the State. Each legislature has to balance public benefits with the taxes to pay for them. But because Congress can take on more debt, partly by printing money, it opens the door to fiscal recklessness. That is an argument *in favor of* federalism not against it. It is absurd to say that government must have a way out of being fiscally disciplined by being allowed to take on enormous debt.

It is more likely that welfare programs run by the States would be much more sustainable compared to the profligate Federal entitlement programs that have accumulated massive amounts of debt and jeopardized the economic security of future generations. Asking future generations to pay for current entitlements is every bit as immoral as theft; in fact it is theft; that is what happens when a person takes money from another without asking their permission. In addition, the ability of future generations to care for *their* vulnerable will be severely jeopardized if they have to pay for *our* generation's vulnerable as well. This illustrates how it is self-defeating to disregard core values and the rule of law.

Not only has nationalization of entitlement spending lead to unsustainable debt, but it also assumes that Americans are incapable of deciding what is best for them, or what they are willing to pay for. It is not incumbent on Congress to enact nationalist programs to make up for what they perceive as the shortcoming of the State legislatures. Each government has its own sphere of responsibilities. When the Federal Government encroaches on the States, it creates a more centralized and powerful government more likely to result in tyranny. A federalist system, with power dispersed among fifty democracies, is much more capable of balancing social needs with the discipline needed to sustain them than one democracy with centralized power.

Another instance to which we might apply these arguments is child labor laws. It is often claimed that without federal action, children would have continued to suffer in poor working conditions, and that those who complain about federal usurpation would have condemned millions of children to unsafe and unhealthy hard labor. Much in the way it did with civil rights in 1964, Congress enacted child labor regulations in 1916 by asserting a broad interpretation of the Commerce Clause. The legislation was rejected by the Supreme Court.[9] Yet again, this shows how wrong the *Wickard* Court was to ignore the Commerce Clause precedent up to the time of its ruling. It also provides yet another example that the General Welfare Clause was not interpreted to allow Congress to act in the general welfare independent of enumerated powers. Otherwise, Congress would have claimed the power to regulate child labor using that clause.

The transformation of attitudes toward child labor in the early twentieth century refute the claim that federal action played any role in bringing about the changes. Federalism once again shows that Congress was not needed. By 1933, all 48 States had some form of child labor and compulsory schooling regulations on the books.[10] Between 1900 and 1930, child labor declined from 18.2% of the child population to 4.7%; and the vast majority of remaining child laborers were children working on a family farm.[11] These trends can be credited not only to state regulations, but also to the advancements in technology made by private businesses and the efforts of private organization such as The National Child Labor Committee, founded in 1904 by concerned citizens.[12] In spite of these trends, the new dealers seized their recently awarded, court-granted powers and passed the Fair Labor Standards Act in 1938, which regulated child labor among other labor-related issues. Typical of politicians, they celebrated their long-fought-for "victory" when the legislation was passed. The truth is that the victory had already been won through the efforts of the States, private businesses and private initiative. The victory should not be legislation. The victory should be the changing of hearts and minds brought about through the free exchange of ideas.

It wasn't only child labor that improved without Federal legislation. Labor for adults transformed as well. The entire progressive era of the early twentieth century is characterized by significant advancements in labor conditions while the Court still held to a correct reading of the Constitution. Once again, claims that Federal legislation was necessary are inconsistent with the facts. The truth is that no significant Federal labor regulations were passed prior to 1933, the year the New Deal began. Yet consider this list of significant improvements which took place prior to that year:

- By 1920, workmen's compensation laws were in effect in 43 States[13]
- The average number of hours worked per week in all industries shrank from 57.3 in 1900 to 49.8 in 1926[14]
- Average hourly earnings increased more than three-fold over the same time period from $0.22 to $.71 in spite of minimum wage laws being struck down as unconstitutional.[15]
- From 1913 to 1933, workplace fatalities decreased from an estimated 61 deaths per 100,000 to 37, a 40% decrease.[16]

These improvements can only be accounted for by a combination of state regulations, technological advancements and a voluntary shift in the practices of private businesses, exemplified by the establishment of The National Safety Council in 1913, which sought to improve work-place safety. These improvements did not stop Congress from usurping power in the 1930s to fix a problem that was already being eradicated naturally by free citizens and State governments. This is not to say that federal legislation produced no results or that its effects have been all bad; nor does it suggest that societal norms at the time were all desirable. However, the data prove that change was happening without federal intervention, undermining one of the primary contentions made in its favor.

This point is further strengthened when we examine what happened once the New Deal hit full stride in 1937. Once the Court began putting a rubber stamp on New Deal legislation, rather than recovery and salvation for the unemployed, the country relapsed and sank deeper into the depression. The National Labor Relations Act (Wagner Act), the National Industrial Recovery Act and newly implemented Social Security pay roll taxes, among other things, combined to have a debilitating effect on employment.[17] In 1938, unemployment shot back up to nearly 20%.[18] After all the clamor and uproar over the Supreme Court's rejection of "essential programs," when it finally did capitulate, all we were left with was a Constitution in tatters, a government with drastically fewer restraints and just as much suffering and poverty as before. In 1939, FDR's Treasury Secretary Henry Morgenthau admitted "We have never made good on our promises."[19]

It must be stressed again that the merits of particular legislation should not justify violating the law. "The good sought in unconstitutional legislation is an insidious feature," said Howard Taft, because when those legal barriers are broken down, very little stands in the way of further government intrusion which is increasingly dubious in value and dangerous to liberty. Thus, we find that the Federal Government has taken it upon itself to regulate not only child labor and discriminatory practices, but a broad array of other subjects which have complicated our legal system, smothered entrepreneurship and left us with enormous amounts of debt. The "serious breach" the Court made in the "ark of our covenant" has needlessly condemned future generations to the endless train of abuses that have come about from the resulting explosion in the size of government, chief of which are a $17 trillion debt at the time of this writing, and trillions more in unfunded liabilities.

Whatever suffering may have been alleviated by the New Deal; and it would be generous to say that it alleviated any; must be weighed against the suffering that will be brought about when your children and grandchildren are forced to pay those debts. Whatever compels us to act on behalf of the less-fortunate cannot justify passing the bill on to others who have no voice. If the country truly believed that federal action was absolutely necessary and proper for the alleviation of poverty, and other societal ills, then we should have passed Constitutional amendments. That would have been the honest thing to do, and it would have been likely to produce more moderate changes which likely would have demanded discipline from Congress.

Perhaps the most prominent argument in favor of a big central government is simply that it came about by the will of the people. FDR, Lyndon Johnson and other progressive leaders were democratically elected and they carried out the wishes of those who elected them. If we don't want big government then we are free to vote against it in every election. Because we still have big government, it must be the people's will. It is democracy that serves as the source of government's power and keeps it in check.

There are four points to be made in response to this argument. First, the Constitution does not give us a democracy in which majority rule is the only factor in determining policy. The Founders were well-versed in classical history and they knew the pitfalls of many of the world's early democracies. Thus, Madison warned against "...the superior force of an interested and overbearing majority."[20] They also were all too aware of the danger of despotic monarchs. It was Hamilton who wisely stated that "Real liberty is neither found in despotism or the extremes of democracy, but in moderate governments."[21]

Seeking the proper balance, the Founders gave us a Republic, governed by three out of four bodies not intended to be directly elected by the people: the Senate, the Executive and Judicial. The President was to be chosen by the Electoral College, which were supposed to be a group of educated voters, chosen by the State Legislatures. The Senate was to be chosen by the State Legislatures directly, and the Judicial was to be chosen by the President and Senate. This is very far removed from a democracy. Presidents were to be chosen by a process designed to resist an impetuous political process. In early presidential elections, campaigning for oneself was seen as undignified. Unfortunately, presidential elections evolved to take on more populist tones and came to be dominated by political parties. Today, the original Electoral College is virtually non-existent.[22]

Virtually the same was true of the Senate. The Founders wanted in the Senate a group of leaders who would be wiser, more stable, and more likely to vote their conscience rather than pander to an unstable political process. The Founders were so adamant about this that they voted 10 to 1 against electing senators by popular vote.[23] Alexander Hamilton echoed the sentiments of the convention while debating about the design of the Senate when he said: "There ought to be a principle in government capable of resisting the popular current."[24] The Senate was also expected to protect the powers of the States. This is why they were given longer terms and were to be chosen by the State Legislatures. This all changed with the adoption of the 17th Amendment in 1913, which provided for the popular election of Senators within each State. This development certainly made it more likely that senators would vote to expand government handouts, as they were now tasked with winning popular approval rather than being accountable for protecting state sovereignty.[25] However, at least this change was done the right way: by Constitutional amendment.

In any event, these developments do not change the fact that all elements of government were to be bound by law, not majority rule. In his timeless book "The Road to Serfdom," F.A. Hayek dismissed the argument that because we get to vote for our federal politicians, it must be that government is acting within legal rules.

There is no justification for the belief that, so long as power is conferred by democratic procedure, it cannot be arbitrary; the contrast suggested by this statement is altogether false: it is not the source but the limitation of power which prevents it from being arbitrary.[26]

The source of government power is the Constitutional law, not majority vote. This brings us to the second point. Turn your attention again to the phrase "rule of law" and contrast it with "majority rule." In a country governed by rule of law, *the law rules,* regardless of what the majority wants. The majority may change the law by invoking the proper Constitutional means, but until that is accomplished, the law rules. To change the law by usurpation or judicial decree upon the demands of majority will is invalid. The purpose of this is to prevent popular passions and impulsive reactions from becoming the driving force behind legislation, and to ensure a steady and predictable legal system which, in turn, ensures the safety of natural rights to life, liberty and property. Of course, majority rule is an important mechanism in our system, but it is not, and should not be, the only means of determining policy.

Democracy has been described as two wolves and a sheep voting on what to have for dinner. This illustrates the reality that no one really believes in democracy because the minute it becomes destructive of natural rights the victims will abandon it with force. As Milton Friedman once said, "if 55% of the people vote for the other 45% to be shot, we would not think it just and would certainly fight it."[27] What is clearly shown in this extreme hypothetical is that we all understand the binding force of natural laws over and above the will of the majority. We only believe in democracy as long as the majority does not vote to take away the natural rights of the minority. The same concept holds true in a constitutional republic. Democratically elected officials are first bound to uphold our natural rights, which are partially (see the Ninth Amendment) enshrined in the Constitution. This would ensure that the majority could not simply vote to oppress the minority by, for example, confiscating a portion of their earnings and forcing them to participate in a retirement program against their will. James Madison referred to this danger when he warned of "faction[s]" in which "a number of citizens, whether amounting to a majority or minority of the whole, ...are united and actuated by some common impulse of passion, or of interest, adverse to the rights of other citizens..."[28] Thus, pure democracy, or any other system which fosters factious government, does not create a safe environment for freedom and is not an effective way to govern. The Founders understood this well and crafted the Constitution so as to limit the likelihood of citizen's rights being diminished by majority rule.

Here is the third point in rebuttal to the argument that big-government was the will of the people: no it wasn't. Many big-government programs, now considered popular, were not the result of popular demand when they were first conceived. They were either crammed down the throats of the American people or were a late response to popular movements that had already largely fixed the problem. Let's examine a few specific examples.

Public education may be cited as the ultimate government benefit which enjoys very popular support. But public, more accurately government, education was a movement begun by government officials and pushed along by teachers rather than being the result of unsatisfied parents. Contrary to popular belief, education was nearly universal and very few parents complained before government monopolized it. Early movements to establish government (common) schools were initially intended only to fill in the gaps left in primarily rural areas where few private schools existed. One report on the school system in the State of New York in the 1830s said:

> Under any view of the subject, it is reasonable to believe, that in the common schools, private schools and academies, the number of children actually receiving instruction is equal to the whole number between five and sixteen years of age.[29]

The vast majority of these students were educated in private schools. Gradually, the common schools began to grow as government followed the all-too-familiar pattern of expanding public benefits with little evidence showing a need for the expansion. Although the arguments for public education touted public benefits, the real motivation was supplied by newly formed teacher's associations interested in job security and steady pay.

Government officials seeking to make themselves more useful also led the charge for "free" schools. Horace Mann, largely credited with being the father of public education, was the first secretary of the Massachusetts State Board of Education established in 1837. Mann repeatedly argued that education was a good public investment and that it would increase economic output. After years of struggle and vigorous opposition, most of Mann's vision was implemented by the late 19th century.[30] Today, it is taken for granted that government-run schools are the best way to educate children. But history shows that rather than spurring government education, parents were mostly ramrodded into the system. Only now are parents beginning to see the stagnating effects of centralization as school choice movements continue to build momentum across the country.

Another example that shows many big-government programs were not in response to popular demand is the Occupational Safety and Health Administration (OSHA), a federal agency, founded in 1970, tasked with regulating work-place safety. Was there a spike in work-place accidents in the 60's? Were there nation-wide protests and strikes calling for more work-place safety? Not at all. In fact, work-related deaths were falling steadily both before and after the creation of OSHA.[31] But of course, OSHA loves to point out the decline only *after* its creation. The numbers show that OSHA has contributed *nothing* to the rate of reduction of work-related deaths, yet they have saddled businesses with numerous and costly regulations. This is not to assert that government programs cannot or do not produce desirable results; it is simply to show that many big-government programs have not been the result of popular demand as some have argued.

These examples highlight a common pattern with government. Politicians must constantly make themselves seem useful. So, they spend their time concocting schemes that make sense on paper (and even some that don't). It sounds good enough to voters: "Who could be against education and worker safety?!" and so the programs pass. As time goes on, it is taken for granted that voters "wanted it" so, politicians expand the programs as they compete to be more generous. As the program becomes entrenched over time, a lobbying group forms around it and people come to depend on the program's benefits. It then becomes nearly impossible to remove or even modestly cut the program as opposition to such initiatives is well-organized. In addition, it is easy for defenders of these programs to point out the supposed "victims" of such cuts, while it is difficult to demonstrate the tangible benefits of spending restraint, particularly when a small program is considered in isolation. And so the notion that such programs are the result of the people's will is solidified. Such is the pattern of many government programs which carry the façade of popular support.

Recall that one aspect of the argument in favor of big government is that if you don't like it, you can vote for someone else. Of course, this ignores the difficulty of removing government programs once they become entrenched. But let's examine another flaw in this argument in the context of the rule of law: politics.

This is the fourth point in rebuttal of the "will of the people" argument favoring big government. When the rule of law is strong, politicians at the federal level should only be responsible for a narrow set of issues which we get to influence through them. When the rule of law is weak, government expands its powers over time and politics, often used interchangeably with majority rule or democracy, comes to dominate nearly every aspect of our lives. In a majority-rule society, unrestrained by law, there is almost nothing which politicians will not eventually convince the majority to allow them to manage. Don't you *want* more safety? Security? Education? Jobs? Don't you *want* less fraud? Crime? Poverty? Rarely is it ever considered that these issues can be addressed with little or no involvement from government. Too many of us have simply become accustomed to the paradigm that government must play a central role in setting "national policies" such as job creation and social welfare. Benefits, particularly in the short-term, can be easily touted, while the long-term dangers are harder to use as arguments against government action. The more that is managed by politicians, the less is managed by the people. Increasing numbers of people and businesses are forced to deal with the government's various agencies while some are even robbed of the freedom and responsibility to fully manage their own lives.

The rule of law stands in stark contrast to simple majority rule. It ensures against an arbitrary government dominated by politics. When the rule of law is strong, politics are restrained because issues that might otherwise become political are left outside the domain of government. This ensures that most issues will be worked out by people operating through free exchanges in markets of commerce and ideas. In such an environment of freedom, cooperation and harmony are more likely to thrive. In contrast, when the rule of law is weak, politics dominate as those seeking for power pit one group against another; taxpayer against welfare recipient, old against young, Democrat against Republican etc. Issues that should be left in the hands of private citizens are co-opted by government, often crowding out private initiative.

A good indication of how far removed our government is from the rule of law is how politicized nearly every subject has become. Can you think of more than a handful of issues that have not been impacted at all by some government policy? In this environment, a class of demagogues has come to dominate the national discourse. The best ideas we can come up with are not based on reason or on centuries of human experience but rather on emotion, stirred up by cute slogans, pithy punch lines and dishonest 30- second commercials. Richard Nixon summed up how politics work when he told an aide: "I don't give a good g—damn what Milton Friedman says.   He's not running for re-election."[32] What is shown in this quote is that in the world of politics, the hard data and research of a Nobel Prize-winning economist is meaningless if it can't be sold to the public. Thus, anyone that stands in the way of government intrusion using facts, studies and history is more easily dismissed in the world of politics. It is much easier, in politics, to promote emotionally charged anecdotal stories of supposed victims suffering from any number of problems which government must fix. An elderly widow can't get along without Social Security; an underwater homeowner must have more "consumer protections" and on and on ad nauseam.

And of course, those of us who are suspicious of government are easy targets in the world of politics. If you believe that individuals would be better than government at providing their own retirement, it must mean that you have no heart and you want old people to "fend for themselves." If you want to get rid of OSHA because it violates the Constitution and does nothing to benefit work-place safety then you must want workers to die. If you believe that private markets are better than government at providing low cost, high quality health care and education, it must mean you are a greedy Scrooge who cares nothing for children. And we cannot forget about the political power of the race card. If you oppose the subsidy for colleges who graduate more minorities in agriculture it must mean you are a racist and don't want black people farming. A particularly disgraceful example of cheap politics was when Senator Chris Murphy of Connecticut told a television host that if you don't support gun control legislation, you want children to die.[33] And who can forget the commercial showing granny being wheeled off the cliff in response to a good-faith effort to reform a health care program that is trillions of dollars in the red.

As a result of this type of demagoguery, our freedoms have been diminished as government has virtually monopolized education, distorted housing markets, incentivized unemployment, confiscated wealth, and regulated health care to the point where it is prohibitively expensive for millions of Americans. Many go without insurance because the Federal Government does not allow insurance companies to provide affordable plans that fit individual's needs because bureaucrats must decide what goes in an insurance plan. The government's "solution" is to force those people to buy insurance which they cannot afford under threat of a fine which they can afford no better. That solution was passed using a level of demagoguery and dirty politics perhaps unsurpassed in our country's history, and signed into law by a President surrounded by children, as if to say that anyone who opposes the law must oppose children's health.

The *Helvering* ruling opened the door for the Federal Government to control people's retirement, and they soon followed up by intervening in nearly every other aspect of our lives and businesses, culminating most recently with a massive disruption of the free exchange of health care and insurance. We now live in an age of unfathomable government complexity and largesse. The dominance of political parties limits our choice of candidates. The vast power of government and attendant entrenched special interests limits the impact our chosen representatives can have. Masses of uninformed voters choose the politicians that can appeal to them in the most cost-effective way, which usually means little cognitive effort is involved. One year, when my wife went to vote, she told me of an 18-year-old coming in to vote for the first time. She didn't know what to do so she simply copied her friend's ballot. In this environment, do you take comfort in the fact that you can vote for your representatives in Congress?

The political process is an unwieldy way to run a country. Many people seem to have a difficult time understanding why our politics have devolved to such a level of divisiveness and downright silliness. The reason is simple: that is the nature of politics. Silliness and divisiveness are not a problem in Washington any more than a foul smell is a problem for a dairy. It is simply its nature and it has been that way since the founding of democracy. Any student of political history knows that our politics today, contrary to popular belief, are tame compared to the viciousness of campaigns in past decades. The real difference between then and now is not in the politics but in the number of issues that politics affect.

The Framers of the Constitution were all-too-aware of the corrupting influence of politics. That is one of the primary reasons they limited the Federal Government to the enumerations in Section 8. That is why they did not want political parties to develop. That is why they designed a Republic and not a pure democracy. The political process leads to short-sighted solutions based on election cycles with little regard for the long-term good of the country. If we want to avoid the damaging effects of politics then we must keep them contained within as narrow a sphere as possible by limiting democratic government.

In Federalist #62, James Madison explained the importance of structuring the Senate in a way that would ensure politics would have as little influence as possible in its operation. This is why Senators were to be chosen by the State Legislatures and were to have longer terms than members of the House. He said:

> The necessity of a senate is not less indicated by the propensity of all single and numerous assemblies to yield to the impulse of sudden and violent passions, and to be seduced by factious leaders into intemperate and pernicious resolutions.[34]

The amount of legislation brought about by "sudden and violent passions" would be difficult to calculate. The bulk of New Deal legislation certainly falls within this category. Once those had been passed, the Constitutional barriers were broken, and the precedent was set for politics and majority rule to dominate the law-making process, leading us to the enormous and complex legal and regulatory environment in which we now reside. This prompts the placement of a subsequent point made by Madison in the same paper:

> ...It will be of little avail to the people that the laws are made by men of their own choice if the laws be so voluminous that they cannot be read, or so incoherent that they cannot be understood... Law is defined to be a rule of action; but how can that be a rule, which is little known and less fixed?[35]

In an age where 1,000-page laws are passed through an impulsive process led by "factious leaders," we should take little comfort that we get to choose our representatives. The law-making process is something in which all good citizens should participate vicariously through their elected representatives. But when the laws cannot be understood by teams of dedicated experts, our votes become severely diluted as most people have little understanding for what lawmakers are doing. That lack of understanding creates greater separation between citizen and representative, which, in turn prompts even more government scheming as voter participation and involvement wane. The rule of law serves as a barrier to keep the political process from dominating large swaths of American life. A government, securely bound by legal limits on what it can do, helps to ensure that many divisive political issues are left to private individuals to work out on their own. When this happens, divisiveness is more likely to be replaced with cooperation or at least a "live and let live" attitude.

When we examine closely the arguments in favor of big-government, we find one strand that interconnects them all: more power for government. Progressive philosophy, no matter how noble its intentions, depends on greater government power. The very nature of its political ideology demands more power so that government can scheme, plan, control, regulate, tax, and redistribute. Of course, it is always claimed to be for good purposes, but there has never been a despot who did not claim he was trying to achieve noble ends. President Obama once remarked that you should reject the warning voices of those who claim that government power is dangerous.[36] He said this just weeks before the IRS and NSA scandals began making headlines. When someone in power is telling you to trust them with power that is the precise moment you should be suspicious. An excerpt from Thomas Jefferson's writings in the 1798 Kentucky Resolutions bolsters this point:

> It would be a dangerous delusion were a confidence in the men of our choice to silence our fears for the safety of our rights... Confidence is everywhere the parent of despotism... it is jealousy, and not confidence, which prescribes limited Constitutions to bind down those whom we are obliged to trust with power... Our Constitution has accordingly fixed the limits to which, and no further, our confidence may go... In questions of power, then, let no more be heard of confidence in man, but bind him down from mischief by the chains of the Constitution.[37]

Although it was crafted in response to government weakness, the Constitution was carefully designed to be a legal barrier against expansive government power. Power, particularly in the hands of government, should *always* be suspiciously held because we know from sad experience that it is the nature and disposition of nearly all men and women, as soon as they get a little authority, they will immediately begin to expand and abuse their power. Government is full of self-interested humans just as the rest of society, but there is a crucial difference: government makes the rules for the rest of us. No other private entity enjoys that power. Thus, we carefully guard against the abuse of this unique power by exalting the rule of law as opposed to putting our trust in the fickle discipline of the humans who hold it.

Government action gradually embraces a wider scope as time goes on. Madison observed: "Since the general civilization of mankind, I believe there are more instances of the abridgement of freedom of the people by gradual and silent encroachments by those in power, than by violent and sudden usurpations."[38] The isolated effects of each deviation from the rule of law may be small, but the cumulative effect can be catastrophic. That these deviations are gradual and silent lends credibility to President Obama's, and others', dismissal of government's potential to abuse power. That makes vigilance for the rule of law all the more important.

Another clever tactic used by statists to expand government is to simply redefine the core principles of the founding documents. The pernicious and common argument is that government must be empowered to act so that it can provide the things which the Declaration of Independence and Constitution claimed were the ends of government: life, liberty, equality, general welfare and domestic tranquility. These, they say, must be provided by government because not everyone can enjoy them equally due to a myriad of adverse and random circumstances beyond the control of individuals. This is a gross and deliberate misinterpretation of the Declaration's reference to our rights, ostensibly meant to mask big government with the façade of principled legitimacy. The sleight of hand is in equating "life, liberty and equality" with "shared prosperity." Those terms were never meant to signify prosperity nor were they meant to suggest that government should guarantee it.

First, a distinction must be made between the natural rights the Declaration talks about and the various unnatural privileges which make life more comfortable. We have a natural right to live, uninterrupted by the harmful actions of others. We do not have a right to be protected from natural diseases and random life circumstances to which we are all equally subject. We have liberty to work for the things we need and want such as cars, phones and a bigger home. We do not have a right to be provided with those things simply because they may enhance our liberty. We have a right to what we earn and produce. We do not have a right to what others earn and produce. The terms liberty and equality were not used in the Declaration to infer that government must provide things that would help us overcome the adverse effects of random circumstances.

Jesus' parable of the talents is instructive on this point. In life, some are given two talents, some five and some ten. What matters is not how many talents we are given but what we do with them, so that even the two-talent person is under condemnation if he does not use his freedom to make the most of what he has been given. The perverse teaching that we must take talents away from the one with more and give it the one with fewer does nothing to fulfill the promise of equality, nor does it enrich the life of either the "giver" or the receiver. Under this arrangement, the "giver" is encouraged to resist the confiscation of his property and is less likely to give willingly to those in need because his voluntary action has been partially replaced by coercion. Meanwhile, the receiver is robbed of the chance to earn what he has, and to learn the lessons that only struggle and self-reliance can teach. Worse, he has less opportunity to be the beneficiary of the genuine charity which would give him a deep sense of gratitude and kinship with his benefactors, as well as an obligation to make good use of it and eventually spread some charity of his own.[39]

When government is the distributor of "charity," not only is it woefully inefficient, but it builds a wedge between benefactor and beneficiary, which prompts the latter to disassociate the benefit from the beating heart that produced it, and to thereby feel more at ease remaining on the dole; while the former comes to resent the use of his property as a means to perpetuate indolence.

Liberty and equality under the law often lead to prosperity but it does not follow that government must provide prosperity in order to enhance liberty and equality. Liberty is not a system or a means to a higher political end. Freedom is the end in and of itself. Liberty is its own reward. We do not defend liberty because it produces prosperity. We defend liberty because we love liberty. People may well fail when given liberty, but if they have it, they have the most important thing the social compact has promised them. Prosperity, or, a basic level of income, is not a prerequisite for liberty and equality to exist. Those rights exist naturally regardless of our economic standing. Government's primary end is to protect rights, not make us comfortable.

Nor does the articulation of natural rights mean that the government should be involved either in imposing cooperation through welfare programs, or in prohibiting it through onerous regulations. It is true that domestic tranquility and general welfare were two of the main ends of the Constitution as articulated in its Preamble. But the misunderstanding is in the source of the prosperity which provides welfare and tranquility. The framers set up a Federal Government of limited powers because they understood that the source of prosperity is a free people who enjoy equal protection under the law, administered by a constitutionally limited government where property rights and freedom of contract are strong. They did not give the Congress the authority to preside over huge wealth transfer programs or to do anything else they thought necessary for prosperity.

It may be argued that some things conducive to prosperity, other than protecting property rights and freedom of contract, are worthy pursuits for government. It is true that when people suffer through no fault of their own, it becomes our duty to help. But to claim that people have *a right* to these things, protected by the Declaration of Independence and Constitution, is something very different. To make that assertion is to enter a realm of government vigilantism where Congress and the President are empowered to be the judge of what each person should have. Such a philosophy turns the Declaration and Constitution on their heads by assuming narrow individual liberty and expansive government power.

Those documents did not pretend to empower government to provide a job, an education, health care and anything else deemed necessary to live "equally" prosperous lives. Equality means that we are all equally free to pursue our own dreams. It does not presume the cynical attitude of envy which teaches that because someone else might have more wealth, it somehow diminishes a person's equal right to toil in their pursuit of happiness.

Tocqueville warned us that "The principle of equality ...predisposed men to endure" extensive government programs and "often to look on them as benefits."[40] The principle of equality is hard wired in all of us as an essential feature of a just society. But as the term is used in the Declaration, it made no reference to equality of material wealth or even of opportunity. If we make the claim that it refers to equality of opportunity, we are forced to concede that government should provide job training, or a myriad of other things necessary to equalize people's opportunities to succeed.

Equality never meant to protect people from random circumstances. It means that even if you are a "victim" of chance, you will still get the same treatment and protection from government. It means whether you appear in court wealthy or poor, you will have the same opportunity to defend yourself. It does not mean you are guaranteed a portion of the wealthy person's money. Equality means you get the same treatment from government regardless of your political persuasions. It means we are equally free to pursue our goals without infringing on the rights of others. It means that each individual is equally sovereign and independent over their person and property, regardless of the value of that property. The things most offensive to the equality spoken of in the Declaration of Independence are not the disparity between rich and poor, but rather the unholy influence that the rich often have on government, and the special treatment government gives to various industries and well-connected businesses, which, ironically, is precisely what makes income inequality greater than what it would be under more pure free-market conditions.

Those of us who love liberty are often falsely caricatured as hermits with no desire to cooperate with others. Because we see no legal role for government in redistributing wealth, it is claimed that we have no sense of community or of mutual support. Nothing could be further from the truth. In fact, *free* exchange and *voluntary* cooperation are invigorated by liberty and vice versa. Free people who have skin in the game through legally protected property rights and profit incentives will cooperate with others to the benefit of all. We rely on others to grow our food, make our clothes, build our homes, assemble our cars and a host of other things that free us to use our own talents for the benefit of others. That level of cooperation and mutual benefit is a function of capitalism, not government coercion and redistribution. Everywhere we look throughout history and our present world, it is the governments which exalt individual property rights that minimize poverty, maximize wealth and produce the most cooperation.

It is government that often stands as an impediment to cooperation through various regulatory schemes, rather than allowing rational, consenting adults to decide for themselves the terms of their economic relationships. Is it seriously contended that coercive government transfers make us any more benevolent and cooperative? Not only does government fail to accomplish that, but its extraconstitutional programs fail at having any significant impact on poverty reduction, the very reason it seeks to redefine equality in the first place.[41]

Inevitably, these philosophies are attacked as "social Darwinism" and as being offensive to our better natures because they supposedly leave people to "fend for themselves." Far from it. The real Darwinism was the era when those with the most weapons and manpower constantly sought to accumulate wealth by enslaving and conquering others. For thousands of years, humans lived in a brutal world where property rights only belonged to royalty; then came the Age of Enlightenment. We began to recognize natural rights and that governments, instead of plundering resources, should allow people to be free and to retain ownership of the things they earn, protected by law. We established republican government, not to ensure an equal distribution of goods, but to ensure that property rights and liberty would be protected. We established the rule of law to do away with arbitrary and forceful seizures of property. That created a system which demanded that people provide value to others through free exchange in order to accumulate wealth. It is this system of free markets and capitalism which requires cooperation in order to succeed, the opposite of "dog eat dog." Of course, competition plays a vital role in this system and that means some will fail. But it is precisely the threat of failure that drives progress and makes everyone better off in the long run. We did not institute republican government to protect people from competition. We did it to protect competition, without looters and plunderers, especially the government kind, arbitrarily intruding on the property rights which allow all of us to fairly compete. Competition, within the framework of property rights, contract enforcement, and bankruptcy protections, guarantees that individuals have equal protection to pursue their happiness by exchanging their talents.

Government does not ensure equality by manipulating the outcomes of exchange. Government ensures equality by neutrally enforcing the terms of the exchange. Complaints of large companies or wealthy individuals with too much "bargaining power," whatever that means, are simply unfounded.[42] When one takes advantage of another, there are always effective means to remedy the situation without relying on government compulsion: complain, spread the word, go somewhere else, unionize, boycott, strike, start your own company, etc. These methods aren't always the quickest, but they are far more powerful in the long run. Most importantly, they preserve freedom and avoid the inevitable negative unintended consequences of government coercion.

Of course, in the case of fraud or negligence government should act swiftly as these are in violation of the natural rights of others. The guiding principle for government should always be to protect natural rights, not to tip the balance of the scales when they judge something to be unfair. Not only is government not empowered to change the outcome of exchange, but it also cannot legally *compel* exchange where it feels it should exist. This is precisely what it does through Social

Security and various other welfare programs. Government does not ensure equality, and certainly not liberty, by forcing people to cooperate. Government ensures equality and liberty by protecting people's right to choose whether or not *they want* to cooperate and by enforcing those agreements; not by imposing its own agreements on people under the guise of making them equal.

Of course, any philosophy taken to the extreme can be dangerous. I do not mean to suggest that there is absolutely no role for government to play in poverty reduction or other prosperity-promoting policies. I mean to suggest that the primary ends of government are to protect natural rights, not to invent new ones, and that the bulk of domestic legislation, including anti-poverty measures, was to be reserved to the States or to the people. Constitutional legitimacy cannot be claimed by redefining equality and liberty to mean that individuals only have those rights when government sufficiently redistributes enough material wealth to them. Those concepts do not imply an active government involved in redistributing, scheming, planning and coercing people into the do-gooder's vision of material equality. They imply exactly the opposite: a passive government which only acts in the event a citizen's natural rights are infringed by another. Unfortunately, the lust for power will drive those who seek it to adopt nearly any philosophy which will aid them in their pursuits of it, regardless of how obviously it distorts the truth.

Fortunately for us, there was a group of men who resisted the lust for power: the Founding Fathers. Toward the end of the revolution, King George III inquired about what Washington would do after the war. He was told that he would go back to farming. The King replied that if Washington did that "he will be the greatest man in the world."[43] The Founders were of a select group of people who did not seek for power. Their lives coincided with a unique time in history which allowed them to serve as stewards over the transition of power from the old world to the new. They, particularly Washington, could have seized much more power and schemed to their hearts' content trying to fix society's problems; but they didn't. Instead, they dedicated their lives, their fortunes and their sacred honor to the task of creating a free, *self-governing* society with a government of laws, and not of men, which was to endure for generations.

Self-government does not mean simply that we get to vote for representatives who have nearly unlimited power to come up with ways to take care of us and regulate our lives and businesses. Self-government is not the freedom to choose your master; it is the *freedom to be your own master* and to have that freedom protected by law. It is a curious attitude, held by many progressives, which seems to suggest that our most sacred freedom is found in the political process in which we get to vote every few years for the kind of society we want. In a truly free society, we get to vote *every day* with our decisions about what kind of society we want, free from government coercion or manipulation. These decisions, made in markets of ideas and commerce, have a much more profound impact than any government policy could ever dream.

Free people tend to be more virtuous. That is why the Constitution created not only the wealthiest society in history but also the most benevolent. The rule of law helps to secure our self-governing way of life by checking government and thus, providing the incentive to cooperate and act charitably. On the other hand, arbitrary government, driven by politics, often creates division as it picks winners and losers through schemes of redistribution and regulation with a variety of negative unintended consequences. Those who would tout the virtues of democratic government would do well to realize that there is nothing more "democratic" than freedom itself. Our cumulative choices are what dictate prices, employment, education, charity and virtue. There is little rationale for turning these choices over to self-promoting politicians.

I have said that the prosperity of America is due to the liberty that has been afforded its people, but that is really incomplete. Liberty can only be pure enough to result in prosperity when it is properly harnessed by the rule of law; a law, which carries the consent of the governed rather than one that has been imposed by usurpation and judicial decree; a law which protects private property, the right of contract, and freedom of conscience; a law which maximizes freedom while maintaining order. These are what made the Constitution, and our nation, the most successful experiment in Republican government in the history of the world.

The rule of law, both natural and constitutional, is fundamental to a stable and prosperous society. No amount of feigned virtue should excuse us from following the Constitution when it hurts as well as when it comforts. Any supposed good that has come from the Federal Government's vast unconstitutional powers has been, or soon will be, offset by their negative consequences. We cannot ignore principle without sooner or later paying the piper. The virtues of the rule of law and of adhering to core values have shown the futility of trading long-term stability for a mirage of short-term benefits. Arbitrary rule by a politically-driven legislative process, by executive order, or by judges declaring what they think the law ought to be rather than what it is, have destabilized our society and created a system destined for collapse unless major reforms are enacted.

CHAPTER SEVEN

THE SOLUTION

We have spent a great deal of time up to this point establishing the correct diagnosis for our government problems. This was extremely important for determining the best way forward. To sum up, the diagnosis is this: the Federal Government has abandoned the rule of law by ignoring the limits placed on it by the Constitution as originally written. The Supreme Court had its opportunities to enforce Constitutional restraints but capitulated to FDR's New Deal programs. This has led directly to a massive, inefficient, redundant, debt-ridden, politically gridlocked, interventionist central government that has compressed liberty, burdened businesses, distorted markets and put future generations on the hook for tens of trillions of dollars in debt and unfunded liabilities.

The dilemma now is what to do about it. Before choosing among some viable alternatives, I want to address what might be called the "main stream" view of how to fix things. Of course, this view does not fully consider the diagnosis. It is caught in the wrong paradigm and, therefore, cannot be the correct way of solving the problem. It takes for granted that Congress is empowered to run the thousands of federal programs in existence. Democrats talk of raising taxes on the wealthy and cutting out fraud, waste and abuse to be more "fiscally responsible." Republicans talk about trimming government spending and returning some programs to the States. Both are caught up in an endless and predictable cycle of political gamesmanship that is poorly suited for producing substantive reforms. Party politics is simply not the proper arena to address the country's problems. We are fast approaching fiscal and economic collapse. Both parties are to blame for our mess and neither party has shown any real willingness to tackle the problem. The threshold is at our doorstep. Whether two, five, ten, or twenty years from now, we cannot afford to have a cross-your-fingers attitude and hope that Republicans will slow down Democrats just enough to keep us breathing until the next election cycle; or that Democrats will finally find that "fraud, waste, and abuse" and actually eliminate it.

We also have to consider the natural course of governments over time. Things will only get worse if we do not put in place more lasting changes. It was Jefferson who warned that "The natural progress of things is for liberty to yield, and government to gain ground."[1] No stronger evidence for this exists than our own history. If we extrapolate that history out into the future, imagine where we will be another 20 or 50 years from now if we continue with business as usual. No. We cannot continue to do the same thing we've been doing and expect a different result. As the definition goes, that's insane.

We have become too reliant on the political process to fix government. The political process is part of the problem and cannot safely be relied on to produce meaningful change. We should always seek to elect honest politicians who are seriously committed to liberty and constitutionally limited government. While it is conceivable that a large grass-roots movement strong enough to accomplish such a feat may take place in America, I'm not holding my breath. I would welcome it if it happened and I will be its strongest advocate, but the political process, as previously explained, is simply too unreliable for anyone to hope that it will produce a perennial limited government.

Yes, vote for every honest candidate. In the meantime, we have to also be working toward something more substantial in order to achieve the needed changes. Even if we were to elect a congress and president with honest hearts and a respect for limited government, we must understand how the current structure will work against them. Even the most capable of leaders will fail in an impossible scenario. There comes a point when we have to realize that the system is broken and that, no matter how talented and principled the people we send to Congress, there is simply too much dysfunction, partisanship, special interest and corruption. But even if they could succeed, how long would it be before another Congress came in to undo what had been accomplished? The structure of government is at least as important as who runs it. While we will have to depend on the political process to a certain extent, we must be fighting for more lasting structural changes.

With that, let's examine some more viable options for addressing our government's root problems. There is significant disagreement among those who accept the basic diagnosis of a government operating beyond Constitutional limits. Some have given up entirely and are simply living out what they see as the last days of the United States the best they can. Others are pushing for more extreme measures such as nullification or even armed rebellion. The truth is that most options beyond giving up and short of armed rebellion should be used in conjunction rather than in competition with each other. But not all methods are equally effective.

Some continue to hold on to hope that we might eventually get a Supreme Court to overturn the New Deal Court's decisions, or at least qualify them with meaningful restrictions on Congress. If this were to happen we could achieve the structural changes to government necessary to restore meaningful limits. Under this scenario it is possible that a new string of lawsuits may arise challenging many big-government programs. All or parts of these programs may then be overturned. That is a radically simplistic description, but simple does not mean impossible. There would be many details left to be worked out but the principle is not unprecedented. After all, it was the New Deal Court itself that paved the way for radical shifts in jurisprudence which overturned long-standing precedents. The difference here of course, would be a justifiable return to the text of the Constitution rather than an unjustifiable departure from it.

One might argue that the Supreme Court's hands would be tied, even if they decided to hear a new case challenging say, Social Security. But lawyers put too much stock in precedent, at least in comparison to the stock they should put in the Constitution. When deciding a Constitutional question, the first thing a judge should look at is the Constitution itself, not some previous judge's interpretation of it. Only in extremely difficult cases, where Constitutionality is ambiguous, should a judge have to rely on previous court precedent. A judge's oath is to uphold the Constitution, not the jurisprudence which has decimated its meaning. It should also be noted, that many times in history, the Court has chosen to override precedent when a particular policy was clearly unconstitutional, as in the case of *Brown v Board of Education* overturning *Plessy v Ferguson*.[2] Where would we be now, if the Court had simply ignored the text and spirit of the Constitution and accepted every decision that was handed down from previous Courts who got it wrong?

There are serious flaws with relying on the Courts. First, hopeful predictions about what will happen with the Supreme Court are about as reliable as winning the lottery. Judges usually don't turn out as statist or as Constitutional as their cheerleaders had hoped, as in the case of John Roberts and his bizarre decision on the Affordable Care Act. Then there is the question of what would happen if a program like Social Security were suddenly overturned. This could potentially produce disastrous results for the people who rely on the program, depending on the particulars of the law suit. For these reasons, hoping that the Court will have a change of heart is about as useful as hoping that Nancy Pelosi will come to understand the meaning of the General Welfare Clause. If it happens, we would welcome it, but the Court is not likely to suddenly change their tune, at least not to the degree necessary to restore meaningful limits on Congress.

Another option considered by some is nullification. This doctrine, advocated by Thomas Jefferson in the 1798 Kentucky Resolutions, asserts that States have a right and a duty to refuse to enforce or comply with unconstitutional federal laws, effectively rendering them null and void within that State. Recently, there has been quite a spat between conservatives who advocate for nullification and those who want new Constitutional amendments. This is puzzling because there is nothing in either method that contradicts the other. Both methods can be used.

However, nullification, in its extreme forms, is a fool's errand. Amending the Constitution will certainly have its difficulties, but the key difference however, is that Article V (the part of the Constitution which prescribes the method of amendment) is actually written in the Constitution, whereas nullification is merely implied. We cannot get the courts to enforce the *text* of the Constitution which limits government let alone an *implied* theory. In any event, I am all for using any peaceful and lawful method that enforces Constitutional discipline on Congress including nullification. What defies sense is why any friend of Constitutional government would be opposed to either method other than a disagreement as to which is the best tactic. Even then, there is no reason we cannot pursue both courses simultaneously. If I were a state legislator, I would vote to nullify the Affordable Care Act one day, and vote to apply for a convention on the next to make sure that such an act could never be passed again. If the courts strike down the nullification, as they almost certainly would, then we would be right back to the option of calling for an amendments convention, which, as it turns out, could be used to put nullification, or something similar, in the text of the Constitution.

Given the proper diagnosis for our government problems - that the Constitution has been largely abandoned - we must look to our government charter for the right remedy. The reason we have an out-of-control government, with its attendant political gridlock, is because the Congress, the President and the Courts have ignored the plain text and meaning of the Constitution. If our problems originate with the Constitution, that is, the Court's misguided interpretations of it, then so too will our solutions. We need a series of amendments which will clarify its meaning, restore its significance, and re-establish meaningful restraints on the Federal Government.

Other than the first ten amendments, the Constitution has been amended 17 times over our history. Some of those amendments were a bit trivial, such as the 26th, which set the voting age at 18. Others were much more foundational, such as the 14th, which guaranteed equal protection under the law for all citizens. It is insightful to go back and read 19th century and even early 20th century political speeches. Most of them are replete with references to and discussion of the Constitution. Today, nearly every policy discussion in Washington is completely void of reference to the Constitution. Somewhere along the line we swept it under the rug.

The Founders implored their posterity to use the amendment process if we thought government needed more powers or needed powers taken away. James Madison, and his successor James Monroe, both vetoed internal improvements bills then asked for Constitutional amendments to allow that type of federal activity.[3] George Washington, in his farewell address, gave us this parting counsel:

> If, in the opinion of the people, the distribution or modification of the Constitutional powers be in any particular wrong, let it be corrected by an amendment in the way which the Constitution designates. But let there be no change by usurpation; for though this, in one instance, may be the instrument of good, it

is the customary weapon by which free governments are destroyed.[4]

There are some who would view the Constitution as sacrosanct. They would contend that changing the Constitution would be tantamount to heresy and that the better path would be to adhere to its meaning as is. To this Thomas Jefferson responded:

> Some men look at Constitutions with sanctimonious reverence and deem them like the ark of the covenant, too sacred to be touched. They ascribe to the men of the preceding age a wisdom more than human, and suppose what they did to be beyond amendment... I am certainly not an advocate for frequent and untried changes in laws and Constitutions... But I know also that laws and institutions must go hand in hand with the progress of the human mind.[5]

The process of amendment is what should have been used by Roosevelt in the 1930's. Instead, he and Congress used the "customary weapon by which free governments are destroyed," and the Court let them get away with it. Rather than use the properly established method of amendment, progressives in the early 20th century concocted the contemptible doctrine of a "living Constitution"; the idea which basically contends that the Constitution can be re-interpreted to fit the needs of whoever is in power. This is the opposite extreme of those who think the Constitution should not be touched. The term "living Constitution," a phrase wrought with patronizing insult, was part of a tactic deliberately designed to side-step the Constitution's barriers to government overreach and is still used by nearly every modern-day progressive.

Upon closer examination, the inherent contradiction in this phrase becomes apparent. What gives the Constitution life is our strict adherence to it, and our wise decisions to surrender to its boundaries. The Constitution is living only as long as we heed its clear meaning and amend it when that meaning does not align with proper legislative objectives. The moment we try to get around it by sophistry and judicial decree is the moment of its death. None other than Rexford G. Tugwell, a previously cited architect of Roosevelt's New Deal, had the moral fortitude, later in his life, to recognize the error of the "living Constitution" doctrine.

It [the Constitution] was interpreted to allow the establishing, and the enormous growth, of many presently existing institutions without any Constitutional authorizations whatever – such as the massive regulatory system. There are many public activities not contemplated in any of the Constitution's clauses – education, social insurance, and the system of national highways to name a few... The authority for them has been extrapolated, sometimes without any Constitutional reference. This, like other extensions, is elaborately justified by legal theorists who speak of a "living Constitution." What they mean is that the Constitution can be made to mean anything thought necessary to getting on with public and private business. But what then becomes of the law...? It vanishes, of course, except that the Supreme Court takes its place... This decline of trust in Constitutionality can, of course, only be remedied by reconstituting the process of amendment.[6]

It should be noted that Tugwell remained an ardent progressive all his life. He wanted a new constitution which would have explicitly granted more power to government. But what he recognized was the importance of adhering to the people's charter, the government's permission slip to do certain things and no more. He knew that gaining power by usurpation undermined credibility and loyalty to social institutions. The fact that he arrived at these conclusions is a testament to his honesty, which, if imitated by other progressives, would provide fertile ground for a higher form of debate and problem solving.

Unfortunately, most progressives will not admit that they have no use for the Constitution, except for the parts that align with their beliefs. Thus, we hear Barack Obama complaining in a 2001 radio interview that the Supreme Court did not go far enough to overcome the Constitution's restraints, or that the Constitution does not say what government must do on behalf of citizens, such as redistributing wealth to them (which, by the way, is essentially an admission that redistribution is unconstitutional).[7] To be sure, progressives aren't the only ones who ignore the Constitution when it suits them. When "conservatives" passed the Patriot Act, it was every bit as offensive to the Constitution as Social Security. But there is no question that the Constitution's limits on power are most destructive to progressive tenets. Thus, the charade of a "living Constitution" is put on to justify extra-constitutional programs while garnering the political advantage of appeasing those who still respect that charter. If you don't like what the Constitution says, then admit it and let's debate a possible amendment. As the quotes from some of our leading Founders indicate, there is nothing wrong with changing the Constitution to meet our needs. But to obscure your true opinions for political gain is destructive to honest and productive debate.

Even more destructive is sweeping the Constitution under the rug and continuing with the illusion that government acts with Constitutional authority when it has none. A 2011 Time Magazine cover asked if the Constitution still matters. The question was superimposed over an image of the Constitution being put through a shredder. The basic conclusion from the author was that it does still matter, but we shouldn't let it get in the way of "progress."[8] Translation: it matters only when it suits us. Can that really be said to be a living Constitution? These attitudes mock the rule of law and undermine self-government; part of which means that we the people should ratify changes to the Constitution; not judges, not the President and not Congress without the approval of the States.

Some have coined the term "originalist" or "strict constructionist" as labels for those who interpret the Constitution according to its original meaning. Such labels should be rejected because they imply that there is some other legitimate way to interpret the Constitution. If a judge were asked to enforce a modern contract between two private parties, we would find it strange to refer to the judge as a "strict constructionist" for enforcing the text and intent of the contract. When a judge reviews a statute, she explores the debates in the legislature to understand the language and intent of the legislation in question. What kind of chaos would ensue if judges neglected to find legislative intent in the statute under review and simply substituted it with their own judgment about what they thought was expedient? The entire legislative process would be corrupted beyond recognition. Why would interpreting the Constitution be done any differently? Indeed we find that in numerous cases throughout the 19th century, judges labored to review founding documents in search of original intent; a practice all but forgotten today. The only reasonable and legitimate way to interpret *any* legal document, especially a constitution, is to construe it according to the plain meaning and intent of its text according to its authors. Anything else is to substitute the rule of law for the arbitrary rule of politicians and lawyers.

We must do away, once and for all, with the patronizing nonsense of the "living Constitution" doctrine. It is not a poem subject to the interpretation and feelings of the reader. It is a legal document with clear and specific intent. It either means what it says, or it is meaningless. Instead, let us revive a truly living Constitution by passing a new series of amendments which will renew its force and re-establish it as a strong barrier to government power. This approach will not perfectly restore all of its original intentions, but it will have several advantages.

First, the process does not rely on Washington. Article V of the Constitution provides a method by which the States can call for an amendments convention independent from the control of Congress. Expecting Congress to fix Congress is futile. Congress is the problem and cannot be relied on for the solution. Therefore, any process that doesn't involve Washington should be considered the best choice.

Second, Constitutional amendments will produce powerful and lasting changes. It is not good enough to hope for politicians to statutorily restore Constitutional government. Such measures have already proven to be pitifully inadequate. A perfect example is the debt ceiling. Congress has imposed on itself a statutory limit of how much debt they can pile up. But what happens when they get close to that limit? You guessed it, they raise the limit; something they have done *75 times since 1962.*[9] When Democrats enacted a "pay-go" system in 2007, a provision which requires new spending to be offset by cuts in other areas or revenue increases, Congress had no difficulty waiving the requirements any time they wanted to increase spending without discipline.[10] Any self-imposed limits on what Congress can do are useless and underscore the need for deep structural change from without.

I wrote earlier in this book about the endurance of the Bill of Rights and how it has come to be more significant today than it was when ratified. This is because its language is simple, direct and usually in the negative; that is, it says what government cannot do. One of the reasons our government abandoned the Constitution was because of the ambiguity surrounding the General Welfare Clause, which resulted in disagreement about what government *can* do. Simply worded amendments that plainly spell out what government cannot do are much more difficult to get around than simple grants of power.

For example, when government is authorized to levy taxes, what exactly does that mean; all kinds of taxes? Can they tax for any reason they want? Can they levy a poll tax? Can they tax you if you don't buy health insurance? These types of questions surrounding the Federal Government's authority to tax have been brought up and debated literally from the founding up to this day. A negative power, on the other hand, would not yield the same result. Consider the language of the second amendment: "the right of the people to keep and bear Arms, shall not be infringed;" simple, direct and unmistakable. This is not to suggest that the right to bear arms has not been without encroachment, but in comparison to other parts of the Constitution it has remained firmly intact since its ratification. Therefore, if we want lasting and meaningful restraints on the Federal Government, we should pass negative amendments which explicitly delineate what government cannot do. These will be subject to far less misunderstanding and will guarantee additional barriers against government overreach for generations to come.

Third, this approach will have the potential, as far as it is possible, to transcend politics. The Constitution still retains the healthy respect of most Americans. If there is any one thing that can bring political opponents together, it is the Constitution. Left, right or center, any fair-minded person will admit that our government is out of control, and Constitutional amendments may be necessary to get the structural changes which most people know we need.

Most good Americans value liberty as well as the many good and necessary things government does. If we attempt to work through the Constitution, we can have a much more constructive debate on how to achieve a balance between liberty and government power that will suit modern realities. This may get us beyond the politically driven gridlock that frustrates so many Americans. There must be compromise from conservatives and libertarians, and there must be an admission from progressives that we have indeed abandoned the Constitution and should, therefore, work to re-establish constitutionally legitimate government. Doing this will shift the focus of the debate on the real issue that divides us; the proper role of government, while minimizing, as much as possible, the debilitating influence of politics.

Fourth, this process will restore a healthy respect and attention to the Constitution and to the rule of law. We cannot sustain the system which would give to government whatever authority it requests during an election or during a crisis, with no thought of Constitutional restraints. The amendment process is itself an additional check on government power. We the people have granted to government the power to do certain things through the Constitution. If they want more power, or if we feel they need more power for a specific purpose, then it should be granted in the proper way. If it cannot be done that way then it shouldn't be done. This guarantees that if we are going to error, we will error on the side of freedom. It also ensures a greater respect for social institutions which must carry the consent of the governed. It has been suggested by many economists that respect for social institutions plays a vital role in how effective they can be. With so many federal agencies spread out over the country making and enforcing increasingly burdensome laws, a deep distrust and resentment of these institutions is growing rapidly. It will only end in disaster unless deep Constitutional reforms are enacted. Our consent must come from more than just an election. It must come from the Constitutional framework which dictates predictable and understandable rules for government.

Fifth, from a strategic perspective, using Constitutional amendments to achieve structural change will have the advantage of playing on the one thing all politicians want: power. We can use that to our advantage by getting State governments to take some of it back from the Federal Government. The goal would be to restore some semblance of federalism as part of a new modern system. One of the principle barriers to centralized power was the operation and power of the States. This has been completely eroded today and must be restored at least far enough to put a stop to the Federal Government's unsustainable growth. Alexander Hamilton, when writing about the amendment process in the Federalist Papers, said: "We may safely rely on the disposition of the State Legislatures to erect barriers against the encroachments of the national authority."[11] Rather than hoping that Congress will relinquish its own authority, it is much more practical to hope that Governors and State Legislatures will wrest back some of the broad authority assured to them by the Tenth Amendment. If we can play on the nature of politicians to our advantage then we should do so. The design of the separation of powers is partly to rely on the jealousies of the different branches. Those jealousies can and should be incited in the States to restore a proper balance of power between them and the central government.

The amendment process has been used successfully numerous times throughout our history; the 13th banning slavery, the 14th guaranteeing equal protection under the law, and the 19th guaranteeing the women's vote among others. These amendments have been lauded with great fanfare as crucial advancements in Constitutional law as well they should be. We have the opportunity to add to that legacy with new amendments that can help fulfill the vision of liberty and limited government.

Of all the amendments, the 18th and 21st are the best examples of how the process should be used, or rather, *that it should be used in the first place.* The previous three I mentioned were really overdue manifestations of previously unachieved Constitutional ideals. But the 18th and 21st Amendments, the prohibition of alcohol, and then the repeal of it, give us a perfect example of how to proceed when we see a problem which has no provision for federal intervention, and for which we believe federal intervention may be necessary. We saw alcohol consumption as a national problem which broke up families, led to unemployment and destroyed lives. We recognized that the Constitution did not allow the Federal Government to deal with the issue, so we amended it as provided by Article V. A few years later, we saw what a disaster that policy was, so we went back to Article V and amended it back to the way it was. We could have dug up the long-since dismissed arguments of Hamilton and Story, and used the General Welfare Clause to pass prohibition laws without amending the Constitution, but we didn't. When we realized prohibition wasn't working we could have simply removed the law-enforcement agencies and not enforced it, but we didn't. We did it the right way. We saw a problem, we made an attempt to fix it through an amendment; it didn't work, so we amended it again. Now, we simply sweep the Constitution under the rug and take it for granted that the Federal Government has the authority to prohibit the sale and consumption of marijuana and cocaine, as well as a long list of other powers deemed to be for the "general welfare."

Had we used this process to bring about other changes in government, we likely would have suffered much less abuse and might not be under such a heavy burden of debt. The amendment process would have brought the debate into a more honest light and would have allowed provisions for checks and limits on the newly granted power as well as guarantees against certain other encroachments. With Social Security, for example, we might have been guaranteed the freedom to opt out, or to consider other options such as a state run or private system where we could retain full ownership of our earnings. At a minimum, we might have avoided the blatant treachery of Congress in raiding the Social Security trust fund and leaving behind government bonds in its place.[12]

To our condemnation, we did not use the properly prescribed Constitutional method for changing government. This has led to massive debt, out-of-control regulations, corrupted legal and tax codes, and consolidated power in Washington. The only way we will fix these problems is by revitalizing the Constitution by reconstituting the amendment process to achieve structural changes in government. The political process and the courts are too unreliable. We will need the political process to gain a foothold. Sooner or later, we cannot achieve what is needed without good and honest men and women who will put the long-term interests of the country before their own ambitions. But once those people are in office, we cannot simply settle for a temporary cutback in government. We must seize the opportunity to leverage the power of the States to call a convention.

CHAPTER EIGHT

THE NEW CONVENTION

The process of calling for a convention will be a long and hard struggle. It will require unity of purpose from those committed to limited government. Unfortunately, many *conservatives* are wary of amending the Constitution. If this process is to have any chance of success, there can be no division among conservatives so let's address some of their concerns. Their three main arguments are; 1) the convention might produce unwanted amendments, or rewrite the Constitution altogether in a "runaway convention"; 2) they contend that if Congress does not follow the Constitution now, there is no reason to believe they would follow any constraints from new amendments and; 3) the problem, they say, is not with the Constitution but with the government's refusal to follow it.

The first flaw in these arguments is that the first two contradict each other. Why should we fear dangerous amendments if Congress won't follow them? If government ignores the Constitution now, there can be no harm in new amendments which will not be followed. Congress already claims a power to do virtually anything it pleases. A government that ignores new amendments is the same as a government that ignores the current Constitution. A runaway convention is no less desirable than the runaway government we already have. In essence, we have nothing to lose but much to gain by calling a convention.

A more punctilious rebuttal to the idea that a new convention might produce dangerous amendments, or rewrite the Constitution altogether, is the process of ratification. A minimum of 38 States must ratify any proposals made by an Article V convention for it to become the supreme law. In addition, Article V does not allow for a new Constitution to be written but only allows amendments to be *proposed*. The convention cannot do anything authoritative on its own. Even if, in the unlikely scenario the convention went rogue, whatever changes they propose would have as much effect on the Constitution and our form of government as a hill of beans (subsidized of course). In essence, it can only make suggestions to the States on how to amend the Constitution. Law professor Robert Natelson has compared a convention to what we might call a task force.[1] It is simply a body of chosen delegates whose purpose is to consider an issue and propose solutions. The *implementation* of those solutions rests with the States that called for the convention. A whopping 75% supermajority is required to make the convention's proposals into law. The implementation, or the ratification process, is where the real struggle takes place. There is simply no way that any radical or dangerous amendment, let alone a new Constitution, would be ratified by 38 States.

The second argument, that new amendments would not be followed, is equally unfounded. This belief ignores the current context of the government's Constitutional delinquency. For 150 years, the Constitution was respected and was largely effective in checking government power. Congress did not simply decide out of the blue to blatantly ignore the Constitution. It took decades of political and legal struggle, spurred by cultural and economic changes, to undo Constitutional constraints. While it is conceivable that some future crisis after a long string of Court rulings might impel a departure from any new amendments, it is unlikely that Congress would simply thumb their nose at them immediately after their ratification. The nation's familiarity and closeness with the new amendments would certainly be a powerful political deterrent to any tendency to ignore them. In addition, we can and should place enforcement mechanisms in the amendments themselves, such as giving States standing to sue in court over any violations. These additional safeguards would effectively close the door on any concerns that new amendments would quickly be set aside.

The third argument against a new convention is that the real problem is not with the Constitution but in the government's refusal to follow it. First, *there are* flaws in the Constitution. The 16th and 17th Amendments drastically altered the original formula, and have greatly contributed to an out-of- control government. Without the income tax, we would not have the government we have today. That necessarily implies that if we want to fix our government, we must address these changes through Constitutional amendment. Second, our current government ignores the Constitution because it has decades of precedent and legal acquiescence which give it the pretense of legitimacy. So, in effect, the government *thinks it is following the Constitution;* but they are really following a warped version of it. This tells us that a healthy respect for Constitutional government still exists and lends further support to the assumption that new amendments would not be simply ignored by Congress. What we are seeking to do with new amendments is to replace *the Court's misguided interpretations* of the Constitution, not its original text.

The best and surest way of overturning bad jurisprudence is to use the amendment process. That is what the progressives did after the Supreme Court struck down the income tax. It is what we should do to overcome *Helvering v Davis* and other bad Court rulings. Another good example of this is how the 14th Amendment overturned the infamous *Dred Scott* decision in which the Supreme Court declared that African Americans were not citizens and could therefore not sue in federal court.[2] The problem was not the Constitution. There were many African American citizens prior to the *Dred Scott* ruling. The problem was the court's *misinterpretation* of the Constitution. This could only be remedied by the passage of a new amendment, the 14th, which gave citizenship to all those born in the country, and subject to its jurisdiction, regardless of color.

These examples provide an excellent historical precedent showing what should be done to overcome misguided judicial review. New amendments would have the same effect in correcting, not flaws in the Constitution, but the mistakes of the Court's rulings, particularly during the New Deal. This process, brought about by a national movement, would set a *new precedent* of palpable constitutionality which would realize the goal of limited government.

It is not clear whether conservatives who are against new amendments are going too far or not far enough. If you love liberty and constitutional government, but are *not* in favor of new amendments, it must mean that you believe the Federal Government should simply follow the Constitution as written and return to its 19th century form. In this sense, you are going too far. If you are opposed to new amendments because you believe the process is too dangerous, and we should rely solely on elections, then you aren't going far enough. Federal elections are never going to result in lasting change, and the dangers of the amendment process are overstated at best. We should not let fear keep us from trying the Constitutional method the Founders put in place to rein in a usurpative Federal Government. As for the former line of thought, the smallest Federal Government possible would be ideal, but we cannot let our vision and values blind us from what can reasonably be expected.

It is one thing to talk about Constitutional government, as many Tea Partiers and some Republicans do. But how do we actually achieve it? How do we make the Constitution meaningful again? Honesty and adherence to the Constitution would demand that we phase out every federal program that does not have at least a plenary relationship to the Constitution's enumerated powers. This would include Social Security, Medicare, Medicaid, welfare of every form, subsidies of all kinds, education, housing, etc. But is this achievable? Do we really believe that there will ever be enough votes in Congress to abolish the Department of Energy or Education? As desirable as that would be, it is simply too unlikely to be relied on.

So how do we balance between restoring some semblance of the federalist vision given to us by the Founders and the modern reality that we will never again see a Federal Government less than 10% the size of the economy? The success of the Constitution was predicated to a great extent on balance. A new convention can only be successful if we seek balance and compromise for our time and circumstances. We are not going to restore the original understanding of the General Welfare Clause or of the Commerce Clause. But we can do some things that will limit those powers. In the following chapters, we will discuss specific amendments. You will find that none of them would preclude us from continuing to fight for as small a government as possible. All we are fighting for now is to save the Republic from disaster. The fight to limit government will go on forever.

We cannot let our respect for the Founders evolve to such a level of reverence that we believe their work should not be touched. We must govern ourselves according to our time and circumstances just as they did. Any new amendments should apply founding principles to modern realities. We will never again have a 19th century Federal Government. We should not constitutionalize the federal leviathan, but to believe we can abolish it through elections and nullification would lend it just as much longevity. Those methods alone will never produce the needed structural changes. Why not use every method at our disposal, *especially a Constitutional provision*, to realize the principles of limited government and rule of law?

Of course, this discussion would be greatly enhanced if we knew the specific amendments being proposed. But before we get into those, we have to discuss the process of calling for a convention. One hurdle to calling a convention is simply the fear of the unknown, which can only come about through misunderstanding. Many are skeptical of State conventions. Not much is known about them, and they seem a little radical because they are not used often. Few seem to know what to expect. So let us plainly lay out the facts.

Though the practice is virtually forgotten, the States retain the power to call for a convention just as they did in the late 18th century. Not only is the right of convention guaranteed in the Constitution itself, but it is an inherent right of any State, in concert with others, to select delegates and assemble them for the purpose of amending the charter which they themselves created. Conventions have been an integral part of American legal tradition and problem solving. There have been at least 15 conventions since we declared independence, with the last one taking place in 1922.[3] There have been numerous other interstate meetings intended to resolve various issues, such as the one that produced the Delaware River Basin Compact between Delaware, New York, Pennsylvania and New Jersey.[4] Based on our history, calling for a convention is a predictable, safe and practical process for solving big and complex problems.

What would a modern convention look like? Surprisingly little has been written about this subject in comparison to other Constitutional issues, but there is plenty of scholarly work to draw on which gives us a fairly clear understanding of how the process will work. I will spare the reader of most of the legal and technical triviality, favoring instead a general overview of what is most important. Of course, law and procedure are important (that is why I wrote this book!), but if we understand the problem, and are resolved to fix it, we can work through the technicalities. Those interested in the legal nuance can consult the work of Robert G. Natelson.[5]

Article V of the Constitution prescribes the manner in which amendments can be added. It is very simple. Either two thirds of both houses of Congress or two thirds (34) of the States can apply for a convention. At the convention, amendments are suggested, debated, refined and then officially proposed. The amendments must then be considered by the State Legislatures or by conventions in the States for ratification. Three fourths (38) of them must approve an amendment before it becomes part of the Constitution.

There have been numerous and convoluted excuses which have attempted to thwart the state convention process: Congress will interfere, runaway convention, can't trust the State legislatures, we don't know the rules, the President would issue an executive order, and on and on. These complaints arise because of misunderstanding. Even if a few of them have merit, it is not a valid excuse for abandoning a convention. We do not stay in the house because we might get in a car accident. We venture out to get things done and deal with the obstacles as they arise. Regardless of what the obstacles might be, here are the relevant facts:

1. The State Legislatures control the process for calling a State-led convention, including the selection of delegates. Congress and proponents of big government may very well try to interfere with the process when the convention gains momentum. In the end, it may all come down to a lawsuit decided by the Courts. Understandably, that might make some people skeptical, but the language of Article V, and the history and jurisprudence behind it, are unmistakably in favor of an amendment process free from congressional manipulation. Even if the Courts did manage to get it wrong, it would be equally wrongheaded to let that fear deter us. We have a duty to do our part and let the Court do theirs.

2. Congress has no discretion over any part of the process other than to choose between two predetermined methods for ratifying the amendments; whether by the State Legislatures or by conventions in each State. The one time Congress chose to use State ratifying conventions, for the 21st Amendment, the States were left in complete control of delegate selection.[6] Once the requisite number of applications is reached, Congress has no discretion. They are compelled to call a convention. The State convention process was designed specifically to bypass Congress.

3. Neither the President nor any governor has any say in the process. We know this from the operation of past conventions and from the language and intent of Article V. The legislatures may authorize their governors to play a role, but that is up to them. An executive

order trying to interfere with the process may as well be used as fire-starting material. There is no pretext or legal rationale for the President to interfere.

4. The convention procedures are decided by the delegates, or by instructions from the state legislatures. The delegates choose the leaders, committees, rules of debate and voting. They may alter the one-state, one-vote system used in previous conventions by, for example, using a voting procedure that mimics the Electoral College. Whatever the rules, there is no warrant for using this uncertainty as an excuse to not hold a convention.

While, in one sense, these are important issues, they are trivial compared to the overall mission of the convention itself. The enemies of limited government want us to be conflicted and hesitant. If our resolve is where it should be, no procedural issue will stand in the way of the process. In that spirit, we must keep in mind four important points as we work to call for a convention.

First, delegates must NOT be chosen by popular election. Any movement calling for popular election of delegates should be rejected with force. The legislatures are calling for the convention. It is their privilege alone to choose the delegates. Our country has been brought to the brink because of politics. We cannot allow the pettiness of partisanship and election grandstanding to ruin the convention. We do not need the best campaigners and orators in the convention; we need the best minds, honest hearts and sound principles. The politics of this country have become too destructive to allow such an influence to taint this undertaking. The State Legislatures are not perfect but are more likely to choose delegates wisely than a misinformed public.

Second, we must set aside our pride. We cannot allow our personal ambitions to derail the process. We must be more focused on the end goal and less focused on who gets the credit. There are plenty of intelligent minds and honest hearts to choose from as delegates. Ambition and competition among ostentatious and glory-seeking individuals may be as big a danger as any to the success of a convention. The reason the Constitution was successful is partly because those who created it set aside their vain ambitions in a spirit of problem solving and a sense of higher purpose. We must do the same.

Third, the convention must be held in secret with strict rules of silence from the delegates and tight control over access to the meetings. The Framers held the 1787 convention in secret because they knew that public opinion about what they were doing might taint the proceedings. The same holds especially true in our day of ultra-fast mass communication. The delegates must feel at complete liberty to speak openly and honestly so that all ideas can be completely vetted and deliberated according to conscience. There will likely be great opposition to this as many will complain that the process should be open to all. But if we understand the nature of a convention as a sort of task force that can only make *proposals,* then we will understand that it is more proper for the delegates to operate independently and in secret. Modern task forces routinely operate this way. Open and public debate will play its role during the struggle for ratification.

Fourth, there must be compromise and inclusion. The movement for a convention has already begun with conservatives. That, in and of itself, will be pointed to as a reason to discredit it by those on the left. We cannot be baited into fulfilling their stereotypes. Always and everywhere we must reach out, in a spirit of compromise, to all honest and sincere Americans. That means we must concede some ideas which we will not like. We simply cannot gain the numbers we need for ratification without honest Democrats. The good news is that there are some issues which can naturally gain widespread support such as an amendment that might strengthen privacy rights in this age of technology and terrorism. Whatever the substance of the compromise, we must keep an open mind while maintaining focus on the overall mission of limiting the Federal Government's powers.

We can look to the 1787 convention as a model for the new in terms of the spirit that must prevail. Back then the debates were contentious and interests were divided. Many of the framers marveled that the Constitution was able to be completed at all. But because the majority of them made their interests secondary to solving problems, they produced perhaps the greatest legal document known to mankind. We know the consequences if we fail to gain control of this Federal Government. Nothing the new convention produces will be perfect, just as the Constitution was not perfect. But if we focus on honest problem solving and the dire consequences of failure, we cannot help but find a way to come together.

What specific changes should be made? Most apprehensions about a convention (at least from conservatives) would be greatly diminished by a discussion of what amendments should be made. So, let's begin:

Amendment 28

Article V of this Constitution shall be amended as follows: The Congress, whenever two thirds of both Houses shall deem it necessary, shall propose Amendments to this Constitution, or, on the application of the legislatures of three fifths of the several States within ten years, shall call a Convention for proposing Amendments, provided that the requisite number of applications be concerning the same subject, which, in either Case, shall be valid to all Intents and Purposes, as Part of this Constitution, when ratified by the Legislatures of two thirds of the several States; Provided that no State, without its Consent, shall be deprived of its equal Suffrage in the Senate; and Congress shall have no power to regulate the state conventions, applications or ratification process in any manner.

One of the biggest flaws in the original Constitution was the process for amendment itself. The Founders wanted to provide a way for the States to amend the Constitution, independent of Congress, so that they could act as another check on federal power. However, they simply made the requirements for this too strict by calling for three fourths of the States to ratify new amendments. During the ratification debate, the Anti-Federalists raised this concern. One of them, writing under the pseudonym John DeWitt, said this:

> ...such is the difference of interest, different manners, and different local prejudices, in the different parts of the United States, that to obtain that majority of three fourths to any one single alteration, essentially affecting this or any other state, amounts to an absolute impossibility.[7]

Patrick Henry, one of history's greatest champions of liberty, pointed out how easy it would be for good amendments to be thwarted:

> ...a trifling minority may reject the most salutary amendments. Is this an easy mode of securing the public liberty? It is, sir, a most fearful situation, when the most contemptible minority

can prevent the alteration of the most oppressive government; for it may in many respects prove to be such: Is this the spirit of Republicanism? ...If, Sir, amendments are left to the twentieth or tenth part of the people of America, your liberty is gone forever.[8]

Once again, the warning voices of the Anti-Federalists have proven to be prophetic. Not one amendment has been passed by way of the States calling for a convention in our more than two-century history, in spite of the many abuses which the States have endured. The Federal Government has bribed, intimidated, pressured and cajoled the States into becoming mere administrative arms of Congress. The difficulty of passing amendments through the States is compounded in our day by the increased number. Getting three fourths of thirteen States to pass an amendment is much easier than getting three fourths of fifty.

The original Article V calls for two thirds of the States to call a convention and three fourths of the States to ratify amendments. These requirements should be changed to three fifths for a convention and two thirds for ratification. This would make amendment more achievable while still requiring a super-majority so that frequent changes would be avoided. Remember, three fourths requires 38 States and two thirds 34, while three fifths would require 30. 38 States is extremely difficult; 34 is plausible, but 30 is practical. The point is to revise Article V so as to give the States a real chance of becoming a more probable check on federal power. Requiring any more than 34 States to achieve this would render the process virtually useless, as history has shown.

Further changes are made in the proposed amendment which would unmistakably deny Congress the ability to regulate or impose conditions on a state-held convention. These may prove unnecessary depending on how the next convention goes, but history has shown that it is smart to word Constitutions in unmistakable terms. It is not lost on me that we will have to get 38 States to ratify these changes. We will need one monumental push so that we can make further changes possible.

The Founders envisioned a federalist system in which power would be divided between the States and a national government. The principle provisions they put in place to preserve that balance were the Tenth Amendment, the state legislature's power to choose the President and Senate, and the portion of Article V which allows States to create amendments independent of Congress. As we have seen, all of these provisions have either lost their original character or have been set aside altogether.

The strict requirements of Article V have prevented the passage of some potentially good amendments, such as one allowing Congress to regulate child labor. After the Supreme Court ruled against federal regulation of child labor in *Hammer v Dagenhart,* Congress was forced to try to amend the Constitution. They should not have tried to regulate child labor in the first place, knowing it to be unconstitutional, but once they were checked by the Court they did what should be done when we want to make a change to government. Eventually, 28 States ratified the Child Labor Amendment (8 shy of the 36 of 48 States required at the time), but when the Court abdicated to broad Congressional power in 1937, the need for ratification dissipated as Congress assumed broad regulatory powers in contradiction to the Court's long-established precedent. Congress gained by usurpation what was then in the process of being granted by Constitutional amendment; the way George Washington advised us to make changes. It is interesting to note that the Child Labor Amendment is still pending before the States.[9] In *Coleman v Miller* (307 U.S. 433, 1939) the Court declared that proposed amendments could be ratified over any time period as long as Congress did not specify a time limit. An extreme example is the 27th Amendment, which was first proposed in 1789 and ratified in 1992 without a new convention. This admits an almost comforting thought that once the convention finishes its work, we may have plenty of time to win the ratification fight, though the window for reform is narrowing.

Another important example showing the requirements of Article V to be too strict was that 33 States had passed resolutions calling for a balanced budget amendment in the early 1980s, only one shy of the 34 needed for a convention.

Because of the difficulty of passing amendments, the proper channel for changing government has been virtually abandoned, and government fell for the allure and ease of usurpation to make changes. Going all the way back to Madison's call for an internal improvements amendment up to Johnson's "war on poverty," one is left to wonder how much mischief may have been avoided had the amendment process been practical enough to invite changes through the proper channels, rather than concocting preposterous legal theories such as a "living Constitution," or even going ahead with changes without any legal theory whatsoever.

This amendment will do much to realize the wise, but poorly executed vision of allowing the States to amend the Constitution. We have seen and learned from more than 200 years of experience that this is a desperately needed change. The balance of power, so carefully crafted by the Founders has been completely thrown off. This amendment will help to restore that balance by giving the States a more practical means of changing the structure in which Congress and the President operate.

There have been other suggestions for a State check on Congress, such as giving the several legislatures a veto power over federal laws. Some have also proposed to repeal the 17th Amendment and return the choosing of Senators to the State Legislatures. I am not totally opposed to these but amending Article V as I have outlined would still be important for one reason: constitutions matter. Governments must operate by rules which dictate its limits. We need to be constantly aware of the structure under which the Federal Government operates. That is much more likely to happen when it is more practical to amend it without federal involvement. Part of the reason our political system is broken is because of Constitutional neglect; not just that it isn't followed, but that it isn't even discussed. The 28th Amendment, as proposed here, is designed not just as a State check on federal power but also as a means to make the Constitution more meaningful in political discourse. If the States could more easily change the rules Congress has to follow, it would have this effect. Restoring the Constitution to national prominence and to a central role in policy debates is one of the key points of amending it.

If we do not loosen the requirements for amendment outside of Congress then we will subject our posterity to the same difficulties under which we are now suffering and perhaps worse. We should make it easier for them to change the form of government without having to resort to more extreme measures.

CHAPTER NINE

SPENDING AND ENTITLEMENTS

Amendment 29

1. Congress shall not spend more than twenty percent of the average real gross domestic product, from the three years prior, of the United States annually, except any amount used to extinguish the debt.

2. Congress, when they shall have declared war, or upon the approval of three fifths of the State Legislatures within one year, may remove this cap for a period of two years, after which it shall resume force; and in the case of war all expenditures above this cap shall only be for the war effort.

3. This amendment shall apply to the unified budget of the United States. Congress shall have 10 years to make necessary provision for the implementation of this amendment, after which it shall take full effect.

4. Each of the several States, jointly or individually, shall have standing to sue Congress for any violation of this amendment.

Once we have achieved a greater likelihood that States can amend the Constitution, this amendment is the most important and desperately needed of any. It is out-of-control spending that makes government the biggest threat to the country. Controlling the money is the most effective method of controlling what government can do; so if we want to get Washington under control we must start with the money. If we cannot limit the Federal Government by holding it to specifically enumerated powers then the next best thing is capping the amount of money it can spend.

Here is a brief recap from Chapter five. In 2013, the Federal Government spent $3.6 trillion.[1] That is about $40,000 for each family of three in the country. It is more than double what we were spending in the year 2000.[2] Most troubling is that over the last three years, the Federal Government has eaten up between 22% and 24% of the economy, the largest share in history during peace time.[3] While spending has currently leveled off, it is poised to start climbing again soon, reaching the onerous $4 trillion mark in 2016.[4] From there, federal spending will reach 31% of gross domestic product by 2030 and 37% in 2040.[5] Combined with State and local spending, that would mean government would be consuming more than half the country's income. The urgency for a spending cap could not be higher.

There are several ways which we could use to limit federal spending. We could attach spending to revenue growth, as the Swiss have done, or we might limit spending growth to inflation. Certainly the convention would prescribe the remedy they would think best. However, capping spending as a percentage of GDP is the preferable method. This is because it is a more stringent and definite limit, and does not admit an easy means of manipulation. Considering the nature of governments, it is wise to put limits in unmistakable and easily discernable terms. In any event, any spending cap must be based on a crucially important principle which is immediately and plainly clear to any reasonable person: government should not grow faster than the private economy which supplies its revenue. Economist Dan Mitchel has called this the golden rule of economics. A spending cap is a simple and straightforward way to implement this wise rule as it will force Congress to grow the economy before it can consider expanding its programs.

Because there will be inevitable screams of "extreme, draconian, and heartless" let's put this amendment into a bit of perspective. If GDP is $15 trillion, that gives government a maximum $3 trillion budget.

Quite simply, a budget that large leaves no room for the complaint that government cannot meet its obligations, particularly considering the fact that much of what it does is unconstitutional and destructive to private markets. In any event, we are not saying we cannot take care of the less fortunate or regulate the economy. And for the John McCains and Lindsay Grahams out there, we are not saying we cannot meet our national security obligations.   We are simply contending that government be restrained to 20% of GDP.

A 20% cap is not a totally arbitrary number. It is both a moderate proposal and one which will impose badly needed discipline. A 10% cap would be better but is not possible.   Anything over 25% would be pointless because it would not do enough to bring real discipline to Congress. The best guide we can use to choose an appropriate cap is the historical average. From 1947 to 2012, federal spending averaged 19.8% of GDP.[6] A 20% cap, therefore, is a good number based on history, and shows what a moderate proposal this is, especially considering the burden of government spending before Roosevelt's New Deal, which averaged well below 10% in peacetime.[7]

Of course, a spending cap only makes sense if you understand the source of the country's prosperity: the private sector. Any complaint that is raised against capping the government's ability to spend on "badly needed public services" is simply based on a misunderstanding of where prosperity comes from. It is exactly backwards to think that we should strengthen government so it can strengthen the economy. The government depends on the economy, not the other way around. Politicians who grandstand about creating jobs, helping the vulnerable, policing the world and a myriad of other activities should be forced to realize that it is the growth of the economy that makes all those things possible. That will only happen if a cap is imposed on them.

Before going any further it will be useful to address somewhat of a competing amendment: the balanced budget amendment. A balanced budget amendment is deceptively dangerous. For starters, a balanced budget amendment eliminates deficits, but it does not necessarily eliminate the ability or desire of Congress to spend. If we had a balanced budget right now, but were spending the same amount of money, we would be much *worse* off because in that case, the government would be taxing another trillion dollars out of the economy.   An over-emphasis on debt, rather than the size of government, paints us into a corner of accepting tax hikes. If we cap spending then the debt problem will take care of itself. (I will show later that only modest spending restraint, without cuts, is needed to balance the budget.)

Tax increases on the wealthy are much easier to achieve politically than most spending cuts, and would therefore likely become the preferred method to balance the budget. This is exactly what we have seen from European countries which have passed balanced budget or low-deficit requirements. Perhaps most pertinent is Spain, which amended its constitution in 2012 to require a balanced budget by 2020 and beyond.[8] The result was that the Spanish government made Spain one of the highest taxed jurisdictions in Europe with a top marginal rate of 52%.[9] Not surprisingly, the economic situation in Spain is a disaster, with unemployment at around 25%.[10] Something very similar happened in Italy, which also passed a balanced budget amendment in 2012. Once again, the focus on deficits and debt led to far more tax increases than spending cuts. From 2009 to 2012, 80% of Italy's deficit reduction came from tax increases.[11] The country's GDP then shrank 2.4% in 2012 and a further 1.8% in 2013.[12] Taxes and the size of governments all over Europe are threatening bankruptcy and economic collapse because their fiscal rules have focused on debt and deficits rather than spending. When we focus on debt, we open the door for massive tax increases, which are always easier to achieve politically than spending cuts. In turn, those tax increases only justify politicians spending more rather than paying down debt. This vicious cycle has been repeated many times and will continue until spending restraint is practiced.

Of course, most balanced budget amendment proposals recognize this danger and carry a super majority requirement for any tax increase, implying that the budget would almost have to be balanced by spending cuts. Even if we suppose that a super-majority requirement for tax increases is successfully implemented into a balanced budget amendment, the danger would not be removed. In fact, this might even create a more dangerous situation. A balanced budget amendment will not stop government from wanting to spend, and politicians have demonstrated extraordinary creativity and resolve when they want more money. If a super-majority is required to raise taxes, Congress will get around that requirement by multiplying and increasing fees and fines to squeeze more money out of the populace. We will find higher fees for airline tickets, cell phone service, permits and everything else the Federal Government can get its hands on. We will find an increase in duties and tariffs which will restrain trade. Congress will also likely empower the IRS even further to shake down people and businesses for every penny, making that agency even more thuggish than it already is.

Most certainly, Congress will raise taxes indirectly by removing loopholes. Given the choice between cutting a program or eliminating a loophole for corporations and the wealthy, it is clear what Congress would choose. Even without a balanced budget requirement, we have seen in recent years how strong the desire for tax increases on the wealthy has become. Congress is addicted to spending. If we tell an addict that he can continue indulging in his vice so long as he does not use debt to finance it, all we will have accomplished is to add thief to the title of addict.

Finally, we could rest assured that tax rates would never come down under a balanced budget amendment, meaning the U.S. would permanently be home to some of the highest corporate tax rates in the developed world. If Congress becomes even more revenue aggressive than it is now, keeping rates high and eliminating credits and deductions, it is clear what would happen to investment and economic performance. The wealthy have a number of good choices around the world for their money. This is not the time to back Congress into a corner and give it little choice but to find more revenue.

We might mitigate some of these dangers with a tedious wording of the balanced budget amendment but a much simpler and easier solution is simply to cap spending. Attempting to limit spending by making it contingent on revenue will only cause government to look for every possible way, oppressive or otherwise, to get revenue. The better alternative is to cap spending *independent* of revenue and thereby remove any need or incentive on the part of government to get more money out of the economy. It is certainly possible that Congress would restrain spending under a balanced budget requirement, but under a spending cap, it would *certainly* restrain spending – and a spending cap has the added benefits of simplicity and being void of any danger comparable to that of a balanced budget amendment.

Unrestrained government spending is a direct cause of harm to an economy. Debt is a mechanism for governments to merely delay that pain. Why go after that mechanism when we can go directly to the source of the problem? A balanced budget amendment may do no more than make the pain of government spending more immediate and acute because it does not directly require restrained spending. A spending cap would remove the ability of Congress to cause the pain in the first place, whether it comes about immediately by taxation, or later by debt.

To summarize, there are four reasons a Constitutional spending cap is the best option for improving the long term fiscal outlook of the

United States. First, it focuses on the *real* problem: out-of-control spending. Deficits are bad, but they are a symptom of a much deeper problem: a big government. If we get rid of the underlying cause of debt, then debt will naturally diminish. Second, a spending cap amendment would draw a definite barrier of how far government can grow; gaining us significant economic benefits while holding us true to the bedrock American principle of limited government. A balanced budget amendment would do little to ensure the private sector that more money will not be taken away, and, in fact, will actually increase the determination of Congress to get more revenue. Third, and perhaps most important, this amendment would have the added benefit of forcing Congress to reform entitlements, which will be the biggest drivers of spending and debt in the near future. Fourth, a spending cap will allow government to pay down the debt, something a balanced budget amendment will not likely achieve. When Congress gets a surplus with a spending cap, there is only one thing they can do with it: pay down the debt. Under a balanced budget amendment, surpluses are not likely to be achieved because Congress would much rather fund a program for political gain than pay down the debt. Congress will most likely spend every dime they get, unless they are blocked by a cap.

Let us continue making the case for a spending cap by showing in detail why government spending is the real problem. There are three main reasons for governments to spend money: 1) to carry out basic functions such as to ensure property rights, guarantee contracts, and operate a criminal justice system; 2) to stimulate economic activity; 3) to redistribute wealth for purposes of "fairness" or "equality" or "social justice." No serious person calls into question the first purpose for government spending so we proceed immediately to a discussion of government's ability to stimulate the economy in order to show the necessity of a Constitutional spending cap.

There is widespread disagreement among economists as to government's ability to stimulate economic activity in the short term. We can divide the debate among those who follow the theories of John Maynard Keynes and those who adhere to the theories of Ludwig von Mises or Frederick A. Hayek. In 1936, Keynes published his famous "General Theory of Employment, Interest and Money" in which he advocated for government spending during recessions in order to "jump start" the economy. He reasoned that since consumers don't spend a lot of money during a recession the government can make up for the shortfall in demand by spending on infrastructure and other projects.

This would restore overall demand to "normal" levels and would return the country to a healthy economy.

On the other hand, Hayek and Mises argued that recessions are part of natural market corrections. Recessions then, are not necessarily the problem, but are necessary adjustments following a period of malinvestment. They contended that if the economy were left alone, it would naturally rid itself of whatever was causing the recession, and would recover much more rapidly than if government got involved.

Most of the debate between these competing theories occurs because of the sheer complexity of the issue. Many factors affect economic prosperity, and because there is even disagreement about how to properly measure economic prosperity, it is very difficult to prove the causality of any single factor. Not only that, but politics muddle the debate as well. Of course, politicians would rather be seen as doing "something" to help the economy rather than nothing, particularly when people are out of a job or are otherwise struggling. The issue becomes further complicated by a variety of factors that influence the effectiveness of fiscal stimulus, such as the causes of the recession or the manner in which the stimulus is implemented.

In spite of the murkiness of the debate, there does seem to be a general consensus among economists that fiscal stimulus can be effective. This should not surprise us. It is clear that economists are better served by making fiscal stimulus out to be an effective policy. If the right policy is to do nothing, as Hayek would have argued, then economists and politicians both have much less useful roles to play. If there are no plans, no formulas to solve, or no management decisions to be made then economists become much less important in national debates.

Nevertheless, we will accept the moderate consensus for our purposes here. This does not diminish the case for a spending cap. In fact, it may even strengthen the case. The consensus on the effectiveness of fiscal stimulus comes with many caveats. For starters, even most Keynesians agree that, *on average*, the positive effects of fiscal stimulus are mild.[13] Then consider that a stimulus package, according to Keynesians, must be delivered with the right amount, at the right time and in the right way in order to be most effective. The likelihood of achieving this through a slow political process with 536 squabbling politicians is very low. Perhaps most pertinent for the present state of the U.S. economy, nearly all economists agree that the effectiveness of fiscal stimulus diminishes significantly in relation to a country's debt. The higher a country's debt, the less likely fiscal stimulus will work. This is because people and businesses tend to save more and spend or invest less if they anticipate taxes going up in the future to pay for the increased debt, implying that the stimulus may only have a further depressing effect on private sector consumer spending and business investment. This is likely the primary reason so many attempts at fiscal stimulus have been ineffective, including our own in 2009.[14]

This is why Keynes himself advocated for *spending restraint* during times of prosperity. This is the part of Keynes theory that is typically ignored by pundits and politicians. Spending restraint during prosperous times would allow for *surpluses* to be available for economic stimulus during recession without accumulating debt over time. Keynes never argued for large deficit spending in the same way that today's Keynesians do. His theory was a countercyclical approach that advocated for spending restraint and surpluses when the economy was strong in order to finance deficit spending during a recession.

All of this highlights the need for structural restraints on government's ability to spend. Politicians cannot be trusted to restrain spending on their own while revenues are increasing during prosperous times. If spending is left unchecked, accumulating debt will diminish the effectiveness of fiscal stimulus if and when it is tried. A spending cap will lower debts over time and, thus, potentially make fiscal stimulus more effective. Whether or not the theories of Keynes or Hayek are employed by government, long-term spending restraint plays a vital role in both. The bottom line is that a spending cap should be structured in a way that allows for fiscal stimulus in the short run but also enforces discipline in prosperous times. As someone who subscribes to Hayekian principles, this is more a matter of compromise to get the amendment passed. The political process will still allow for the possibility of laissez faire.

The 29th Amendment proposes to base the cap on the average GDP of the previous three years. When a recession hits, the higher GDP of the previous three years allows for government to spend a higher percentage of GDP in the current year so that a recession will not lower government's ability to spend when stimulus is needed. It should also be considered that stimulus would be much more effective under a spending cap because the fears about stimulus becoming permanent will dissipate. Part of the reason stimulus may be ineffective is because of the uncertainty about the size and growth of government. A spending cap however, will signal to the economy that government will not grow past a certain point unless the economy itself grows.

Most economists recognize that free and open markets are the most powerful drivers of prosperity, and that the basic functions necessary for successful markets, such as the protection of property rights, can be effectively managed by *small* governments.   Large governments, on the other hand, eat up a greater share of the private economy and, thus, tend to be a drag on economic growth.   Let's examine a few studies which show this to be true.

In 2009, Harvard economists Alberto Alesina and Silvia Ardagna put together an extensive study of 21 Organization for Economic Cooperation and Development (OECD) countries covering a nearly 40-year time period from 1970 to 2007. They set out to determine the effects of government spending and taxing on economic performance and debt. They summarize their results quite simply:

> Fiscal stimuli based upon tax cuts are more likely to increase growth than those based upon spending increases. As for fiscal adjustments, those based upon spending cuts and no tax increases are more likely to reduce deficits and debt over GDP ratios than those based upon tax increases. In addition, adjustments on the spending side rather than on the tax side are less likely to create recessions.[15]

> ...The evidence from the last 40 years suggests that spending increases meant to stimulate the economy and tax increases meant to reduce deficits are unlikely to achieve their goals. The opposite combination might.[16]

In other words, if a government wants to reduce debt and provide for better economic prosperity, it is more likely to achieve these ends by cutting taxes and cutting, or least restraining, spending. It seems a bit odd that these studies even need to be done in order to show this, but let's continue.

In 2011, European Central Bank economists Antonio Afonso and João Tovar Jalles produced a working paper exploring the relationship between government size and economic performance. They studied 108 countries' economic performance from 1970 to 2008. Their results showed a significant *negative effect* on growth by the size of government and that government consumption is consistently detrimental to output growth regardless of the country. They also found that the positive effects of quality government institutions are stronger when governments are smaller.   Most pertinent to our discussion of a spending cap is that Afonso and Jalles found statistically significant evidence that having strong fiscal rules improves GDP growth. Not only did these authors conclude that large governments have a long-term negative impact on growth, but they also found that institutional fiscal rules which limit a government's ability to spend have a positive impact on growth:

> Our results show a significant negative effect of the size of government on growth. Similarly, institutional quality has a significant positive impact on the level of real GDP per capita. Interestingly, government consumption is consistently detrimental to output growth irrespective of the country sample considered (OECD, emerging and developing countries). Moreover, i) the negative effect of government size on GDP per capita is stronger at lower levels of institutional quality, and ii) the positive effect of institutional quality on GDP per capita is stronger at smaller levels of government size.[17]

The part most pertinent to a constitutional spending cap is this snippet from the authors of the study:

> Finally, and for the EU countries, we find statistically significant positive coefficients on overall fiscal rule and expenditure rule indices, meaning that having stronger fiscal numerical rules in place improves GDP growth.

In 2012, Indermit Gill, chief economist at the World Bank, and Martin Raiser released a 500 page report analyzing economic growth in Europe. In Chapter 7 of their report, they discuss the impact of the size of government on economic growth. The following chart, recreated from their data, clearly illustrates the relationship between government size and growth.

Growth is Slower as Government Gets Bigger

Median growth by average government size as a percent of GDP for EU
countries, 1995–2010

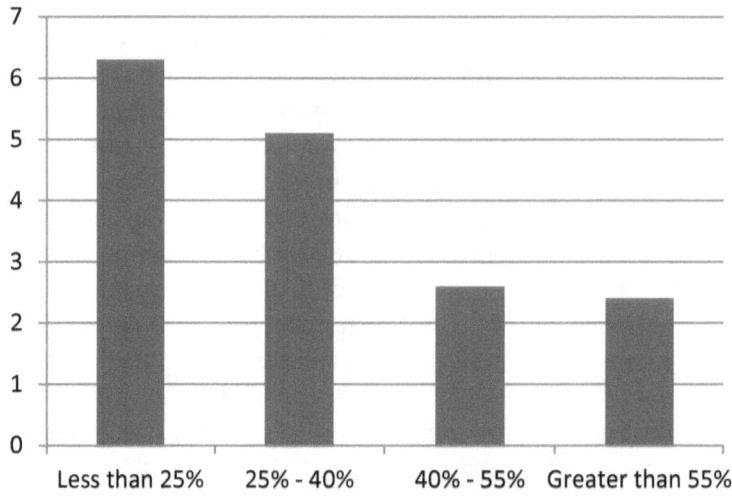

Recreated using data from Gill and Raiser, *Golden Growth*, 364

The authors found a much less pronounced relationship for the
world average. But it is important to note that it is much more useful to
compare developed nations such as the United States and Germany
than it is to compare Canada to Zimbabwe. The suggestion is that the
need for spending restraint is much greater in developed nations such
as the United States. As the chart and the authors of this report
indicate, a tipping point of government spending of 40% of GDP seems
apparent, meaning that the negative relationship between government
size and economic growth becomes more pronounced near this level of
spending. Given that the United States currently has a burden of
government spending of about 40%, when state and local government
spending are factored in, the impetus for a spending cap becomes
stronger; and this percentage will only continue to grow without
reform.

Gill and Raiser stated several reasons for why big government is bad
for growth.[18] Chief among them, of course, is the taxes required to
support it. Taxes cause producers and consumers to adjust their
behavior in order to avoid paying them, meaning that some activities
are discouraged. People might work less or may not have as great an

incentive to acquire new skills while businesses may turn down opportunities to expand. Also, as government grows bureaucracies give rise to special interest groups which are more determined to expand their own power and influence rather than work for the public good. Government growth is largely driven by social transfers. This creates dependency among a growing share of the population which, in turn, increases the political pressure to expand the programs and their attendant taxes. As those taxes slow the economy and decrease the number of good-paying jobs, the calls for more transfers grow louder, leading to a vicious cycle. Finally, government spending tends to have a crowding out effect on private sector investment, meaning that when government spends on certain activities, private entities decrease their investments in those areas. Decreased investment from the private sector prompts its own vicious cycle as government continually tires to make up the difference. Significantly, Gill and Raiser also note that the essential functions of government, such as the protection of property rights and the rule of law, can be carried out by small governments.

Similar to Afonso and Jalles, Gill and Raiser also found that deep structural changes in the form of fiscal rules may be necessary to get better government. Constitutional amendments are the only way to achieve the "profound change in institutions" spoken of by these authors.[19] This speaks to one of the central premises of this book, which is the idea that the solution to our government problems cannot be solved by simply voting in a fresh batch of politicians who promise to make government more efficient. We need binding structural changes to our Constitution in the form of fiscal rules which limit government's ability to spend. Only then can we realistically hope that Congress will truly get its fiscal house in order.

The crowding out effects of government spending alluded to by Gill and Raiser merit special attention. Remember, government can only spend what the private sector produces. The more money they spend, the greater the tendency to crowd out private sector employment and investment. This implies that government spending, intended to help the private economy, at some point becomes counterproductive. In a recent brief, David Ranson from the National Center for Policy Analysis explained some of his findings about government's crowding out effects from studying U.S. federal spending from 1929 to 2012:

> the data ...show that not only is the cumulative private-sector response to changes in federal spending consistent, inverse and

proportionate, but it appears also that a $1 increase in federal spending reduces private spending by more than $1.

The economy has limited economic resources that federal spending cannot evade for long. On average, each additional dollar that the Federal Government spends on consumption or investment is soon offset by a reduction of at least a dollar in what the private sector spends. ...This phenomenon has long been known as crowding out, but it seldom plays the role it should in government policy discussions. Conversely, a cut in federal spending is made up quickly by a gain in private-sector spending crowding in.[20]

Economist Livio Di Matteo from the Fraser Institute conducted an extensive study of the relationship between government size and economic growth. He reviewed 14 *additional* studies spanning several decades which generally found a negative relationship between the size of government and economic growth. In other words, as governments grow larger, economic growth tends to slow, particularly beyond a certain threshold and in developed countries such as the United States. Here are the conclusions from Di Matteo:

Ultimately, whether a large public sector—and by extension a large tax burden—has a positive or negative effect on economic growth is an empirical question and numerous studies have examined the relationship.

A survey of the literature shows that numerous studies document a negative empirical relationship between government size and economic growth rates.

Regression analysis leads to the conclusion that over the first decade of the twenty-first century ...there is a hump-shaped Scully curve relationship between the government expenditure to GDP ratio and the growth rate of per capita GDP. All other things given, *annual per capita GDP growth is maximized at 3.1 percent at a government expenditure to GDP ratio of 26 percent*; beyond this ratio, economic growth rates decline. This demonstrates that there is an optimal size for the public sector when it comes solely to the effect on economic growth. Naturally, what size the public sector should be is also about broader societal outcomes but, even then, the evidence suggests that there are few additional benefits once the public sector reaches 30 to 35 percent of GDP.[21] (emphasis added)

These findings are consistent with those of Gill and Raiser which show that a certain threshold exists beyond which government spending becomes increasingly self-defeating. Di Matteo gives an even lower estimate for that threshold; 30% to 35% of GDP as opposed to 40%. What is particularly interesting about this report is that it identifies 26% of GDP as the level of government spending which optimizes per-capita economic growth. Per capita growth rates are much more pertinent to a discussion about prosperity because they tell us the improvements felt by individuals. Remember, total government spending in the U.S. is already over 40% of GDP.

Based on what we have discussed so far we can build a solid case for spending restraint enforced by Constitutional amendment. But it is clear that we must take into consideration more than just the amount of money government spends in order to understand how the economy is affected by government. We must also consider the rate of government growth, the burden of government spending as a percentage of GDP, debt/deficits, and taxes. When we take into consideration all of these interconnected factors it becomes even more clear that restrained government spending is generally better for economic performance. In spite of the evidence, government predictably balks at meaningful cuts in spending or even at reducing the rate of growth of spending. The chief argument used against spending cuts is that it will cost people their jobs. In order to refute these claims and to get a broader view of government's impact on the economy, let's look at specific examples of countries whose governments spent relatively modest amounts while enjoying strong economic growth.

Progressives love to point to Bill Clinton's presidency in the 1990's in an attempt to show that increased taxes will not hurt the economy, or that they will even help it to grow. The U.S. did enjoy an economically strong decade during the Clinton years, and he did raise taxes early in his presidency. But what also happened is that the burden of government spending fell from 21.4% of GDP in 1993 to 18.2% in 2000.[22] It is clear that this happened because government grew at a very slow pace during this time. In fact, among modern presidents, overall federal spending grew at the slowest rate during the Clinton years.[23] This also caused deficits to fall, signaling to the private sector that taxes were not likely to increase any time soon. Indeed, a small tax cut actually occurred in 1997. At a minimum, we can certainly conclude that the slow rate of government growth did not negatively affect economic growth.

This is important to understand because currently, when we debate "cutting" government spending we are actually debating how fast government should grow. A cut is when less money is spent in one year than in the previous. But when politicians talk about a cut they usually mean spending less money than they previously planned to spend. This is like giving your family a spending budget of $100,000, then reducing it to $50,000 and patting yourself on the back for being financially responsible even though you spent $40,000 the previous year. By this definition of a cut, Bill Clinton took a chainsaw to the federal budget during the 90's.

It has been shown that the U.S. could achieve a balanced budget within five years without any real spending cuts or tax increases.[24] All that needs to be done is to simply reduce the rate of government growth to the rate of inflation; no cuts, according to the real definition of a cut, no tax increases, balanced budget in five years. This demonstrates the power of spending restraint to achieve fiscal and economic goals and undercuts the case for a balanced budget amendment. Debt and balanced budgets will take care of themselves if spending (and taxes) is capped. Let's look at some more examples.

Something very similar to our experience under Clinton happened in Canada during the 90's, only they actually *cut* government spending. From 1995 to 2000, the burden of federal spending in Canada fell from 22% of GDP to 17%.[25] The Canadians cut defense, unemployment insurance, business subsidies, and aid to provincial governments (equivalent to our States) among other things. Many on the left today would have denounced such proposals as "draconian" and "immoral". But the effects on Canada's economy were anything but. Unemployment in Canada fell from 11% in the early 90s to 7% late in the decade.[26] And, unlike in the U.S., Canada's burden of federal spending continued to fall after 2000, bottoming out at 15% of GDP in 2006.[27] (Not quite the progressive utopia we all imagine) This led to rapidly falling debts and allowed for tax cuts which further boosted economic performance. The International Monetary Fund recognized the enormous success of Canada's economic and debt-reduction achievements throughout this time period.[28] This episode shows that not only can a government grow slowly and still have strong economic performance, but it can actually shrink and still achieve that result.

There are other important lessons to learn from Canada's experience. Many of the spending reforms were enacted by the *liberal* party as they were forced to face the reality of their fiscal situation after decades of out-of-control spending. There was also a movement, not unlike our Tea Party, which pushed both major parties toward reform. Perhaps most encouraging, was that the party that enacted the spending cuts was re-elected, indicating that shrinking government can be politically feasible as well as economically wise.

Perhaps the best example of spending restraint we can point to for our present purpose is that of Switzerland. In 2001, more than 80% of its voters approved a de facto spending cap commonly referred to as a "debt brake." This mechanism prevents the government from expanding faster than the trend line revenue it receives over a period of years. Before this measure went into effect in 2003, the Swiss government was growing by 4.3% annually.[29] After the debt brake, government has grown by 2.6% annually and total government spending has decreased from 36% of GDP to 34%.[30] (Total government spending in the U.S. went from 36% to 41% in the same time period.) Federal Government spending in Switzerland is now lower than 20% of GDP.[31] Has this spending restraint been devastating to the Swiss economy as many on the left might have predicted? No. Switzerland is one of the few countries who made it through the financial crisis relatively unscathed. They continue to have one of the highest per capita GDPs in the world and unemployment is steady at around 4%.[32] And of course, Switzerland does not have near the fiscal problems of many of its European neighbors.

These examples, and the studies cited clearly show, at worst, that restraint in government spending is compatible with strong economic performance. More likely, spending restraint is actually conducive to strong economic performance, particularly in the long run. *Given this, and what we know about free market economics, a solid empirical case can be made that economic prosperity is more likely under a government which restrains spending.* This debunks the falsehood that cutting government spending, whether a real cut or a politician's cut, is bad for the economy. Most important, it gives a strong, evidence-based case for a Constitutional cap on spending.

This is not to say that cutting government spending will not cost people their jobs; of course it will. But the goal of lawmakers should be to accomplish the greatest amount of good for the greatest amount of people in the long run, rather than please a narrow constituency of government workers within the context of a two-year election cycle.

What's more is that those workers will likely be far more productive in the private sector and will boost economic growth over time. Of course government spending creates jobs; I can create jobs if you give *me* a trillion dollars. But which would create more jobs: a trillion in the hands of politically motivated politicians operating through an inefficient maze of bureaucracies, or a trillion in the hands of self-interested investors and businesspeople who have to *earn* the money they spend/invest? We need jobs that are useful, seek to produce or build what is demanded in a free market, and are not as likely to be the result of favoritism or political necessity. That means job creation should belong to the private sector.

This leads us to a more philosophical discussion comparing government spending to private sector spending. Does any fair-minded person seriously believe that government is better than the private sector at effectively allocating capital? One need look no further than the embarrassing amount of redundancy and waste in the Federal Government to answer that question. How many reports of lavish conferences, ridiculous programs, and bankrupt government investments have to surface? The retort that these are "meaningless" amounts of money is simply insulting. No dollar honestly earned by the taxpayer who funds this type of corruption is meaningless. To contend otherwise is to suffer from the same disease that overtakes every politician who shows nothing but contempt for the money which they so carelessly spend but do not earn. On this philosophical basis alone we would have ample justification for a spending cap which would tell politicians and bureaucrats that their contempt for other people's money can only go so far.

There is simply far less incentive for bureaucrats to spend other people's money wisely than there is for private citizens to spend their own money wisely. One politician says "We need to spend on X." Another says "We need to spend on Y." But nothing stops them from lumping X and Y into the same bill and we spend money on both because there is nothing imposing discipline on the process. The result is that we spend money on things which would only get a fraction of popular support if it were forced to stand alone. Does that make sense to anyone? Only a spending cap would force Congress to prioritize. If it cannot get majority approval we should not be spending money on it. Is not that how representative democracy and republicanism should work?

With a spending cap, we would guarantee that only a limited amount of money will go to the less-efficient government sector. Every dollar in the private economy is either saved, spent or invested, all of which is good for the economy, and we get to skip the step of sending the money to Washington and letting them filter it through the bureaucracy with its attendant broker's fees. Therefore, we ought to ensure that as much money as possible remains in the hands of the people who have the greatest incentive to spend it wisely.

Government spending, usually driven by politics, has less to do with wise investing and more to do with putting on a show for constituents. As politicians seek to hand out the most goodies to their voters they accumulate an ever larger list of projects and services for their States and districts. This then leads to businesses competing over tax dollars in the form of contracts, grants, and subsidies designed to fulfill political priorities instead of behaving like entrepreneurs and seeking to fulfill the priorities of market participants. In turn, this has created the special interest lobbying scene that we have all come to despise. The despicable growth of wealth in and around Washington D.C. is a testament of this trend.[33] Once these private contractors are hooked on government money, the outcry against spending cuts becomes louder and a vicious cycle ensues. A spending cap will not completely eradicate this cycle, but it will force discipline on government and will free more businesses to do more productive work meeting the demands of consumers rather than seeking rent in Washington.

Of course all of this assumes that it is even legal for government to attempt to boost economic activity. In fact, the Constitution provides for no such authority, and, for the reasons just cited, it is simply not a proper role for government to play. This is why the Founders made no provision for government influence over the economy other than to be a neutral arbiter between States by regulating commerce among them. The notion that we have somehow progressed to a new set of circumstances that renders this Constitutional reality obsolete is false. True enough, we have become much more interconnected. Interstate commerce now constitutes a much greater share of all commerce and it should be expected that the Federal Government would have to play a correspondingly increased regulatory role. But there is absolutely nothing based in economic fact which suggests that a government limited from managing the economy or spending wildly is outdated or unwise. The Founders limited the Federal Government not because they understood that commerce was mostly local at the time; they limited government because they understood that it is motivated by politics, and politicians are not to be trusted with arbitrary power to spend and regulate because their political goals would likely supersede sound economics.

However, restoring 19th century government should not be our goal with these amendments. There may well be a good case for fiscal stimulus in times of recession or for more extensive regulation, *relatively speaking*. But spending restraint, in the long run, is necessary to amplify the positive effects of fiscal stimulus and to force government into prioritizing and limiting what to regulate and enforce. We may not turn back the clock and keep government from spending on the general welfare, but we can and must limit how far government can go in order to give permanent confidence to markets, ensure that more money is kept in the private sector, and to force discipline on an out-of-control bureaucratic blob.

As we continue to build the case for a Constitutional spending cap, let us now move to consider the third reason for government spending: redistribution of wealth. This comes in many forms. The idea of these schemes is to take money from one group and give it to another. The proponents of these programs justify them on the basis of three principles: equality/fairness, charity, and for economic reasons.

The equality argument cannot be sustained. For starters, leftists confuse equality with *material* equality, which as explained in chapter six, is completely misguided. Their attempts to justify government-enforced material equality using the language of the Founders are either ignorant or dishonest. The Founders clearly had no intention to redistribute wealth from the rich to the poor for purposes of "equality." Equality to them meant equality of liberty, equality before the law, and equality in the eyes of God. This is the only equality that should be enforced by government.

Even if we accept the progressive definition of equality we are left with the problem of how to achieve it. Do we guarantee everyone the same amount of income? The same home? The same amount of vacation time? The same fill in the blank with your particular material wants? But then again, if you have unique material wants, how do we create material equality among more than 300 million unique individuals? And if we do not guarantee the same amount of material wealth to all can we truly say that we have achieved "equality?"

Material equality is unachievable in free market systems, and even in socialist systems over time as history has shown. There is simply no common rationale for even defining material equality let alone making it a reality. The reason the word equality is used is because of its political value due to its ties with America's founding ideals. What progressives really want is simply more fairness in a world of vast wealth disparity. This is a noble goal but we are left with similar questions. How much redistribution is enough to be considered fair? Can government be trusted to do what is really fair or will they more likely do what is in their own best interest?

Wealth disparity is a natural occurrence in a free market. Some have more talent, some work harder, some were born into wealth, and simple luck plays a role as well. But is all of this unfair? Suppose, for example, that my wishes come true and millions of people buy my book. Who should get the earnings from all that revenue; the people who invested in its promotion; the person who wrote it; Jane Doe, a teacher from Maine or John Smith, a janitor from Ohio? A presidential candidate would probably say "absolutely give it to John Smith he is in a crucial battleground State!" How could it possibly be "fair" for anyone to get money they did not earn? I frequently remind my wife of this every time she displays disgust at another athletes' $100 million contract. Who else should get the money people pay to watch those athletes? And so what if luck plays a role? Maybe I'm lucky enough to have an uncle that works at a big publisher (I don't). Does that now justify Jane Doe getting more of the money from my book sales?

A progressive would likely argue that because Jane Doe, or someone like her, taught me English that she should in fact get a portion of my book sales. How else could I write if it weren't for her? And it would only be fair for John Smith to get some of it too, since he worked the night shift at the plant that built the computer on which I am writing this book.

These arguments are pure nonsense. John and Jane did not agree to a portion of my earnings when they agreed to their employment. They voluntarily agreed to the salaries and wages offered to them. It is not government's role to retroactively impose a new contract between me and my high school English teacher because they decide that I have earned "too much." Should Jane also share in the *failures* of her students for purposes of "fairness"? Or should John share in the losses of someone who got hooked on internet gambling on a computer from his plant? It is true that many people contribute to an individual's success; but true fairness demands that individuals only be compensated with what they agreed to, not what is bestowed upon them after the fact by vote-seeking politicians.

Another justification for redistribution is charity. Once again, progressives suffer from an inability to properly define what they claim to espouse. Charity is giving of one's self for the benefit of another in need. There is nothing charitable about giving *another's* substance for someone in need. Government does not earn a dime of what it spends. It cannot, therefore be called charity when it spends on others in need. This is especially true when we consider that politicians stand to gain more votes as they give away more money. What is called charity is more like a bribe from politicians seeking re-election.

The only principle which has even a slight chance of justifying government redistribution is economics. A prosperous society may do well to offer a basic safety net for those who fall on hard times and are truly in need. This would help to combat poverty and create more opportunity. When looked at in this light, we are more likely to consider the effect on the people using the safety net. If it is structured in a way that incentivizes people to remain on the safety net then that is what we will get. Good economic policy should incentivize people to work rather than find ways not to. Good political policy is to keep people on the dole so that they vote for you to keep the dole alive. If voters place upon government the responsibility to offer charity and fairness, in terms of wealth distribution, with no limit, then there will be no end to using other people's money to achieve these ends. This is why charity and fairness belong in the private sector where wealth goes to the people who earn it and random luck falls on everyone with no bias or political agenda; and where free people are likely to be charitable. A social safety net should not exist to right the supposed wrongs of the free market. It should be there to simply help struggling people; which will inevitably exist in any system; get back on their feet, and that implies a strict limit on its use.

Helping others in need is a noble thing and all of us have a duty to give of our time and resources to those who are less-fortunate. But where the money comes from and how it is spent matters. The great economist Milton Friedman explained that there are four ways to spend money.[34] Each of these is placed into one of the quadrants in the following table.

	High Discipline	Low Discipline
High Value	Spend one's own money on self	Spend others' money on self
Low Value	Spend one's own money on others	Spend others' money on others

The table shows the different value and discipline levels people assign to the use of money for the four different ways it can be spent. As government only spends other people's money on other people, it falls in the low discipline/low value quadrant. The way in which government inefficiently doles out various forms of welfare through an over-bloated bureaucracy operating more than 120 separate programs, and the lackluster effectiveness of all that spending, is proof of government's low-discipline and low-value spending nature. While we cannot change that government will always spend other people's money, we can impose discipline on them with a spending cap.

Once again, these arguments assume that it is even legal for the Federal Government to provide a safety net; and once again, the Constitution provides for no such authority. However, rather than attempting to turn back the clock and completely and abruptly end all federal welfare spending, a better and more practical solution is to limit that spending. These arguments are not an affront against all welfare spending; they are a plea to enforce discipline on an undisciplined government. We cannot afford to allow politicians to continue spending other people's money in the name of "charity" and "fairness" with no restraints. They must be forced to prioritize with a limited budget, and to structure welfare programs in a way that benefits the truly needy, incentivizing them to move forward rather than permanently living off the dole. In the end, that will prove to be the more compassionate policy, as more people working and achieving independence is the surest and best way to combat poverty. If government wants to stimulate the economy through fiscal stimulus and provide a safety net it can do so if disciplined and limited by a

Constitutional spending cap. If we do not impose that discipline then all of us, especially the poor, will be in peril.

Thus far in this chapter we have justified a Constitutional spending cap by exploring the two reasons governments spend money for which there is some dispute: to stimulate the economy and to redistribute wealth. However, we have shown that a spending cap will not inhibit government's ability to stimulate the economy and that in fact, it will improve economic performance by allowing for more effective fiscal stimulus, guaranteeing that more money remain in the private sector, and by instilling confidence in the private sector that government cannot grow faster than the economy. We have also shown that redistribution of wealth for purposes of "charity" or "fairness" is not justified because of politician's ulterior motives and undisciplined nature. It is, however, wise to keep in place a basic safety net for the vulnerable. Thus, a spending cap would still allow government to maintain a safety net but would enforce desperately needed discipline on such spending in order to curtail political influence, reduce the allure of the dole and direct money to where it is truly needed. The diagram on the following page sums up our case thus far.

The Case for a Constitutional Spending Cap

Which Affects

- **Unrestrained Politics Determines Spending**
  - Politicians aim to please key donors and contituencies rather than pursuing economically sound policies
  - Politicians would rather appear to be doing 'something' even if it doesnt work

Which Affects

- **Speed of Government Growth**
  - Signals to private sector that taxes may soon rise, discouraging investment

Which Affects

- **Burden of Government Spending**
  - More money in government means less money saved, invested or spent in the private sector, crowding out
  - Redistribution creates a sense of entitlement to and dependence on other worker's production
  - Bureaucrats have little or no incentive to spend other people's money wisely
  - Government workers are usually paid more for less productive work
  - Large bureaucracies constantly work to make their jobs seem more important rather than fulfilling genuine needs

Which Affects

- **Taxes**
  - If taxes are raised to cover the burden of government spending then businesses have lower profits and less money to grow
  - Higher taxes in the U.S. discourages foreign investment and encourage business to move their money off shore causing capital flight

Ignites more political bickering and repeats the cycle

- **Debt/Deficits**
  - Higher debts discourage outside investment and make stimulus less effective
  - Debts must be paid in the future. It is taxation without representation, and it is immoral to ask future generations, who have no voice, to pay our debts

Perhaps the most compelling reason for a Constitutional spending cap is the desperate need for entitlement reform. Aside from defense, spending on Social Security, Medicare and Medicaid combined are, by far, the biggest drivers of government spending. Under current policies, in just 15 years the Federal Government will be spending approximately 30% of the country's wealth.[35] That means, if State spending remains constant, then total government spending in the United States will be *over* 45% of GDP by about 2030. That is not far off. I remind you of the results from the studies we discussed which demonstrate slower economic growth with bigger governments, particularly beyond 40% of GDP. We simply cannot sustain a government, at these levels, which grows faster than the economy.

The largest share of federal spending, 39%, goes to Social Security, Medicare and Medicaid. Those shares will continue to rise as more retirees leave the workforce in the coming years. Over the next decade those programs will consume 50% of all federal spending.[36] The growth of government must be reversed, and everyone knows we cannot do that without entitlement reform. Gill and Raiser put a particular emphasis on social transfers (entitlements of all kinds) while discussing the size of government related to economic growth. Their regression analysis found that social transfers have a consistently negative effect on growth.[37] Contrary to popular opinion on the left, social transfers hinder growth, which disproportionately harms the poor, as fewer and lower-paying jobs are the result. Predictably, the reaction is to blame the free market and income disparity, prompting further calls for more taxes and transfers, leading to more dependence and less work.

The reason entitlement reform has not been accomplished by politicians is because of the political pitfalls surrounding the issue. Under our current paradigm, any attempt to reform entitlements necessarily must include a reduction in benefits in some form and/or an increase in revenues in some form. Both of these measures are political poison to whoever suggests them. But here is one point that must be understood as a prerequisite to debating entitlement reform. *By 2050, these three programs alone will consume every tax dollar received by the Federal Government.*[38] That means everything else the Federal Government does, from defense to national parks, would have to be paid for by more debt or additional taxes. *We cannot possibly tax enough money to meet these obligations.* If we tried to tax our way out of this problem, the amount required would devastate the private economy. Businesses would move to other countries, lay people off, move money around, report less income and invest elsewhere or not at all. Funding that spending with debt would be equally devastating as default would assuredly crush us given our current levels of debt.

While some tax increases may be inevitable, *the bulk of reform must come through some type of reduction in benefits*, at least in terms of what is guaranteed by the government. No amount of fanciful accounting can change this simple fact. ENTITLEMENT BENEFITS FROM GOVERNMENT WILL BE CUT! IT DOES NOT MATTER HOW MUCH WE TAX OR HOW ELSE WE CHANGE THE PROGRAMS! GOVERNMENT BENEFITS WILL BE CUT WHETHER WE WANT IT OR NOT! POLITICIANS HAVE PROMISED OBLIGATIONS THAT CANNOT BE FULFILLED! No matter how Bernie Sanders and the progressives try to spin it, there is not enough wealth to fund entitlements in their present form without decimating economic growth. The only thing we can decide is whether we will make manageable reforms now, or wait until catastrophic reforms are forced upon us in the future.

There have been bipartisan warnings about the unsustainability of these programs going as far back as the mid-90s, yet politicians continue to drag their feet.[39] The political gridlock with entitlements centers on the familiar debate between tax increases and spending cuts. Of course, Democrats believe that the situation is not as dire as some believe and that we can tax our way out of future obligations. Therefore, it becomes necessary to show that benefit cuts, enforced by a spending cap, are the only option for entitlement reform that will *not* destroy the economy. A Constitutional amendment, imposed by the States, is the best way to force Washington to come to the table and solve this mess. An analysis of each entitlement program will show the desperate need for reform and that tax increases will do little to solve the problem.

<u>Social Security</u>

Social Security was the catalyst for the Supreme Court's regrettable decision to allow Congress a nearly unlimited power to spend. This discussion of entitlements now demonstrates more clearly than ever how unwise that decision was; and how wise the Founders were to limit the power of the national government to enact such programs, knowing that they would likely bankrupt the country. This context gives us more clarity when discussing options to deal with these programs. Here are the facts.

To begin with, it is important to understand that Social Security is not a social insurance plan in the technical sense; it is rather a type of welfare program. That retirement benefits are calculated based on payroll contributions does not change the fact that Social Security redistributes money from the working class to the retired class, making them welfare recipients. Too many Americans still believe the government's misleading claims about the nature of Social Security. When the money is taken from your paycheck it does not go into an account with your name on it. It is given directly to a beneficiary. No American has a legal right to their benefits. As soon as the money is taxed it becomes government property and can be appropriated any way Congress wishes.

By law, Social Security cannot consume funds from the regular budget. The program can only pay out in retirement and disability benefits what it receives in payroll taxes. Any money collected by pay roll taxes in excess of payments must go into a trust fund to be used to meet future obligations. Over the last 80 years, the program has accumulated a trust fund of about $2.7 trillion.[40] *But the trust fund does not have any real assets in it that can be used to pay benefits.* Because payroll contributions are government property, all the excess payroll tax receipts have been spent by previous congresses in order to pay for other budget items and to make the deficit seem smaller. The trust fund has been replaced with Treasury bonds which are essentially IOUs. The only way to use the trust fund, which is nothing more than a figment of accounting gimmickry, is to raise more debt or taxes to pay for its bonds. So, while Social Security cannot take directly from the general budget it can take money indirectly by receiving payments on the bonds left in the trust fund by Congress.

Just a few years ago, the Social Security system began to draw on the trust fund as pay roll tax receipts became insufficient to pay obligations. That means Congress has to add more debt or raise other taxes in order to replenish the trust fund when it is drawn on to pay obligations. Because of this backdoor tactic, Congress has exposed the general budget to Social Security's cash shortfalls. Anyone who says, and there have been many, that Social Security does not add to the debt or deficit is either lying or does not understand how the program works. In fact, Congress had to borrow $37 billion in 2010 from the budget in order to make up for the shortfalls in that year.[41] Congress will end up borrowing or taxing another $355 billion to cover the shortfall for the period 2011-2015.[42]

These shortfalls are expected to continue until about 2035, when the trust fund, or the IOUs, will be exhausted.[43] At that time, if no reforms are enacted, benefits, *by law*, will have to be cut by about

25%.[44] That means retirees like myself would see a negative rate of return from our contributions to Social Security. The stock market, even after 2008, doesn't look so bad. Thus, the trust fund is meaningless in terms of determining the true solvency of the program. The only thing the trust fund determines is at what point benefits will have to be cut. When the fund is exhausted, Congress will no longer be able to use the backdoor tactic of filling it with bonds because they cannot give money directly to Social Security from general revenues. The total cash shortfalls for Social Security over the next 75 years, or the amount that will be added to our debt, will total a present value of about $10 trillion.[45] It is important to note that this projection varies widely for a number of reasons. But this number is a conservative estimate from Social Security's own actuaries and covers a relevant time period, making it the most useful number.

Now that we know the scope of the problem the question becomes whether we can tax our way out of this mess. Consider what is driving Social Security's shortfalls. When Social Security began in 1935, the contributions of 17 workers paid for the benefits of one retiree. In 2035 the estimated ratio will be 2.1 workers per beneficiary.[46] That startling statistic should be enough to answer the question. We simply cannot ask 2.1 workers to fund what was previously funded by more than eight times their labor capacity.

To be thorough, let's dig deeper into the option of raising taxes. Remember that Social Security cannot get money from the general fund, which means we can't simply raise income taxes or tariffs to pay benefits. If we want to raise revenue to help pay these benefits we will have to raise payroll taxes. But Social Security is a unique program that calculates benefits based on what a beneficiary contributed throughout his working life; the more you put in, the more you get out. Raising more revenue by increasing payroll taxes will simply increase the benefits that have to be paid out. This will not give us nearly enough additional revenue to cover unfunded obligations. It will only make our obligations bigger.

The only option available to overcome this problem is to change the structure of Social Security by taking away the relationship between what a worker puts in and what they can take out; at least for higher income earners. Currently, annual income over $117,000 is exempt from payroll taxes.[47] Some have suggested that this exemption be completely removed and that no additional benefits be given for those additional contributions. Under this provision, all that additional revenue could be used to help pay future unfunded obligations without creating more obligations.

This would be extraordinarily unwise for several reasons. First, this plan would still not do much to solve the long-term fiscal imbalance. Proponents of this measure like to claim that eliminating the cap on payroll taxable income, without giving additional benefits for those contributions, would make Social Security "solvent" for 75 years, meaning that contributions and the trust fund will be able to pay out benefits.[48] But calling it "solvent" is very misleading because the trust fund does not contain real assets that can be used to pay benefits. It is full of nothing more than bonds. If Congress were given an additional revenue stream into that fund, it would simply spend the excess cash on other items and keep filling the fund with more bonds. Congress has no incentive to use excess cash to pay down the trust fund when they can count additional bonds (debt) as making the program solvent. Thus, no *real* fiscal surplus would be created for the system as Congress would have to continue to raise taxes or debt to pay for the bonds as they come due. Congress has proven again and again that if it gets the money, it will spend it, especially when they have a proven mechanism which they already use to conceal future obligations. Any plan which seeks to bring Social Security in balance without *imposing spending discipline* on Congress is futile.

It may be said that the program is in balance under this provision, but only by using accounting tactics which would be illegal in the private sector. Many large private corporations have trust funds full of cash set up to pay the pensions of its future retirees. If those corporations took the cash out of those trust funds to pay for current corporate activities, replaced the cash with bonds, and tried to count those bonds as assets in an attempt to mask its future obligations the perpetrators would literally be thrown in prison for fraudulent accounting (not to mention for operating a system which pays past investors with current investor's money, i.e. operating a Ponzi scheme.) This is exactly what Congress does with the Social Security trust fund. Raising additional revenue by removing the payroll tax cap would only give them further license to continue this practice and would not solve the long-term cash imbalance. The following graph from Social Security's actuaries tells the story.

Increased Taxes Won't Solve Social Security's Imbalance

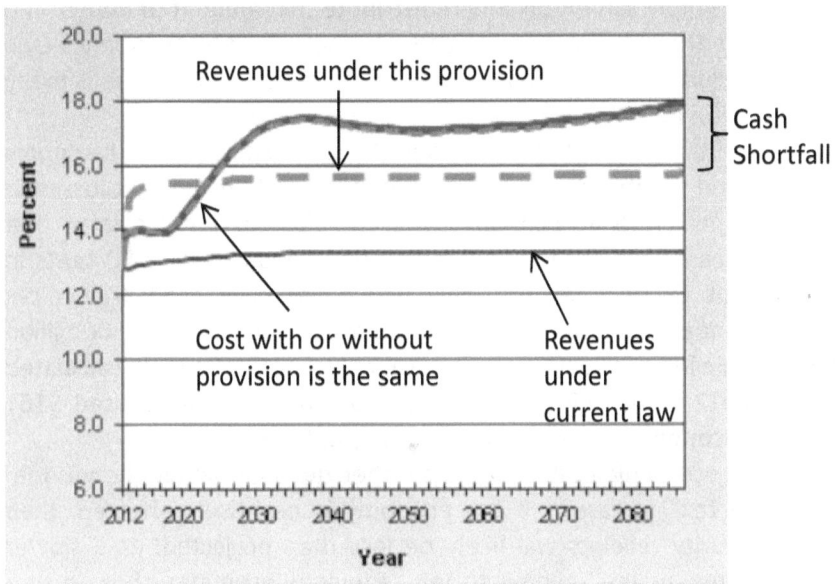

Source:www.ssa.gov/OACT/solvency/provisions/charts/chart_run362.html

As the graph shows, the imbalance would be "fixed" until about the mid 2020's. From there, the program would resume cash deficits which would continue into the foreseeable future. A plan to completely remove the cap on Social Security payroll taxes and not give benefits for those additional contributions is the most radical tax increase proposal for fixing the program. Yet the above graph shows that cash surpluses under this plan will only be restored for a short time, after which deficits will resume indefinitely.

More importantly, we must consider the impact such a radical tax increase will have on the economy. Eliminating the payroll tax cap would create the largest tax increase in American history and would result in more than $1 trillion in tax revenue over the first ten years of its implementation.[49] It would also give the United States, the land of the free, *the highest marginal tax rates in the world*. Progressives say "no problem, the rich can afford it." But it is not a question of affordability on an individual basis; it is a question of affordability for the economy. A person making $500,000 a year could technically "afford" to have 80% of her income taken away, leaving her with $100,000. The question is what effect such confiscation will have on the behavior of that worker. The answer is that she will reduce work, take her money elsewhere or not invest at all. This will, in turn, reduce investment in the country and will slow economic growth, harming the poor. We simply cannot tax and redistribute that amount of money and not expect there to be adverse consequences for the economy. One study concluded that eliminating the payroll tax cap would cost as many as 1.1 million jobs over ten years.[50]

Payroll taxes distort labor markets. These distortions in the supply and demand of labor create what economists call deadweight losses to the economy. Harvard economist Martin Feldstein has calculated that every increased dollar in payroll tax revenue adds another 50 cents in deadweight losses.[51] So, not only would we have a $1 trillion tax increase under this provision, but it would also add *another* $500 billion in economic losses. Social Security expert Jagadeesh Gokhale calculated that in 2012 alone, without this provision, the program caused $161 billion in economic damage from deadweight losses.[52]

These economic costs lead to another question about the wisdom of payroll tax increases. If the economy is negatively affected, then Social Security receipts will likely be less than projected, as a slower economy means less income to tax. Previous estimates showed that Social Security would not run into cash deficits until 2017. But because of the economic downturn, cash deficits actually began in 2010. An adversely affected economy will make the shortfalls in Social Security's receipts relative to benefit obligations even larger than shown in the actuaries' graph from the previous page. Tax increases are notorious for not yielding the amount of increased revenues advertised by supporters. As the increase in payroll taxes takes effect and begins to discourage economic growth, the revenue increases may be lower than expected.

Clearly, raising taxes will not get us near where we need to be to make Social Security truly solvent. And remember this is just one entitlement program for which Congress must pay. *The largest tax increase in American history cannot pay for just one of our many government programs.* We still have to pay for defense, border security, the legal system, and thousands of other federal programs. What does it tell us about the need for spending restraint when the largest tax increase in American history cannot even pay for one program's unfunded obligations? It tells us that it is paramount to getting out of our fiscal nightmare. We cannot meet future unfunded liabilities with tax revenue. The only way to keep Social Security from adding to our debt is to *reduce promised benefits,* at least in terms of what the government promises to redistribute.

The only way to do this, and still maintain or improve retirement security, *is to change the system to one in which individual workers control privately owned retirement accounts.* This creates for the worker a controllable asset which they own and can be inherited by children, unlike Social Security benefits which are owned by the government the moment it comes out of a paycheck. Such a privately owned asset would be a powerful tool for wealth creation, would provide greater retirement security, and could also be used by children and grandchildren to get job training, go to college or start a business.

Some may warn that this is too risky because of the stock market's history. But risk should be determined by a free person who has a right to control what they have earned. It is not up to politicians or a majority vote to decide the level of risk people should take when controlling their own money. Freedom and personal responsibility impose discipline on individuals and thereby tend to improve outcomes.

In any event, the argument that privatization is too risky draws its strength more from a media-driven disdain for Wall Street than from actual returns from long-term investments. "Subjecting worker's retirement security to Wall Street speculation" makes for a great political punch line but offers little insight into what would actually happen in a privatized system. A worker retiring in 2012 is seeing a 2.2% return on their Social Security "investments." On the other hand, a worker who would have invested in the S&P 500 over the last 40 years, including the 2008 disaster, would have received a 6.8% return.[53] And given Social Security's fiscal situation, the return for future retirees is likely to be much lower, if not in the negative as they will be forced to pay more or take fewer benefits without privatization. Even if future stock market returns will be lower, as some argue, there can be little doubt that they will be substantially higher than the return on Social Security contributions.

Some have claimed a much lower rate of return from the stock market after adjusting for risk. But such calculations are meaningless in the real world and are only useful as a dishonest deterrent to privatization. While risk is sometimes calculated into an estimate of future returns in order to help an investor choose among investment options, a return adjusted for risk does not represent a real return. There is no "risk police" who goes around confiscating the difference between what was actually earned and what the return should have been after adjusting for risk. The 6.8% return in the stock market for the last 40 years is not risk adjusted; those are real returns.

Another common argument against privatization is the transition cost. Moving to private accounts would require workers to fund not only their private accounts but also the benefits of current retirees. The claim that this would be too expensive is misleading because it ignores the fact that unfunded liabilities under the current system would be even more expensive. The same sources we would use to pay unfunded liabilities; taxes or reduced benefits; may be used to fund private accounts until current retirees receive all their benefits. In truth, this would be cheaper because private accounts would yield higher benefits to future retirees so that even if a worker were contributing less to a private account than what would be taxed under the current system, she would still receive higher benefits in retirement. One way or another, unfunded liabilities have to be covered either by cutting benefits or raising taxes. Rather than cutting benefits and banishing those losses to oblivion, it would be much wiser to put smaller contributions into powerful private accounts that would likely more than make up the difference over time. Whatever the structure, the feasibility and cost-effectiveness of private accounts has been well-demonstrated.[54]

If the left is so eager to create a society that "works for everyone" then let's start by giving middle class and poor workers back what they already earn by putting their Social Security contributions into a privately owned account. This will give them an asset that can grow in value much faster over time and can help them to accumulate wealth and lift themselves to a higher economic class; something Social Security has never, and will never be able to do in its current form. The left complains that capital generates far better returns than labor, thereby enabling the rich to accumulate wealth much faster. Rather than complaining that the rich are doing it and looking for ways to tax and redistribute their capital gains, we should allow everyone else to get in on the deal.

Why should wealthy Americans be able to secure their retirements and accumulate large trust funds with more lucrative and profitable private investment accounts while poorer Americans are forced to rely on a government program with meager or even negative returns, and whose very taxes inhibit their capacity to save? In essence, like so many other government welfare programs, Social Security is self-defeating. The people it attempts to help are instead depressed from being able to do the things that lead to real wealth: saving and investing. A society that works for everyone is not one in which people are dependent on government's redistribution programs; it is one in which poorer Americans are empowered to participate in the same activities that create wealth for everyone else.

If the complaint is that some unlucky retirees will be left in poverty because of the poor performance of their accounts then we can discuss other ways to mitigate this such as by requiring a certain allocation of investments to be placed in safer bonds. Even so, the bad fortune of a few is not a valid reason for coercing every worker into a broken system where they have no property rights over what they earn. Social Security is often labeled a social safety net but it is not a safety net in the sense that it is only there to help the most vulnerable. The vast majority of its transfers go to middle class retirees who would have been much better off with private accounts. Worse, Social Security redistributes wealth from the poor working class and gives it to the wealthy retired class in an age where technology has made it possible to do productive work well beyond the traditional retirement age.

If we are truly concerned for the most vulnerable then we will devise a system which empowers them to accumulate wealth rather than confiscating it from them in exchange for a promise to pay them back when they retire. We will empower them to independently save and invest for their own retirement using the money they earn. If they fail, then a minimum benefit guarantee might kick in and private charity, family, and churches would play the role they have filled so well throughout our history. We can also make it so that if there are some who like Social Security as is, they can remain in the system with no changes. But it is more likely that most or all would choose private accounts. If we are truly concerned with the most vulnerable then let's offer them the better deal and let them choose.

There have been many proposals put forward to reform Social Security. Some cut benefits, some raise taxes, and some use both in various combinations. *But offering private retirement accounts is the only proposal, which has been evaluated by the Social Security Administration, which will bring the program into true cash flow solvency[55] without further harm to the economy, while at the same time giving poor and middle class workers the natural rights to their property and a path to real wealth accumulation.* This is also the only proposal which brings the system into balance without raising taxes and which would actually result in *higher benefits* for retirees. A reform which would give higher benefits to retirees would be enough reason to offer private accounts even if the current program were projecting positive cash flows for 100 years. No other reform plan comes close to accomplishing all that.

If we do not privatize, we either have to cut benefits, raise taxes or both. Any combination of those actions would be harmful to beneficiaries and/or the economy. It makes no sense to subject ourselves to those limited and harmful options when we have another option which saves us from having to do anything detrimental to the economy or beneficiaries.

These truths transcend partisanship. If we honestly debate how to solve the problem then we will conclude that privatization is the answer. Recent history indicates as much. Before George W. Bush's call for private accounts, President Clinton was poised to call for his own version of privatization late in his second term. Noted liberal Senator Daniel Patrick Moynihan was also in favor of private accounts, calling the plan the "democratization of the stock market." Mollifying fears that a transition to private accounts is too costly or otherwise untenable, a team of advisers in the Clinton administration found that not only were private accounts feasible and safe[56], but a whopping 73% of *Democrats* supported some form of privatization.[57] Unfortunately, Clinton's plans were derailed by the Monica Lewinsky fiasco[58] but this bit of history shows that privatization is practical and moderate. With a Constitutional spending cap it would actually be possible.

We must also consider the economic benefits of the dramatic increase in savings and investment that would occur from private accounts. While no recent studies have attempted to quantify the economic gain, one study from 1997 estimated a boost from privatization of at least $10 trillion.[59] If payroll taxes were redirected from government spending to private investment it would be a boon to economic growth and job creation. That economic growth would, in turn, further improve retirement security by creating more and higher paying jobs, giving more workers a greater capacity to save. This would create an upward spiral toward independence and prosperity contradistinguished from Social Security's downward spiral toward dependence and diminishing returns.

Medicare

Social Security paved the way for the other two major entitlement programs: Medicare and Medicaid, both enacted in 1965 as part of President Lyndon Johnson's "great society" programs. Medicare is essentially a government health insurance program for seniors aged 65 and older. Using an extraordinarily complex array of participating health providers, price controls, plans, and regulations, it assists seniors with a variety of health expenses from hospital care to prescription drugs. Most of the funding for the program comes from the 3% payroll tax you see on your paycheck. About 10% of Medicare's funding comes from small premiums paid by seniors. Unlike Social Security, Medicare can be funded from the general budget, making it easier to fund with debt without having to employ deceptive accounting practices which partially hide its true solvency.

There is no concealing the looming disaster that is Medicare. Nearly all agree that this program is in dire financial condition. Estimates of Medicare's unfunded liabilities range from about $30 trillion to as high as $90 trillion. Part of the reason the range is so large is because of the recent reforms to Medicare from the Patient Protection and Affordable Care Act. There is much uncertainty and controversy as to whether the PPACA will actually deliver a large reduction in unfunded liabilities. The number we will use for our purposes is from Medicare's actuary which is a 75 year unfunded liability of $36 trillion.[60] That staggering amount is, amazingly, a conservative estimate. For perspective, that number represents about $313,000 for every household in America *in addition* to the taxes we will already pay throughout our lives.[61] In 2013, Medicare cost taxpayers nearly $500 billion or about 3% of GDP.[62] Over the 75 year horizon, Medicare will grow to nearly 10% of GDP, making it the single biggest factor driving up the size of government to unsustainable levels.[63] Of course, the thing driving this explosive growth in costs is changing demographics. The number of elderly people in the nation will grow 80% by 2030 while the workforce paying for their healthcare will only grow by 10%.[64]

There are several reasons the cost of Medicare is so high other than the high cost of healthcare and a rapidly increasing population of retirees. First, Medicare beneficiaries are virtually removed from feeling the cost of the care they consume and thus have no incentive to economize. Unlike Social Security, benefits are not contingent on what an individual contributed to the system. As we learn from Freidman's analysis of spending other people's money on one's self, a person has very little incentive to find low prices and every incentive to spend as much as possible. Why not consume all the health care you can if you're not the one paying for it? This overconsumption drives up prices beyond what they would be in purer market conditions. Progressives might respond by asserting that removing the pain of the cost from the consumer and giving them the freedom to purchase all they need is part of the point of Medicare. But ignoring the discipline of the price system is not a solution; it is counterproductive. We cannot lower the cost of things by using government to shift them from one group to another. All that does is conceal and increase the cost as people gradually get the illusion that the benefit is "free."

Doctors are also incentivized by Medicare to prescribe the most costly health care options because they get paid based on the services they provide, regardless of patient's health outcomes. There is also a tremendous amount of fraud, waste and abuse in the system. A 2013 report from the Department of Health and Human Services estimated that about 10% of its payments were made improperly.[65] But given that this is the government's estimate we can be fairly certain it is much higher. Indeed, Malcom Sparrow, a Harvard University professor who is an expert on health care fraud, testified before Congress that improper Medicare payments could be as high as 20%.[66] Those figures, combined with administrative costs and other inefficiencies, indicate that perhaps as much as 33%, or roughly $160 billion every year, is spent by Medicare that *does nothing to improve health outcomes.*[67] The Government Accountability Office for 20 years has designated Medicare a "high risk" program "in part because its size and complexity make it particularly vulnerable to fraud."[68]

This last point is particularly important. The truth is that nobody really knows how much money is lost to fraud because that size and complexity is precisely what allows fraudsters to remain hidden. Medicare processes over *a billion* claims a year, mostly by computer, without scrutiny from human eyes.[69] It is the nature of the program that causes waste. Unless we want to go down the road of real totalitarianism by, for instance, using the military to find the fraudsters, there is no way to put a dent in Medicare's waste without fundamentally changing the nature of the program. The government patted itself on the back for recovering $4 billion in defrauded money in 2011 while fraudulent activities may cost as much as $100 billion a year.[70] And the fact that government continues to increase the amount of money it recovers from fraud may simply indicate that fraud is increasing, not that government is getting better at detecting it.

Medicare's finances make it seem like something conceived right out of the Soviet Union. But the fiscal mess is only the beginning of Medicare's communistic DNA. First, it is falsely billed by some of its supporters as a voluntary program. But those who attempt not to participate are threatened with the loss of Social Security benefits in outright violation of the law. That is nothing shy of tyranny. Medicare enrollees are also effectively forbidden from spending their own money on health services outside of the system because if they do, the health care provider they use is banned from Medicare for two years. Thus, nearly all but the wealthiest seniors are coerced into a government insurance program which is in dire financial condition and is notorious for providing lower quality care. Second, Medicare's price controls, regulations and boards are reminiscent of Soviet-style central planning. An excerpt from the analysis of Cato Institute scholars Chris Edwards and Michael Cannon paints a vivid picture:

> These price and exchange controls fill more than 100,000 pages of regulations and related guidance... Medicare operates 16 different pricing systems for different types of health care services. Physician services provided under Part B, for example, use a complex pricing scheme based on the "resource-based relative value scale" (RBRVS). The government assigns each of 6,700 distinct physician services a value, which is then adjusted for each of 89 regions in the United States and converted to dollars. The result is that the government sets about 600,000 different prices for just this part of Medicare. A 29-member board of doctors sets the "relative values" of medical procedures under the RBRVS. ...Medicare's Part A, which covers hospital services, has its own centralized pricing scheme based on the diagnosis-related group (DRG) classification system, which includes more than 500 different types of patient cases. Other Medicare pricing schemes include those for ambulance services, home health agencies, skilled nursing facilities, and long-term care facilities. Each is a hugely complex price-setting system that generates a range of economic distortions.[71]

If I we replaced "United States" with "Soviet Union" and "dollars" with "rubles" in this excerpt, we might think it came from an economics or history book explaining why communism collapsed. The picture of government trying to formulate a price system that accommodates the vast complexity of individual choice in health care for millions of people is a quixotic exercise of insanity.

Every credible economist in the world understands that price controls cause perverse resource allocation. If prices are set too high then providers of those products or services will be enticed into the market regardless of the demand for them. In the case of Medicare, that means government will end up paying more for those products and services, whether or not they add value to enrollees. This certainly contributes to the massive amount of Medicare spending cited earlier that does nothing to make patients healthier or happier. Medicare's artificially high prices also fail to consider the quality of the product or service offered. Whether the quality of a hip replacement is poor or excellent the doctor gets paid the same. This leads to a trend of lower quality care because doctors have no profit incentive to offer higher quality work.

If prices are set too low then shortages result, meaning more people lack access to those products or services. For example, Medicare pays primary care physicians much less than it pays specialty doctors. This has resulted in a major shortage of primary care physicians for Medicare enrollees.[72] It is these physicians which are so important for detecting illnesses early, which leads to much higher survival rates for a variety of illnesses, not to mention lower costs in the long run.

Worse, Medicare's price controls and regulations have an effect on more than just its own enrollees. Medicare is the single largest purchaser of health care in the country and perhaps, even in the world. As such, its price controls and regulations affect the availability and quality of various health care products and services *for everyone*, as health care providers tend to shadow the prices set by Medicare's boards. We cannot operate a Soviet-style system without reaping Soviet-style results: lower quality, higher costs and a looming collapse.

Clearly, there must be a *fundamental change* to the nature of Medicare if we are to create a better deal for seniors and save ourselves from exploding costs in the near-future. Proposals to increase premiums, raise taxes, cut benefits, or use some combination of these will do nothing to solve the fundamental problems of Medicare. These proposals will do nothing to expand choices, end Medicare's ridiculous maze of communistic price controls and regulations, or improve the quality of care for seniors. Instead, they simply double down on the misguided strategy of fighting against the fundamental laws of economics rather than harnessing them for the benefit of all.

Again we must ask ourselves: Can we tax our way out of this mess? After the analysis presented in the previous section on Social Security the answer should be obvious. If we can't tax our way out of a $10 trillion hole, how could we possibly tax our way out of a $36 trillion hole; let alone tax our way out of the combined $46 trillion hole? It has been estimated that Medicare payroll taxes would have to be raised from 2.9% of each paycheck to 17.8% in order to fund the program's future obligations; a tax increase, which, by itself, would eviscerate employment and economic performance. Add that tax increase with the hike demanded by Social Security, then combine all other federal obligations, and it becomes clear that taxes cannot be raised high enough to fix our fiscal mess. This is not an ideological argument, it is a mathematical fact.

Not only that, but ample empirical evidence shows that countries are more successful at achieving fiscal balance when spending cuts far outweigh tax increases, *and when a large portion of those cuts come from social transfer programs*. In a 2010 working paper, researchers Andrew Biggs, Kevin Hassett, and Mathew Jensen studied numerous successful and unsuccessful attempts at debt reduction (fiscal consolidation). Here is an excerpt from their findings:

> ...lasting reductions in debt stem from expenditure cuts, and less so from revenue increases. To facilitate success in future consolidations, our results and the previous literature indicate that a suitable low-end target for the expenditure share is around 85 percent of the total fiscal consolidation. ...Of the individual expenditure items, our results indicate that social transfer reductions should comprise the largest share of the consolidation; there is a stark difference between the very large transfer shares in successful consolidations and very small transfer shares in unsuccessful consolidations.[73]

In other words, a near 6 to 1 ratio of spending cuts to tax increases should be *the low end* target for successful long-term debt reduction based on decades of experience in other countries. A great portion of those cuts must come from social transfer programs like Medicare and Social Security in order to be most effective.

However, the goal should not be debt reduction but smaller government, the economic benefits of which have been thoroughly demonstrated. When we add to this the fact that the quality and availability of medical services and retirement security for the elderly can actually be *improved* while cutting government spending, it becomes clear that the vast majority of our fiscal adjustments *must come from spending cuts*, particularly by removing government's burdensome control over entitlement programs. Why should we raise taxes to pay for a program which is structured to drive up the very prices which make it so costly, not to mention pay for its enormous waste? The smarter thing to do is to change the nature of the program so that prices fall and waste is eliminated, thus removing the need for tax increases in the first place. The right solutions should focus on restructuring the system so that prices and quality naturally improve.

The way to reform Medicare is to base the system on free market principles. That means abolishing price controls and onerous regulations, along with the central planners which administer them. Every senior should be allowed to opt out of Medicare without any threat of penalty from the government. Every Medicare enrollee should enjoy the freedom to buy whatever health services they wish outside the system, and the providers of those services should not be threatened with banishment from the program for performing the devious task of providing health care.

Of course, all that can be avoided by simply eliminating the role of government as the payer for medical services. Medicare taxes should be redirected, at least partially, to individually owned health savings accounts with no caps. Like a private retirement account, this would give each individual ownership and control of their health care dollars and an incentive to seek the most value for their money. Only a system based on private ownership will bring costs down and quality up as health care providers compete for the dollars in private accounts.

The need for reform is strengthened when we also consider the tremendous impact the Affordable Care Act will soon have on Medicare. The law created a new board that is responsible for finding money in Medicare to pay for ACA, which can only mean that payments to healthcare providers will be lowered. That will inevitably affect quality of care in Medicare for seniors as more doctors will likely stop participating. Medicare's actuaries concluded that ACA's payment reductions would mean that "Medicare beneficiaries would almost certainly face increasingly severe problems with access to care."[74] The actuaries also estimated that as many as 15% of hospitals might end their participation in Medicare by 2020, 25% by 2030 and 40% by 2050.[75] ACA's payment reductions are so severe that the actuaries presume that Congress will act to adjust Medicare payment rates. If that happens, and it likely will, every claim made by the Obama administration about cost savings to Medicare will be dismantled. It would also drastically alter the conservative estimates of the program's future unfunded liabilities while still leaving us with no way to pay for ACA's additional costs. This shows how incapable government is of bringing costs down by attempting to shift them from one group to another. In the end we are forced to choose; either fundamentally restructure the program or double down by attempting more stringent price controls, cost cutting measures and tax increases which only make Medicare, and the economy, worse.

When President Johnson signed Medicare into law in 1965 he predicted "No longer will young families see their own incomes, and their own hopes, eaten away simply because they are carrying out their deep moral obligations to their parents."[76] Like so many other empty government promises, Medicare has only worsened children's ability to care for their parents. Their obligations, collectivized, bloated and abused by politicians for their own purposes are now poised to collapse an entire generation. It is clear now that Medicare has, instead, darkened the hopes and decayed even more of the future incomes of young families as trillions of dollars of liabilities hang over their heads. We should have learned by now that government is incapable of reducing burdens; all they can do is shift burdens around, and in the process they often make those burdens harder to bear.

It is time now to consider the deep moral obligation we have to future generations to fix the mess that has been created for them. The moral failure of burdening future generations with untold amounts of debt is not one we should be prepared to live with. Our Founders fought a revolution in large part over the fact they were taxed without representation. That is exactly what we are doing to our grandchildren. They have no voice and they have no vote, yet they are being saddled with taxes to pay for things they will not benefit from. That is taxation without representation. Future generations will also have poor and sick people to take care of. How will they be supported if future generations also have to pay for *our* poor and sick?

<u>Medicaid</u>

Although not as large as Social Security and Medicare, Medicaid still occupies about 7%, or roughly $250 billion, of the federal budget.[77] The program receives less attention because it is much smaller as a share of the federal budget, but it is important to understand that Medicaid is an enormous program that rivals Medicare in terms of total expenditures. Medicaid is operated by the States, who also pay a share of benefits. When these numbers are added, the country spends about $432 billion a year on Medicaid.[78] That is a huge amount of money displaced from the private economy. One of the pillars of the Affordable Care Act is simply to expand Medicaid partly by finding savings in Medicare. Thus, any downward adjustments in the future liabilities in Medicare will simply be partially shifted to Medicaid. Indeed, Medicaid spending is expected to nearly double to over $800 billion a year by 2021.[79] Without fundamental reform, government can only play whack-a-mole with savings. Given this large growth we cannot ignore Medicaid's future contributions to our debt crisis.

Medicaid is fraught with many of the same administrative problems as Medicare. It is full of price controls which distort markets and cause shortages, resulting in lower quality of care for beneficiaries. Also like Medicare, Medicaid suffers from huge cost overruns and enormous amounts of fraud, caused by the same factors. Medicaid also has another characteristic which may make its cost overruns even worse than Medicare's. Medicaid operates as a sort of federal-state partnership. For every dollar spent by a State on Medicaid, the Federal Government chips in an additional amount to that State, depending on a variety of calculations. The federal share of State Medicaid spending ranges from 50 to 83%.[80] The result is unsurprising. States spend as much money as possible in order to increase the amount of money they get from the Federal Government. This creates a natural spiral of ever increasing program costs and dependency which displaces more people from private insurance.

Many States even go as far as to game the system in an attempt to get more federal dollars. One method is to raise taxes on health care providers and use the funds on Medicaid in order to get more funding from Washington. Health providers are happy to play along because they know that the additional federal money will come back to their bottom lines through Medicaid reimbursements and more than make up for the increased taxes. That is exactly what many States did, including my home state of Arizona, when they agreed to expand Medicaid under the Affordable Care Act. ACA vastly increased the federal share to 100%, and eventually back to 90%, for additional enrollees. The proponents of expansion in the States claimed it was the fiscally smart thing to do and that it would save their taxpayers money. But shifting debt from the States to Washington in the end makes no difference. It was nothing short of a con on federal tax payers and the future generations stuck with the bill, which also happen to live in the States.

Even if States tried to be wise with Medicaid spending they would be prevented from doing so by federal regulations and restrictions, such as those imposing eligibility requirements and caps on the premiums paid by beneficiaries. Essentially then, States are not only incentivized to overspend on Medicaid but are *obligated* to do so. Washington has therefore pressured the States into the same fiscal gluttony which feeds off of debt from future generations.

The solution to Medicaid's problems are not unlike the solutions for its sister programs. The essential component should be private ownership of any funds granted to beneficiaries, giving them the power to dictate the market rather than the government. This could be done through unlimited health saving's accounts.

The tragedy of the commons is a well-known concept of economics. When everyone owns an asset, nobody owns it and, therefore, no one takes care of it the same way a private owner would. A good example of this is one many will recognize. Over the last half of the 19th century, the bison population of the Great Plains was decimated by hunters seeking a profit for lucrative hides. Because nobody owned the bison the attitude was to take all you could before someone else did. As a result, the bison nearly became extinct.

While government ownership and regulation of an asset is preferable to no ownership, both will eventually end the same. Entitlements are socialist programs and a massive tragedy of the commons. This is not hyperbole. Entitlements take what was once earned and owned by an individual (your paycheck) and turn it into public property to be redistributed according to the needs of the state as determined by a massive and complex bureaucracy. Politicians and beneficiaries both adopt the mindset which the commons accurately predicts: take all you can while it's there. Politicians have raided the Social Security trust fund and spent the money for themselves. Medicare and Medicaid beneficiaries, their doctors, and fraudsters see a massive pile of free money ripe for the taking. The resulting frenzy which drives up costs is as predictable as human nature. This is not an insult to those who honestly receive entitlement benefits. They are simply acting in their best interest given the circumstances. People always act in their own self-interest. That is why the lesson of the commons is to create a system which seeks to harness that human instinct for the common good, rather than to be victimized by it. We call that system capitalism, or private ownership.

The argument that we should keep the present system because people benefit from, and depend on, entitlements is no more effective than it would have been to argue that we should have let hunters continue to decimate bison because they depended on it for a living. Of course entitlements benefit people just like the bison benefited those who exploited them. But future generations pay the price. At one time, we had an economy and demographics that could support these massive programs. But the demographics and economics, spurred by the effects of the commons, are now working against us.

The total 75-year unfunded liability for the Federal Government is about $55 trillion, or $478,000 for each household.[81] And these are government numbers which are almost certainly underestimates. One economist calculated the total amount of all future debt, the difference between all projected expenditures and revenues, to be over $222 trillion.[82] The immediate future is equally troubling. Our current $17 trillion debt is poised to drive up interest rates. By 2023, the Federal Government will be paying more than $800 billion a year just on interest payments for our ballooning debt.[83] Think of that; $800 billion every year in government spending that provides no security, no protection, no health care, no education, no benefit to anyone! Interest is a hidden cost to large government programs that is never reported. In 10 years, $.75 of every dollar spent by Congress will go to Social Security, Medicare, Medicaid or interest on debt.[84] Two words: socialism, collapse. The message could not be clearer to any fair-minded person: CAP FEDERAL SPENDING!

You might have wondered whatever happened to the bison. Today herds of bison once again roam the plains ...*on private ranches*. More than 90% of the U.S. bison population is privately owned.[85] Because private owners have an incentive to look after their assets, bison populations have recovered over the years. The same will be true of entitlements when the transition is made to private accounts. Private property rights are the biggest drivers of prosperity. Many will complain of the massive cut in benefits but the truth is that *benefits will not be cut; they will simply be transferred from public ownership (socialism) back to private ownership (capitalism)*. Only this policy will improve retirement and health care security, drive up quality, avoid the fiscal disaster, improve property rights, expand liberty, and grow the economy. No other entitlement reform option can come close to accomplishing all that.

We must fight the ideological tunnel vision that would force us to choose some combination of harmful tax increases and/or benefit cuts. This will require a huge paradigm shift and an accurate understanding of how these programs work (or don't work) and their true fiscal situation. It will take leaders who are committed to changing public opinion rather than conforming to it. The truth is that if most Americans understood the nature of these programs they would clamor for private accounts.

Polls showing large support for entitlements are misleading because they often do not get to the crux of the issue. We shouldn't be surprised that after a career of having their money confiscated by government, retirees want it back. That shouldn't be confused with support for the programs. If we were to ask the American people to choose between a program that confiscates a portion of their money in exchange for a promise from government to pay it back later by confiscating other people's money, and a system that allows them to keep their money to begin with, we all know what the majority would choose.

One of the advantages of a state-imposed Constitutional spending cap is that it forces Congress to make changes which might otherwise be politically impossible to make. Attempts at reform are extremely difficult, as we saw from President Bush's brief attempt to reform Social Security and Representative Paul Ryan's more recent attempt to reform Medicare. It is easier for politicians to cater to voters than to do the hard task of leading and explaining the necessity, let alone the benefits, of private accounts. Whatever you think of Bush and Ryan, they should be commended for their efforts but they are fighting a losing battle. The system is broken, politics rule the day, and within that framework, monumental entitlement reform may simply be impossible. That is why we must change the framework by imposing a spending cap from without. There is hope of getting this done. Bipartisan support for a spending cap from fair-minded people has already been shown. A spending cap of 20.6% of GDP has been introduced with Democratic cosponsors in the Senate (McCaskill and Corker) and House (Cooper and Duncan of TN).[86]

Most Americans want the government to cut spending, until it is proposed to cut the program that benefits them. Once a specific program is targeted, the beneficiaries of that program are able to organize a strong opposition. The general language of a spending cap, with no specific mention of any program, should be able to carry widespread political support, which will be necessary at the state level to prompt legislatures and governors to call a convention and ultimately achieve ratification. Only then will Congress be forced to come to the table and cut spending. Spending discipline must be *imposed* on Washington. We cannot hope that they will do it themselves. It is up to the States to pass an amendment which would force Congress to reform these programs and get its fiscal house in order.

The rationale and empirical evidence overwhelmingly favor the principle of government spending restraint. Capping federal spending by Constitutional amendment is the only sure way to align with that knowledge. Our history shows that monumental progress is achievable without government spending over 20% of GDP. As we are poised to experience massive increases in entitlement spending we have no choice but to enact reforms which would force Congress to make the needed changes. If we do not act, then we subject ourselves to the chaos, tumult and suffering of all the other nations before us who refused to constrain their governments', and their own, greed.

The decision in *Helvering* gave Congress an unlimited ability to spend in aid of the general welfare. That ruling, more than any other, is responsible for the Federal Government's largest and most debt-prone programs. While there is no practical way to restore the original understanding, a spending cap is the next best thing. It is essentially a compromise more than 200 years in the making. Hamilton and Story argued for a broad interpretation of the General Welfare Clause so that government could spend in times of emergency. This cap provides a way for government to meet those needs. For 150 years, government was mostly confined to enumerated powers. We now know from experience that unleashing Congress from its moorings was not without negative effects. As we sit on the precipice of an explosion in government growth, it is time to recognize that something must be done to limit government and replace politics with law. If we concede that Congress can spend in the name of the general welfare beyond the enumerated powers, then we must insist that spending be limited. Such a compromise is moderate, wise and will work for the benefit of all.

CHAPTER TEN

TAXES

"The answer to our problems in this country, even at the national level, is to have a law that says there is a percentage limit of the people's earnings that government cannot go beyond."

"We're the only country in the world where it takes more brains to figure out your income tax than it takes to earn the income."[1]

- Ronald Reagan

Amendment 30

1. Congress shall not tax any person or entity at a nominal or effective rate exceeding twenty percent of income, from whatever source derived, except in time of war which shall have been declared by Congress; and the expiration of the cap shall be determined in the same manner as the spending cap.
2. The taxing power shall not be construed to allow Congress to give credits, deductions, adjustments, exemptions or penalties of any kind to any person or entity based in the United States, and all such adjustments in current law shall be null and void within five years of the ratification of this amendment;
3. Congress shall not have power to raise or collect excise taxes.

4. No religion may be taxed or fined in any manner; and charity organizations and other not-for-profit organizations may be made exempt from taxation.

It is difficult to separate a discussion about taxes from a discussion about spending. After all, taxes are meant to be spent. Consequently, some arguments from the previous chapter are repeated in this one. In effect, nearly every point made in support of a spending cap is just as strong a point in support of a cap on taxes. In fact, the theme of this entire book rests primarily on the proper interpretation of the General Welfare Clause which grants the Federal Government the power to tax. That clause also *limits* the authority to tax by specifying the purposes for which taxes may be levied. Therefore, the *Helvering* case not only granted a nearly unlimited power to spend, but it also removed any meaningful limits on the power to tax. This was confirmed in the Supreme Court's approval of the individual mandate of the Affordable Care Act. Of course, there were other events in our history which led to a greater power to tax for Congress. This chapter will discuss some of that history and will set out to make a case for re-establishing limits on Congress's ability to raise taxes. The case for a tax cap could be divided into three parts; philosophical, political/legal and economic. Let's proceed to examine these in order.

We may start a philosophical discussion on taxes by reciting the following universal principle: *You have a right to what you earn.* Any fair-minded person would accept this declaration at face value without hesitation. What you produce is naturally yours to control. Notice we do not assign a percentage to the amount of your property to which you have a right. Your rights extend to 100% of everything you produce. On the other side of the tax equation is government. Do they have a right to your property? No! Government is merely a representation of the rest of society, which did not earn or produce what you did. In addition, government is only granted the powers we consent to give it. There is no inherent or natural right of the state to control any portion of your property. You are sovereign over your property just as the nation is sovereign over its territory. You have as much a right to resist government taking your property as you do a thief.

Of course, most of us enjoy living in society where we have law and order. Most Americans are perfectly willing to pay taxes in exchange for the basic functions of government. But when we look at taxation through the paradigm of individual sovereignty we see the issue in a different light. We are not subservient to the government. They work for us, not the other way around. Government can tax us because *we choose to let them*, not because they decree that it is necessary. Of course, taxes are necessary and government should have a certain amount of authority to collect them. We cannot simply wake up one morning and decide not to pay taxes because we believe in individual sovereignty. But this frame of reference clarifies our relationship with government and offers a starting point for justifying a tax cap. The government is not, and should not be, our master to determine indiscriminately how much money we must pay them, even if we are "wealthy." Thus, a limit on what the government can take from us is necessary to keep the government within its proper sphere of being our servant and to help protect our natural rights to our property.

Quite fittingly, it was Franklin Roosevelt who demonstrated well government's misguided notions of taxation. While discussing pay roll taxes he said: "We put those pay roll contributions there so as to give the contributors a legal, moral, and political right to collect their pensions and their unemployment benefits."[2] Where does this "legal, moral and political right" come from? Can government bestow on you a moral right to your own property? The deceit of FDR's words becomes more apparent when we understand how Social Security really works. The money government takes out of our paycheck is not set aside for us; it is spent by government and becomes its property. The money we receive when we retire comes from another worker's paycheck. Do you have a moral right to a portion of another's paycheck simply because the government made you a promise? The moral rights to our own property, including what is necessary for retirement and disability insurance, exist perfectly well without government's presumptuous bestowal of them. Politicians have no right to take property from us so that they can create a perpetual constituency of government dependents. The legal, moral, and political right to property predates and supersedes government.

The Founders believed in the philosophy of individual sovereignty. It was expressed in words we have all become familiar with in the Declaration of Independence: "We hold these truths to be self-evident, that all men are created equal, that they are endowed by their creator with certain unalienable rights, that among these are life, liberty and the pursuit of happiness." Originally, Jefferson had listed property as the third of these unalienable rights. "Life, liberty and property" was a commonly used phrase at the time, derived from the great political philosopher John Locke, on whose writings the Founders greatly relied while framing our founding documents. Locke asserted that the primary purpose of government was to protect natural property rights. The next sentence in the declaration is reflective of this: "That to secure these rights, governments are instituted among men, deriving their just powers from the consent of the governed." This was a revolutionary idea at the time; the idea that government should work for us, to secure our natural rights to property. Up until that time, individuals typically existed for somebody else, whether the government, or the church, or the privileged class. Jefferson was saying that each individual exists for his own happiness, that he is individually sovereign and has an inherent right to his property, among other natural rights. The central message of these words in the declaration is that you don't exist for government, government exists for you. More germanely, your paycheck doesn't exist for government, government exists to protect your paycheck.

The legal/political justifications for a tax cap can be found by examining the Constitutional history of taxes in the United States. How exactly the philosophy of individual sovereignty was manifested in the new Constitution with regard to taxes is difficult to discern. Part of the problem is that an inherent paradox is created when governments are formed because it must command a portion of the country's wealth, which naturally belongs to individual citizens, in order to secure individual rights. Therefore, it will take some scrutiny to sort this out but any proposal to amend the Constitution should require at least some of the historical precedent affecting the subject of amendment. The questions we are most concerned with are these: What was the nature of Congress's taxing power as originally written in the Constitution? What, if any, were the limits of the taxing power? How have subsequent treatments of the taxing power altered from the original intention and were these alterations wise?

At the convention, it was agreed by most that the new government would need an independent power to raise revenue. After all, the main issue which prompted the convention was the central government's inability to pay its debts. Under the confederation, Congress could not directly tax the people but could only ask the States for money and they sometimes failed to pay. Thus, one of the primary themes of the convention with regard to taxes was making sure that Congress would be able to support itself without having to rely on the States. So, early on it was proposed to give Congress the power of direct taxation. This power was the source of the bitterest contention during the convention and subsequent ratification debates.

The debate was divided, as we have seen, between the Federalists and the Anti-Federalists. The Federalists generally argued that the new government ought to have broad powers of taxation in order to fulfill any unforeseen needs. They insisted that Congress be allowed to directly tax the people and that the lack of this power may result in the same embarrassments which forced the framers to rework the confederation to begin with. On the other hand, the Anti-Federalists were mostly opposed to creating a national government that could directly tax citizens. They argued that burdensome taxation was the very reason they had just fought a revolution. A central government with broad powers of taxation was certain to oppress the people just as the King had. They also worried that with the States raising their own taxes, Americans would have to pay taxes to, not one, but two governments! They insisted that two different governments with co-equal powers of taxation would be unworkable. Therefore, they argued, the new government ought only to have the power of indirect taxation, that is, mainly, duties and excises (sales taxes).

As you know, the Federalists won the debate, but how they won that debate is important to understand because it gives us insight into how the taxing power was intended to be used. The Federalists generally argued that while Congress would have a strong authority to tax, they wouldn't likely use it much unless there was an emergency. They were able to win support for the new Constitution partly by asserting that there were limitations to the taxing power. The Founders never intended for the Federal Government to exercise an unlimited power of taxation without restraint, although it is conceded that a broad power of taxation in the Federal Government was granted. The limitations on Congress's taxing authority were of two kinds: explicit and implicit.

In examining the explicit limitations we start by going back to where we began this book. We have discussed in detail the first clause of the eighth section which grants Congress the power to "lay and collect taxes, duties, imposts and excises, to pay the debts and provide for the common defense and general welfare of the United States." This is certainly a broad power but it is not without limits. It has already been shown that the term general welfare was nothing more than a limit on the power to tax; i.e. Congress cannot tax for whatever reason they want, they can only tax for certain enumerated purposes. There is no need to add any more to those arguments here. Let it suffice that this was an explicit limitation on the power of taxation as explained by Madison and confirmed by many others including Joseph Story.

Another explicit limitation is found immediately following the clause from the eighth section quoted above; "but all duties, imposts and excises shall be uniform throughout the United States." Thus the use of indirect taxes was to be limited in the sense that they had to be levied equally from state to state. While this may not have been a limitation on how high Congress could raise indirect taxes, it did protect the States from being targeted by punitive taxes and from bearing an unequal share of paying them. This was an important protection as we shall see later.

Another explicit limitation on the taxing power was the rule of apportionment. Most of the early days of the convention were spent debating how the people and States would be represented in the new Congress. As part of this discussion, vigorous debate erupted over how slaves were to be counted when deciding how many representatives the southern States would have. If slaves were to be fully counted toward the southern State's representation in Congress, then the States with heavy slave populations would have comparatively more representation than States with fewer slaves. Many of the delegates from the northern States feared this would give the south too much power in Congress. The south wanted slaves to be fully counted so that they could increase their representation. They were fearful that the power of direct taxation (property tax) would be used to tax slaves and thus force them to pay a greater share of taxes to the central government. A compromise proposal was to count three fifths of the slave population. However, the southern States were still unsatisfied.

Then, Gouverneur Morris, a passionate anti-slavery advocate representing Pennsylvania, put forth a highly respected proposal; to tie the State's representation in Congress directly to taxes. The States with more representation would pay more taxes. This idea would ensure that if taxes were raised on southern slaves, then an equiproportional tax increase would have to be raised from other States, thus appeasing the fears of southerners that they would be the targets of disproportionate taxation.

Several members of the convention immediately remarked how just the proposal was. The added benefit of Morris's idea was that a State would be discouraged from over reporting its population to get more representation in Congress. If a State had a greater population it would have a greater representation in Congress but it would also pay a greater share of direct taxes to the Federal Government. The genius of the proposal was that it intimately linked representation with taxation; a principle which was certainly paramount to the generation that had fought a war to protect it.

The convention decided that only direct taxes would have to be apportioned. It was believed that the apportionment requirement would be cumbersome, and if all taxation were subject to this requirement the government might struggle to fund itself. Thus, Article 1, Section 2 of the Constitution reads: "Representatives and direct taxes shall be apportioned among the several States..." and again in Section 9: "No capitation, or other direct, Tax shall be laid, unless in Proportion to the Census or Enumeration..." The bond between taxation and representation was further strengthened by Section 7 which states that "All bills for raising revenue shall originate in the House of Representatives"; the people's representatives only were to initiate the taxes levied on them.

The rule of apportioning direct taxes achieved three things: 1) It made sure that each State would pay an equal share of taxes to the Federal Government in proportion to its population; 2) It closely tied representation with taxation, a vitally important concept for any just and accountable government; 3) It served as a de-facto limit on Congress's ability to levy a direct tax as it would be cumbersome to administer. All three of these important functions have been undone over the years.

After the convention, the understanding of Congress's taxing power became a bit uncertain. The key to understanding the nature of the power is to understand what was meant by "direct taxes." Surprisingly, to this day, no one is certain what the framers meant by the term. At the convention, Rufus King asked the delegates what the phrase meant; no one answered; and little can be gleaned from letters and other commentary which would give us a conclusive definition. This is surprising because it is such an important question. If direct taxation had a very narrow meaning, Congress's taxing power would be broad. On the other hand, if direct taxation had a broader meaning, then the federal taxing power would be more limited because more taxes would have to be apportioned by State according to population. This had serious implications for future tax law.

Setting aside the uncertainty over which taxes are direct and which are indirect, these two terms encompass every tax which can be contemplated, and thus show that the Federal Government's power to tax was explicitly intended to be restrained. Indirect taxes were to be uniform, direct taxes were to be apportioned and all taxes could only be raised for the general welfare as defined by enumerated powers.

We now turn to an examination of the implicit limitations on the powers of taxation. These were assumed to restrain Congress from exercising a general power of direct taxation, particularly in peace time. One of the main reasons the Federalists won the ratification debate was because they argued there were implicit limitations to Congress's taxing power, particularly on the power of direct taxes. Alexander Hamilton said that "it is impracticable to raise any very considerable sums by direct taxation."[3] He then went on to point out that in Great Britain, most government revenues were derived from indirect taxes. To him, and most of the Founders, it was believed that Congress would rely primarily on import duties for their revenue for the foreseeable future. The message was that Congress needed the power of direct taxation in order to support itself in the event of a war, but it would be politically impractical for any Congress to use it in peace time. Given that bills to raise revenue could only be introduced by the House of Representatives, and not the President or Senate, the Federalists reasoned that overtaxing representatives would be quickly voted out of office. Recall that at the time, only representatives were chosen directly by the voters and are up for re-election every two years. The potential for quick changes in the House was believed to be a significant safeguard against high taxes.

The Founders knew that duties and indirect taxes would be a weak source of income and herein rests another limitation on Congress's taxing power. The cost of duties is passed along to consumers – the same consumers who vote directly for the representatives who alone have the power to introduce bills for raising revenue. Thus, it would be very difficult to raise duties too high without significant political backlash. This was widely understood by both sides in the ratification debates. One anti-federalist said of indirect taxes:

> ...few officers are necessary to be imployed [sic] in collecting them, and there is no danger of oppression in laying them, because if they are laid higher than trade will bear, the merchants will cease importing, or smuggle their goods. We have therefore sufficient security, arising from the nature of the thing, against burdensome and intolerable impositions from this kind of tax.[4]

Edmund Pendleton best summed up the federalist position in favor of direct taxation and its implicit limitation:

> A gentleman has said that the power of direct taxation was unnecessary, because the imposts and back lands would be abundantly sufficient to answer all federal purposes. If so, what are we disputing about? I ask the gentleman who made the observation, and this committee, if they believe that Congress will ever lay direct taxes if the other funds are sufficient. It will then remain a harmless power on paper, and do no injury.[5]

Thus, it is clear that Congress was implicitly limited from extensively using the power of direct taxation. Many were assured that the new government wouldn't use the power but would likely rely on duties which could not be easily abused. This proved to be an effective strategy in winning support for the Constitution.

However, the Anti-Federalists were rightfully suspicious that the power of direct taxation would eventually be used widely if there were not more explicit limitations on its use. Ever jealous of centralized power, here are a few of their complaints in the anonymous words of a few prominent writers (writing anonymously in political matters was very common at the time):

> ...we are told that under the proposed Constitution, "direct taxation will be unnecessary"; that "it is probable that the principal branch of revenue will be duties on imports." Some of those who have used such language in public and private, I believe to be very honest men; and I would therefore ask of them, what security they can give us, that the future government of the continent will in any measure confine themselves to the duties upon imports, or that the utmost penny will not be exacted which can possibly be collected either by direct or indirect taxation? How can they answer for the conduct of our future rulers? We have heard enough of these fair promises for the good behavior of men in office, to learn to doubt of their fulfillment.[6]

And from another:

> I am sensible also, that it is said that congress will not attempt to lay and collect internal taxes; that it is necessary for them to

have the power, though it cannot probably be exercised. I admit that it is not probable that any prudent congress will attempt to lay and collect internal taxes, especially direct taxes: but this only proves, that the power would be improperly lodged in congress, and that it might be abused by imprudent and designing men.[7]

These concerns led five States to propose an amendment, intended to be part of the Bill of Rights, which would have allowed Congress to levy direct taxes only if the other sources of revenue were insufficient. It did not pass, but as we know, the anti-federalist's warnings once again proved prophetic.

Another implicit limitation on Congress's taxing power was the difficulty, referred to earlier, of having two governments collect the same kinds of taxes. The Federalists tried to allay fears of an overtaxing national government by assuring people that it would be difficult for Congress to directly tax the people, to any considerable degree, because they were already paying direct taxes to State governments. Put in another way, the Federalists argued that State governments would have the advantage in any contest for revenue partly because they were the familiarly established powers at the time. Alexander Hamilton, writing in federalist 31 about direct taxes said:

It should not be forgotten, that a disposition in the State governments to encroach upon the rights of the Union, is quite as probable, as a disposition in the Union to encroach upon the rights of the State Governments. What side would be likely to prevail in such a conflict, must depend on the means which the contending parties could employ towards ensuring success. As in republics, strength is always on the side of the people; and as there are weighty reasons to induce a belief, that the State governments will commonly possess most influence over them, the natural conclusion is, that such contests will be most apt to end to the disadvantage of the Union.[8]

Speaking in the debates of Virginia's ratifying convention, Edmund Pendleton said:

But we are told that there will be a war between the two bodies equally our representatives, and that the state governments will be destroyed, and consolidated into the general government. I stated before, that this could not be so. The two governments act in different manners, and for different purposes... if each power is confined within its proper bounds, and to its proper objects, an interference can never happen. Being for two different purposes, as long as they are limited to the different objects, they can no more clash than two parallel lines can meet. Both lay taxes, but for different purposes.[9]

And James Wilson, speaking in Pennsylvania's ratifying convention stated:

I think I may venture to predict that the taxes of the general government, if any shall be laid, will be more equitable, and much less expensive, than those imposed by the state governments.[10]

Thus, it is clear that there were both explicit and implicit limitations on the power of taxation at the time the Constitution was ratified. However, the Anti-Federalists were not persuaded. They echoed and repeated the warning that over time the state governments would become subservient to Congress if the latter were given the power to raise direct taxes. One wrote:

And what are the individual States to do, or how are they to subsist? May they also lay and collect taxes, duties, imposts and excises? If they should, the miserable subject will be like sheep twice shorne; the skin must follow the fleece. ...unless we guard ourselves by much better security, there will be no bounds to the new government. They will not have as much to spare for the separate States to collect as Lazarus picked up of the fragments from the rich man's table. [11]

In spite of these warnings, the Federalist's predictions about taxation proved accurate throughout the 19th century. The Federal Government practiced a light hand when it came to taxation and did rely mostly on tariffs. So it is clear that successive generations understood Congress to have a limited ability tax.

Twice during the 19th century an income tax was proposed, not surprisingly, during the two major wars of the century, that of 1812 and the Civil War. While the income tax proposed to help pay for the war of 1812 was never implemented, the Civil War income taxes were. With the enormous cost of that conflict, Congress, for the first time, began to directly tax the incomes of people and businesses; and they did it without adhering to the rule of apportionment. To the enormous credit of Congress, the income taxes were allowed to expire once they were no longer needed (Could you imagine Congress today giving up a stream of revenue?!). However, many of those who paid the income tax believed that they were direct taxes which had to be apportioned from among the States as called for in the Constitution. Now we must come back to the question of what exactly is a "direct tax."

When one of the Civil War income taxes was challenged in 1868, the Supreme Court upheld it as essentially being an excise on doing business and therefore, they ruled it did not need to be apportioned.[12] In 1894, Congress passed another income tax, which was included in the Wilson-Gorman Tariff act. This income tax, unlike the others, was not to pay for a war. Instead, it was part of an effort to restructure the way the Federal Government got its money. Wilson-Gorman imposed a tax of 2% on incomes of $4,000 (roughly $90,000 in today's money) and also reduced tariffs.[13] This was a radical shift away from relying on tariffs and keeping with the tradition that the Federal Government would only turn to direct taxation in times of emergency. The law would put a much greater burden of taxation on the wealthy, which was just fine with the majority of the population, especially given the severe economic downturn at the time. Not only would the rich have to pay the tax, but their businesses would also be exposed to foreign competition with the reduction in tariffs. As you can imagine, the law was hotly debated.

The Wilson-Gorman Act was a good idea in principle. Tariffs raise domestic prices which disproportionately affect lower-income families who need to buy the high-priced goods. And because tariffs protect domestic industry from foreign competition they partially help the owners of that industry to accumulate more wealth without adding any corresponding value to consumers. Therefore, a small flat-tax on wealthy individuals would be a preferable way to fund the government. However, the constitutionality of income taxes is of utmost importance. The wiser course of action would have been to propose a Constitutional amendment, though it is understandable why an amendment was not proposed given previous Supreme Court rulings on the income tax.

The following year, the issue was left, once again, to the Supreme Court. In the case of *Pollack v Farmer's Loan and Trust* the Court effectively overturned the previous rulings on income taxes. Now, the Court *did* define income taxes as being direct taxes and thus, needing to be apportioned as called for in the Constitution. The Court's basic argument was that the Founders intended to limit Congress's authority to directly tax the people. These limitations could not be avoided by simply defining a tax differently from its real effect. Chief Justice Melville Fuller delivered the opinion of the court:

> Nothing can be clearer than that what the Constitution intended to guard against was the exercise by the general government of the power of directly taxing persons and property within any state through a majority made up from the other States. [Apportionment was] designed to operate to restrain the exercise of the power of direct taxation to extraordinary emergencies, and to prevent an attack upon accumulated property by mere force of numbers.

> ...the acceptance of the rule of apportionment was one of the compromises which made the adoption of the Constitution possible, and secured the creation of that dual form of government, so elastic and so strong, which has thus far survived in unabated vigor. If, by calling a tax indirect when it is essentially direct, the rule of protection could be frittered away, one of the great landmarks defining the boundary between the nation and the States of which it is composed, would have disappeared, and with it one of the bulwarks of private rights and private property.[14]

The simple truth is that an income tax, by any reasonable interpretation, is a direct tax. Whether or not the Founders would have agreed and subjected an income tax to apportionment may be questioned. But one thing on which the Founders agreed was that property taxes were direct taxes. Income is property. That being the case, the 1895 Court got it right.

The 1895 and 1868 Courts both put forth strong arguments for their respective decisions, which necessarily had to be based on their own judgment as opposed to the founder's intentions because we lack any definitive clarification as to everything that should be included by the term "direct taxes." As the early history of the United States has shown, little thought was given to using income taxes. Whether by design or oversight, it was simply left to future generations to decide how the power of direct taxation should be interpreted and applied. But if the country saw fit to change the way the Federal Government funded itself, and in the process break from a hundred years of tradition and legal understanding, then passing a Constitutional amendment was a requirement.

Eighteen years after the Court's ruling in *Pollock*, the nation did just that with the passage of the 16th Amendment, which enabled Congress to directly tax incomes without regard to apportionment. The 1895 Supreme Court courageously upheld what was a clear limitation on the taxing power. To its credit, the government utilized the proper channels of amendment to give Congress a power which was not authorized but which was deemed necessary. This was the properly established pattern for changing the rules of government, and the one for which this book now contends. Using it ensures the legitimacy of government actions, which ought to be particularly important in the case of taxes.

However, 100 years after the 16th Amendment's ratification, it is a good time to evaluate its effects. Such an evaluation will reveal that the limitations imposed on Congress's taxing authority were carelessly set aside. Part of the result has been the political bickering, class warfare and gridlock we see today. This Amendment carved out a specific tax for Congress to levy with no limitations of any kind, a danger which was not intended by the Founders. The Anti-Federalists rightly predicted that the powers of direct taxation would eventually be brought into full use. We would have done well to heed their advice: "[The Constitution] should have marked the line in which the general government should have raised money, and set bounds over which they should not pass..."[15] We can still follow that council by passing the 30th Amendment.

Perhaps what the Federalists did not consider in their arguments was that government would attempt to tax only the wealthy and thereby gain popular support, thus undermining their contention that high taxes would necessarily be punished at election time. Other than true socialists, no one argues for high taxes on the poor and middle class. Our tax debates have really only been about taxes on the wealthy. Of course, those who advocate for high taxes on the rich are in a much better position politically and therein lies the reason for such intense debate in spite of the wisdom of low taxes for all. Masses of voters throughout the country are perfectly content to have the government take money from someone else, particularly to fund the programs that benefit them. An entire political party has virtually made its living playing off this attitude. But it is precisely this type of political gamesmanship that the rule of law was meant to prevent. Restoring a limitation on taxes via Constitutional amendment will help us purge the envy and class warfare that is gaining strength in our country.

For more than a hundred years, congressional restraint and respect for the spirit, as well as the letter, of the Constitution were enough to keep federal taxes low and indirect. But the combination of a massive accumulation of wealth in the hands of a few, and a severe economic recession in the 1890s, proved to be too powerful for the Constitution's restraints. Thus, we set down a path which would transfer to the Federal Government a truly unrestrained and lucrative source of revenue. For all the attention given to the New Deal Court's terrible decision in *Helvering*, it was the income tax which made Social Security possible to begin with. Indeed, no entitlement program, nor big-government itself, could exist without it, and the push for expanded federal action in the 1930s likely never would have begun. The explicit and implicit limitations on the taxing authority, and thus the spending, have been nearly completely removed as a result of the 16th Amendment. After a century of restraint, the Federal Government cast its greedy eyes on the wealth of the nation and abandoned the tradition of tariffs as its primary source of revenue.

The passage of the 16th Amendment has led to a myriad of problems. For starters, without the rule of apportionment, the Federal Government has eaten up the lion's share of revenue from the States, and thrown out of balance one of the key characteristics of our federalist system.

The theme of the Constitutional Convention was one of balance and compromise between the powers of the States and Federal Government. Each ought to have the ability to raise the revenue needed for its own purposes. The great achievement of the convention was to create the right amount of balance in our dual form of government. While the State governments continue to operate, they are but vestiges of their former selves and are little more than administrative branches of the national government. The average income tax rate in the States is 5% while the Federal Government has a top rate of nearly 40%. Of course, controlling the revenue also means controlling the policies for which the money is spent – putting the States in the position of bowing to the Federal Government's wishes in order to get back the money taken from their constituents. The apportionment requirement for direct taxation allowed for the preservation of State authority while ensuring the Federal Government would be able to provide for itself. But with the passage of the 16th Amendment, the State's authority has been vastly eroded as they have been overshadowed by a power they were intended to share equally with Congress.

Another negative effect of the 16th Amendment has been the growth of the IRS and its liberty-offending intrusiveness into the lives of Americans. The Anti-Federalists gave us plenty of warnings about this also. Brutus warned:

> ...it will lead to the passing a vast number of laws, which may affect the personal rights of the citizens of the states, expose their property to fines and confiscation, and put their lives in jeopardy: it opens a door to the appointment of a swarm of revenue and excise officers to prey upon the honest and industrious part of the community, eat up their substance, and riot on the spoils of the country."[16]

Brutus continued that an unlimited power of taxation:

> will watch the merchant in the counting-house, or in his store; it will follow the mechanic to his shop, and in his work and haunt him in his family, and in his bed; it will be a constant companion to the industrious farmer in all his labour, it will be with him in the house and in the field... To all these different classes of people, and in all these circumstances, in which it will attend them, the language in which it will address them, will be GIVE! GIVE![17]

And finally he warned that the power of taxation can be the "great engine of tyranny and oppression".[18] We have seen recently the power of the IRS to harass and unjustly target those who are not in favor with the current administration. The stories of innocent people being harassed by government agents for the payment of taxes have steadily multiplied and show no signs of slowing. Such a scene is perhaps the most offensive outcome of the 16th Amendment.

The power shift between the States and Federal Government is not only dangerous to liberty, but it is completely wasteful and inefficient. Why should the Federal Government raise taxes directly from the people, filter it through their bureaucracy, take out a broker's fee, then give it back to the States to administer as it does with so many of its programs? The States have their own elected representatives capable of raising revenue from their constituents and spending the money in accordance with their will. In this manner, Arizona can pay for the things it deems important the same as Massachusetts. This decentralized system is conducive to more accountable, and therefore, better government.

The accountability part is particularly important. The rule of apportionment was partially designed to strengthen the relationship between taxation and representation by tying a State's representation in Congress directly to the amount of money each State would pay in direct taxes. Now that the rule has been removed, it was only natural that that relationship would be weakened. Take for example, the current case of California, which has an enormous debt in terms of future liabilities. There has been some talk about the Federal Government possibly bailing out that State. Setting aside the issue of its reckless spending, why should any State rely on the Federal Government for revenue? That is to say, why should any State be able to get money from taxpayers in other States, who have no voice in California's legislature? If Californians wants to spend themselves to oblivion then let them do it *and let them pay for it*. No principal could be more just, which is why the Founders enshrined it in the Constitution.

We have also recently seen the Federal Government bailout Detroit to the tune of some $300 million, so far.[19] Again, why should the tax payers of Phoenix, a city which has been comparatively run very well, bail out a city which has been poorly managed by people for whom they did not vote? This example illustrates very well how the Federal Government's spend and tax schemes, fueled by the 16th Amendment, have eroded the crucial link between taxation and representation. While it may be argued that our representatives in Congress appropriated the money, it was not our elected representatives which acted irresponsibly in creating the debt. The Constitution authorizes Congress to levy taxes "to pay the debts... of the United States" not of any state or local government. Each has its own representatives and its own objects on which to spend. Nothing is more just than to have each remain within its bounds and to answer the wishes of their respective voters concerning those issues which are entrusted to them. Nothing could be more unjust than for those bounds to be broken and cause money from one set of constituents to be transferred to another.

The diminished link between taxation and representation is exacerbated by the sheer number of items in the federal budget. Our votes for President, Senator and Representative force us to consider a broad range of issues for just those votes – as opposed to considering a narrower set of issues for each level of government. Having to consider a wider range of issues over which a smaller number of politicians preside erodes accountability. For example, how should we consider our representative's votes on the $300 million for Detroit (unconstitutional), which we might disapprove, weighed against a veteran's pension bill (Constitutional), which we might approve? Such difficulties allow federal politicians to get away with sneaking minor items (as measured in millions as opposed to hundreds of billions) into larger spending bills without any real accountability at the polls. That lack of accountability has eroded the link between taxation and representation. This is a big reason why many elections are a choice between the lesser of two evils. The more say politicians have on what to spend money, the more difficult it is for voters to make informed decisions about the best candidates, as they cannot easily hold their representatives accountable.

A much better system is given in the pre-16th Amendment Constitution. We have three separate and distinct governments; local, state and federal, each with an authority to tax for a given set of purposes; the federal for national defense, regulation of interstate commerce and all others enumerated in the Constitution; the local for our most immediate community concerns; and the States with all others not reserved for the federal. When each stays within its bounds, each will be more effective and more accountable to the people. When the bounds are broken, as they were destined to be with the passage of the 16th Amendment, accountability and effectiveness are both diminished.

Another example will illustrate this point. Arizona's Grand Canyon is a natural wonder which brings in millions of dollars to the local economy. Congress has usurped the power to claim it for itself and use taxpayer money to protect it and run the park. Should I vote out my Congressman and Senator for appropriating too much money to the park or for mismanaging it? Such a decision would be ridiculous considering the many more weighty things Congress does. The result is that no one really gets held accountable for the spending and administration of the park. This is why government spending on these types of issues quietly grows year after year with nobody really scrutinizing whether or not the money is needed or being administered wisely. On the other hand, if local governments were responsible for the park, then those elected to tax and spend for its maintenance may very well be held accountable at the polls for faulty management because the park is so vital to the local economy. There is a natural incentive for local residents to see to it that the park is taken care of because it immediately affects their prosperity. Thus, they are in a far better position than Washington to manage it wisely while taking care of taxpayer's money.

Another primary example of the erosion of the link between taxation and representation is Social Security, made possible only by the 16th Amendment. None living today voted for the politicians who put this program in place. Do you remember having given your consent to Congress to automatically deduct 12.4% of your paycheck?[20] It cannot be seriously argued that because Congress has not repealed Social Security it therefore means the people are accurately represented as wanting the program. The structure of Social Security was set up to deliberately to protect the program from future assaults. The payroll (income) taxes used to fund Social Security were picked specifically so that people would demand they get their money back upon retirement, making it nearly impossible to repeal the program. It is impossible to even reform Social Security without one group or another getting the short end of the stick.

When one of Franklin Roosevelt's advisers suggested that payroll taxes were an economically bad idea, FDR responded: "Those taxes aren't a matter of economics, they're straight politics." "With those taxes in there, no damn politician can ever scrap my Social Security program."[21] In other words, no representative, elected by their constituents; no matter how distant in the future, can determine policy upon republican principles with regards to Social Security (and to boot, damn the economic consequences). Neither you nor I voted for FDR or any congressman that enacted Social Security. Yet we are bound to it because FDR was clever enough to structure the program in a way that would make it political suicide for any congressman to try. Our elected officials should be bound to the people's will, within the context of Constitutionality, not the will of a dead President and Congress who acted outside the Constitution.

Politicians speak of "discretionary" versus "non-discretionary" spending, the latter being spending mostly on entitlements and consisting of nearly half of all spending. Are we to simply accept that our elected representatives have no discretion over half the money they spend, as well as a great portion of the money they collect from payroll taxes? And if they have no discretion over what is taxed then where is our representation for those taxes? We should not be governed by politicians from the past for whom we did not vote, any more than we should have been governed by a parliament across the ocean for which we did not vote.

Another way in which the 16th Amendment has eroded the link between taxation and representation is the enormous complexity it has enabled in the tax code. When the income tax was first passed in 1913 the tax code was 400 pages; it is now nearly 75,000![22] This complexity has been the mechanism which has allowed Congress to presume the power of regulating the lives of individuals – a feat not possible with excise taxes. By using credits and deductions Congress can adjust the amount of taxes owed if an individual or business undertakes a behavior which Congress likes, such as buying health insurance or giving to charity. While that doesn't sound so bad, it has now been confirmed that if Congress can issue credits it can also issue penalties for *not doing* what Congress likes, such as *not* buying health insurance. Congress has long been able to use a carrot to regulate Americans but now they have the stick. Taxes were not meant to be used in this manner. The intention of giving the power to Congress was to raise revenue to pay for legitimate Constitutional ends.

The ACA in turn has produced several offensive examples of how taxation and representation have been split. Part of the ACA calls for health insurance "exchanges" where individuals can go online and purchase a government-approved insurance plan. As with many other big-government programs, Washington needs the help of the States to administer critical parts – in this case, the online exchanges. The ACA entices the States to create the exchanges by offering tax credits for individuals who purchase insurance *only through state-run exchanges*. The problem for the law, recognized early on by Democrats, is that if States refused to create the exchanges, the tax credits could not be made available to individuals and businesses in those States, greatly undermining the ACA. Though an attempt was made to make it so that tax credits would be available through federal exchanges, it did not happen because it could not get the votes in Congress.[23] As was feared, after the law was passed many States did not create an exchange and thus made unavailable the federal tax credits crucial to the success of the ACA. "Never fear!" said the IRS! In a shockingly lawless ploy the IRS took it upon itself to give tax credits to individuals purchasing insurance through *federal exchanges*. On the surface, it may seem like a trivial issue. But this is blatantly contrary to the plain language, meaning, and intent of the ACA as enacted by our representatives in Congress. The IRS has no legal authority to act on its own in violation of the laws passed by Congress. It has been estimated that these tax credits would result in a liability of about $600 billion over the first ten years; *all without congressional approval.*[24]   That money must be taxed or borrowed at some point and the people's representatives in Congress did not authorize it.   Who will be held accountable?   Which Congressman will be on the chopping block in the next election because of these IRS actions? No one. Such a blatant attack on taxation and representation is offensive to the legal foundation of our tax system.

This action by the IRS demonstrates how far we have strayed from the Constitutional vision of keeping taxes and representation closely linked.   It also shows, once again, the danger of abandoning the Constitutional restraints so wisely put in place by the framers. Once those restraints are removed, the tendency for government overreach and abuse is greatly enlarged. The only way back is to revisit the Constitution and renew, in unmistakable terms, meaningful restraints; in this case, abolishing Congress's ability to tinker with the tax code so that a clear line of sight can be established for every taxpayer to know exactly what their liability is and which elected representatives are directly responsible for it. With the 30th Amendment thus established, voters will have a much better ability to hold politicians accountable.

Let's summarize what we have covered so far. First we established that human beings have a natural right to what they earn, and that governments only tax at the will and pleasure of the citizen, not the other way around.   We then showed that the framers of the Constitution attempted to preserve this proper relationship by restricting Congress's power of taxation with both explicit and implicit limitations.   It was of paramount importance to the framers to intimately link taxation and representation as a means of securing accountability at the polls for unjust taxes and expenditures. Unfortunately, the 16th Amendment removed the limitations on Congress's taxing authority, giving rise to the IRS and a big central government which have diminished State power, threatened the freedom and privacy of every citizen's finances, eroded the link between taxation and representation, and countenanced the government with a seemingly unlimited power to regulate the lives of individuals through deductions, credits, and penalties.

No practical amendment could undo the entirety of this mess. Ideally, we would simply repeal the 16th Amendment. This would fix a great deal of the mess but it would be an unwise course for two reasons. The first is practicality. Our government has grown so large over time with so many people now dependent upon it that to think we could return to a system of relying on tariffs and excises is simply not realistic. There is no other source of revenue beside the income tax which could possibly satisfy the enormous size of the Federal Government. They may be the primary point of abolishing it but we cannot hope for a return to 19th century government. The Federal Government should never have been given the power of the income tax to begin with, especially without limits, but they have it now and we must enact amendments that can be reasonably expected to pass.

The second reason is economic. Relying on tariffs and excises would be unwise. Both fall with disproportionate weight on the poor and middle class by raising the price of nearly every product they buy. If we eliminated the income tax and replaced it with a sales tax we would immediately increase the tax burden of scores of people who pay no income tax. Such a course would not be wise. Going back to the original formula is simply not an option. The best alternative is to maintain the income tax with a cap and to remove Congress's ability to make complex adjustments. This will make wide-spread support possible while minimizing the negative effects of the income tax.

Congress has taken it upon itself to use the income tax to regulate the behaviors of individuals. There can be no doubt that such a power was never intended for Congress. It is true that the power to tax was given to Congress and was intended to be used at its discretion. But as Justice Story tells us, it is not right to use a Constitutional power to achieve unconstitutional ends. Over time, Congress has so burgeoned the tax code that it has become something far different from what it was intended to be. Taxes were always understood to be for raising revenue for government. Instead, Congress has created in the tax code a massive regulatory heap of complicated rules intended to manipulate and coerce taxpayers.

The crowning achievement of this effort is the Affordable Care Act. The 30th Amendment categorically is intended to make the ACA, and anything like it, unambiguously unconstitutional (at least unambiguous enough for the Supreme Court to catch on). This is particularly important because we must prevent Congress from using its newly confirmed power of penalizing Americans for behavior which is not approved by them. While some legitimate complaints may be offered against removing Congress's ability to give tax credits and deductions, no such legitimacy can be extended to Congress's ability to use the tax code to *penalize* Americans for unapproved behavior. Such a power in the hands of Congress is so grotesquely offensive to everything we ought to hold dear, I can scarcely believe this law was actually passed in the 'land of the free'. Are we to relegate ourselves into a timid flock of sheep with Congress as the shepherd? Are you willing to expose yourself to Congress's freedom-sapping rules for individual behavior; for what you should do with your land or with your money? Few priorities should supersede the effort of dislodging this power from Congress.

Some may protest that the 30th Amendment would eliminate critical tax credits and deductions, such as those for children or for charitable contributions. But these choices, no matter how universally praised, are personal decisions and should remain outside Congress's scope of manipulation. If the concern is that parents will not have enough money to raise their children then lower the tax rate. If the concern is that charitable contributions will fall dramatically then lower the tax rate and leave it to the people to regulate their own behavior. Americans have always been generous and when the need arises they will give. Taxes are for the support of government, not the regulation of behavior.

The vast majority of Americans would much rather pay a low, transparent tax rather than pay a higher tax and ask the IRS for a refund. Even so, the amendments convention may find it prudent to allow Congress to retain one or two important tax deductions through the course of refining this amendment. What is most important is that Congress be restricted from regulating behavior using the tax code and that the code be dramatically simplified or abolished. Such outcomes are most likely under a Constitutional amendment formed behind closed-door negotiations beyond the influence of lobbyists. Previous efforts to simplify the code have been sapped of momentum by politics and special interests. Nearly everyone agrees that the code should be simplified, yet it does not happen. Even if it could be achieved by statute, Congress would quickly resume piling credits and deductions on top of each other, putting us right back where we are now. This is one reform that almost certainly can only be achieved by changing the Constitution.

Others may protest that government will not be able to offer important tax credits such as those for so-called green energy projects. We might address each tax credit in the entire code and could be accused of assaulting each particular endeavor the given credit or deduction is meant to promote. If you don't want the mortgage interest deduction you must be against people being able to afford a home! But the whole point of removing credits and deductions is to remove the manipulative and tainting influence of politicians and special interests. This effort is about simplifying the tax code and lowering the rates so that people can afford the things they need *on their own*. Taxes are a means for the government to raise money for Constitutional purposes. Taxes should not be used to allow Congress to manipulate and regulate individual behavior. Congress already has the power to regulate commerce, as do the States within their jurisdictions. Let this suffice and let taxes be for revenue. All other policy decisions should be considered separately from taxes. An assault on the tax code is not an assault on everything for which adjustments are offered. It is an assault on the mind-numbing 75,000 pages of confusion, manipulation, coercion, invasions of privacy, inequality and drag on productive work. It is an assault on the thousands of special interest lobbyists which have poisoned our political process as they clamor for the next tax credit for their industry. And it is an assault on a system which unduly favors the wealthy and big corporations who can afford an army of lawyers and lobbyists to navigate the tax code and manipulate it to their advantage.

Most Americans want a simplified tax code yet I have sat in on meetings where those same Americans vote to support another tax credit which they perceive will help their business. Voters cannot change the tax code but they can easily support the candidate that is proposing another tax credit for "new technology investments" so the code keeps growing, special interests keep control, and we all pay the price during tax season. Again we see that the solution cannot come about through the political process. A Constitutional amendment, passed without lobbyists, would be the only way to achieve what we all want: a plain tax system where you simply declare your income, from whatever source, pay your given rate, and move on with your life.

Another regrettable effect of the tax code is the violation of the spirit of equality under the law. This guarantee, enshrined in the 14th Amendment, is of utmost importance to Americans. All should be treated equally by the government regardless of who they are or their personal choices. Yet the insanely complex tax code would favor some and penalize others depending on their life choices, wealth or simply their level of patience with filing taxes. The complexity of the code undermines taxpayer morale by making it difficult to know exactly how tax rates are computed, and by giving the impression of unfairness as some are able to manipulate the system and minimize their tax liability. It also opens the door for criminals to commit fraud and erodes the relationship between taxpayers and government. Many Americans don't even know what they pay in taxes or what bracket they fall in. A clearer understanding of how much is paid in taxes tells a citizen exactly what their contribution to government is and thereby bolster's their sense of pride and participation in government functions. The government should be blindfolded and collect taxes from each citizen without regard to their personal preferences or life choices. We should demand equal and exact justice to all, and that cannot be fulfilled without equal and exact treatment under the tax code.

Finally, we must consider the cost of the tax code's complexity. Consider these staggering numbers from the Taxpayer Advocate Service's annual report to Congress: Americans spend an estimated 6.1 billion hours and $168 billion a year preparing taxes; equivalent to the work of more than 3 million full-time workers. [25] This is particularly alarming when it is understood that the work of preparing taxes is pure waste; it adds nothing of value to the economy. The report also goes on to say that since 2001, Congress has made nearly 5000 changes to the tax code imposing a "significant, even unconscionable, burden on taxpayers." Clearly the tax code must be vastly simplified. Not only does the tax code erode morale, diminish equality and promote crime but it also exacts a real economic cost. The case for reform could not be stronger yet Congress has not acted. Have you sensed the pattern yet? Congress will not act on its own. It is up to the States to make constitutionally mandated reforms.

While the cap on tax rates will not fix all of the problems associated with the income tax it will produce very desirable economic benefits. The economics of a tax cap will prove to be the least ambiguous and most persuasive of any arguments that can be offered in its favor.

The first reason a Constitutional tax cap would strengthen the economy is the stability it would bring to the tax code. Economic fluctuations, regime changes and constantly evolving tax law combine to create uncertainty for investors and entrepreneurs. For example, as government creates larger deficits during recessions, investors tend to delay some activities because they anticipate rising taxes in the future. A long term cap on rates, credits and deductions would create tax certainty for investors, removing any incentive to delay economic activity.

Of course, the more common debate over tax policy is determining the rates that should be applied. Obviously, leaving more money in the private sector is good for the private sector and for the economy at large. The economic benefit of lower taxes has been empirically proven; so much so that the principle hardly needs more explanation. But tax policy demonstrates well the ability of politics to crowd out plain logic and sound economics. Envy and class warfare have caused us to lose focus on what matters most in the long struggle to minimize poverty and care for the vulnerable. While most recognize the economic benefits of leaving more money in the hands of the poor and middle class, there are many who do not believe that leaving money in the hands of wealthier people is as beneficial to the economy. Of course, this sentiment is based more on politics than on economics. When money is left in the hands of the people who earn it, they can do three things with it: save, spend and invest; each of which is good for the economy. Spending gives businesses revenue; investing helps businesses startup, expand and hire workers; saving creates stable retirements, inheritances for children and grandchildren and the capital stock necessary for interest rates to remain low (a greater supply of money means a lower price for that money) thereby allowing businesses and individuals to borrow more cheaply. Because there aren't many people burying their cash in the back yard, it makes sense that allowing the wealthy to keep more of the money they earn is good for the economy.

A progressive might respond that helping the economy is fine but the purpose of a strong economy should be to strengthen the poor and middle class. Thus, redistribution, taking money from the wealthy and giving it directly to the middle class and poor, is justified. While it may be tempting to accept this simplistic view, the evidence has shown that the poor and middle class are helped most by a growing economy, not by redistributing wealth to them. In a working paper for the World Bank, economists conducted an exhaustive study of 118 countries over 40 years and came up with these findings:

> Incomes of the bottom 20 percent and bottom 40 percent of the income distribution generally rise equiproportionally with mean incomes as economic growth proceeds. The finding is good news in the sense that we can expect economic growth to lift people out of poverty and lead to shared prosperity on average.

> We also include variables that might plausibly increase the income share of the poor (measures of agricultural productivity and government spending in health and education). This part of

our work essentially provides non-results: none of the macro country-level variables we consider robustly correlates with changes in the income shares of the poorest quintiles.[26] (emphasis added)

In other words, those who talk about "shared prosperity" would do better to focus on economic growth rather than redistribution in order to achieve their vision. In this study, government spending on things such as health care and education *gave no indication of improving the incomes of the poor.* Bolstering these findings is the staggering amount of money spent in this country since the "war on poverty" began in the 1960s, with little sign of significant improvements for the poor as a result of these programs.

These findings show that governments should focus on the economy, not class warfare, if we truly want to help the poor. Pitting the country against the rich gets us nowhere. While there are many factors that contribute to economic growth, we can say for certain that a high tax rate isn't one of them. More money left in the economy, whether held by rich people or small entrepreneurs, means more is available for growth. If a rich person buys a yacht, then the middle-class worker at the shipyard benefits. If he saves it in the bank, more is available for someone to get a car loan at a cheaper interest rate. If he invests it, the receiving business has money to hire more workers.

Even if we conceded that redistribution is generally beneficial, the case for capping taxes would remain strong. The reason is that there must be some limit which would discourage politicians from engaging in harmful class warfare. The high taxes which large redistribution schemes require cannot be levied without negative consequences to the economy which end up harming the very people whom redistribution is intended to help. The spending cap would discipline the spending while the tax cap would discipline the composition of raising revenue so that punitive taxation, which would discourage investment, could not be used.

Wealth creates more wealth. The more wealth that is left in the private economy, the more jobs and growth can be produced. Not only does this concept serve as a basis for low taxes but it should also prompt governments to consider how to lure more wealth into the country and to stay here. Keeping taxes low is certainly a good starting point. As tax rates rise, we can rest assured that individuals and businesses will do the logical thing; avoid paying higher taxes. There are a myriad of strategies that can be used, legal and illegal, which can reduce an entity's tax burden. These strategies range from simply reporting less income to moving a business to a country with lower taxes. It doesn't take much thought to figure out what happens to our economy when wealthy people and businesses take their money and infrastructure elsewhere. Investment and jobs become scarcer. A marginal amount of additional thought reveals what happens to the economies of countries who receive the new businesses and investment; growth and jobs increase, benefiting all classes of citizens. Governments should therefore find ways to attract wealth not to repel it through high taxation. As higher taxes repel wealth, redistribution schemes become less likely to achieve their intended effects as tax revenues will inevitably fall short of projections.

As financial mobility has increased with globalization a new phenomenon has been created called tax competition – a contest between jurisdictions to create the best business environment. In our increasingly globalized world governments must compete for people and businesses just as businesses compete for customers. Just as it does for appliances in the free market, competition helps to create higher quality government at a lower price. Some decry tax competition as a "race to the bottom" as jurisdictions supposedly get caught in a downward cycle of never-ending tax cuts that result in a shortage of public services. But the empirical evidence does not support these fears.[27]

Low tax rates are not the only thing to consider when exploring a possible move to another country. Contract enforcement, a dependable legal system, and sound regulation are all important factors that help businesses to thrive in a healthy economy. A business considering country A with very low taxes but a week legal system, and country B with higher taxes and a strong legal system, will have a good incentive to choose the latter. Tax competition therefore, does not just induce governments to lower taxes. It pressures them to provide value in return for the taxes they do charge. Some evidence for this comes from a recent OECD study which praised the "efficiency-raising effects of... tax competition on the public sector" and noted that it allows people to "choose the level of public service provision and taxation."[28] The mobility of people and businesses, particularly the wealthy, will only get faster as technology advances. The only wise course is to embrace it and compete to attract the best talent to America. A great way to do that would be to constitutionally cap what the Federal Government can tax.

Unsurprisingly, monopolies, especially the government kind, hate competition and will do everything they can to keep their power. Throughout the history of civilization governments had complete control over the taxation of their citizens and there was nothing anyone could do about it except start a revolution. This inevitably led to government waste, inefficiency and abuse just as it does with private sector monopolies. But tax competition has changed this and the government monopolists who would so quickly decry private sector monopolies are being dragged along kicking and screaming. Few things tend to aggravate progressives more than wealthy people who have the nerve to protect their property by putting money in countries with lower taxes and more privacy. Thus, in 2010, Congress passed the Foreign Account Tax Compliance Act (FATCA). This offensive piece of legislation requires foreign banks to report to the American IRS any U.S. citizens with accounts over a certain balance, including their names and addresses.[29] The preference for tougher enforcement rather than reform is obstinate and costly. FATCA has prompted a large increase in U.S. citizenship renunciations – most of whom are wealthy - and has discouraged a great deal of foreign investment.[30]

The tighter governments try to squeeze their citizens the more will slip through their fingers and into more overtly illegal activities. Empirical evidence shows support for this, along with the converse principle that jurisdictions with lower tax rates have higher tax compliance, meaning fewer people try to cheat the system.[31] Rather than going after "tax cheats" with a cloak of self-righteous patriotism, the wiser course is to embrace tax competition and implement policies which will induce people and businesses to *want to* keep their money here and invest in America.

Globalization and competition have pulled billions of people out of poverty. The next revolution of globalization may well be the imposition of discipline and restraint on governments around the world as they compete for talent and wealth. We want that talent and wealth in America. As Europe continues to raise taxes, let us take the initiative in this new competition and invite their wealth to come here. A Constitutional cap on taxes would go a long way toward increasing our competitiveness and attracting the talent and wealth that generates economic growth.

Another problem with higher taxes on the wealthy is the difficulty of properly defining "wealthy." President Obama has apparently put it at $250,000 a year. But this attempt shows a painful misunderstanding of business and economics. A very small proportion of people who earn that kind of money get it from a consistent year-to-year salary. Most six-figure earners are entrepreneurs or investors. For these people, a $250,000 gain in one year could turn into a $50,000 loss the next. In some cases, they may have to depend on those high earnings for several years. But the high tax rate may leave them short of badly needed capital. This is not to invoke pity except for the people who then have to be laid off as a result of bad tax policy. The issue is not, and never has been, about the "wealthy," it is about the economy; leaving more money in the hands of investors and entrepreneurs for investment and growth. It is much more conducive to job creation to allow individuals and businesses, particularly at the lower end of the "wealthy" scale, to keep more of their money in order to offset possible downturns.

Another impetus for high taxes on the wealthy is the wealth disparity complaint. Some argue that greater wealth disparity is bad for the economy and that we should therefore raise taxes on the wealthy and give the proceeds to the poor and middle class in order to create a more equitable distribution of income. Complaints about income inequality have remained strong for generations and are likely to remain persistent because of their political appeal and superficial legitimacy. But an empirical and reasoned analysis shows unequivocally that these complaints are misguided and, worse, counterproductive.

Proponents of forceful government attempts to remedy wealth inequality have never been able to produce a satisfactory mechanism for *how* wealth disparity harms an economy or hurts the poor. Attempts to do so are usually boiled down to one theory: that inequality somehow reduces opportunities for the poor. But this does not explain anything; it merely restates the purported problem. The question is *how*; how does income inequality create less opportunity for the poor? There is no answer because it does not. No one can explain how, in a market system where people must be persuaded to freely choose to make a purchase, a person can become wealthy *at the expense* of others.

The most sophisticated form of the income inequality complaint is that capital gains (income from investments) produce greater returns than salaries from labor, and are growing more rapidly than the overall economy. If these gains continue to grow more rapidly than the economy, then the rich, who primarily benefit from them, will continue to gain a greater share of overall wealth. Therefore, we should tax the wealthy, perhaps as high as 80%, in order to reduce inequality.

This theory could not be more flawed. First, if the gains from capital are so great, why not allow more people to harness those gains instead of punishing the people who do? That brings us back to privatizing Social Security which could significantly reduce inequality over generations by giving people an inheritable asset. And there are other ways to open up capital gains to the masses such as removing restrictions on crowdfunding for equity investments. Of course, that would require that the poor and middle class be treated like adults rather than a class of helpless victims in need of government support.

Imagine the scenario on an individual level. Suppose your neighbor comes across an ingenious and rather safe way to make good money. Are you more likely to demand that he give you a bigger portion of what he makes, or will you more likely be curious about how you can do it as well? It is strange that any legitimacy is given to the former reaction simply because government, driven by vote-seeking politicians, seeks to demand a bigger share for you. The lesson from this analogy is clear: if capitalism produces such great returns, then we should make more capitalists not tax and redistribute the returns.

Second, the theory assumes, falsely, that capital gains and economic growth are somehow mutually exclusive; that capital gains can take place without economic growth and vice-versa. The reality is that capital gains are intimately connected with economic growth. Where else can the gains come from? An equity investment or loan plus interest cannot be paid back without increased productivity and job creation. When a wealthy person or firm invests in a company, they provide the capital necessary for that company to hire workers and expand business, driving economic growth. To criticize the fact that the investors get a greater return on their capital than the workers get for their labor is as senseless as complaining that a producer gets more out of selling computers than each buyer gets out of having one. The buyers of computers are participating in a free exchange which gives them something they can use to make their life better. Likewise, without the capital investment, and the incentive to get a return, workers may not have jobs at all. The salaries for those jobs, while smaller than the returns provided to the investors, are now part of wealth that did not exist prior to the investment, and have provided the additional benefit of expanding opportunities for the workers, such as to gain experience and save money. The investors therefore, are not simply getting a bigger share of the wealth; they are creating more of it, and in the process directly benefiting workers.

I doubt we could find many people complaining about the investments they receive for their businesses. In fact, receiving an investment is usually a celebrated landmark. The only people who seem to complain about this scenario are the people who stand to gain from exciting natural jealousies (mostly politicians) and the uninformed who buy into their rhetoric; usually unaware of how much they benefit from this capitalist system. An uncanny depiction of this happened when the New York Times, often peddling inequality hysteria, was bailed out with an investment from Carlos Slim, one of the richest persons in the world.[32]

Another problem with the theory is that it is unclear why we should fear that the rich will continue to gain a greater share of the wealth, provided that wealth or income grows for everyone. Suppose the theory is true and that capitalists at the top will continue to gain a greater share of wealth until they have 70%, 80% and eventually 90% of the wealth. If the growth of their wealth is contingent on economic growth, as it must be when based on free-market principles, then the smaller share owned by the rest of us will still be larger in absolute terms than our previously larger shares. In other words, as long as everyone's wealth increases enough, we have no reason to complain. If in a hundred years the richest 1% has gained 99.9% of the wealth there is nothing to worry about so long as the .1% remaining is substantially greater than the 60% share we have today. I understand the difficulty of overcoming the natural shock such a statement might bring but the concept is perfectly rational. (Of course, it must be shown that in the real world wealth and incomes are indeed growing for everyone; we will get to that in a moment.)

In any event, history shows this will not likely happen. Throughout the 19th century, the richest 1% saw their share of wealth steadily grow until it peaked at about 45% around the turn of the 20th century, after which it fell continuously until 1970 when it resumed growth.[33] While the long-term fluctuation of the top 1%'s share of wealth involves many factors, it is not inevitable that it will grow indefinitely. In fact, it is clear that we are witnessing the emergence of a global middle class, indicating that the spread of capitalism is helping more than just the wealthy.[34]

The proponents of redistribution may claim that capital gains for many wealthy people are not the result of direct business investments but merely accumulate from the exchange of stock, and therefore, do not directly benefit job creation or economic growth. This is true in a sense, but we have to ask whether these stock gains come at the expense of others. Imagine you have an antique lamp in your attic. After a number of years you discover from the Antique Roadshow that the value of your lamp grew by 300%! Was that wealth taken from anyone? Of course not. In a similar manner, the wealth of most people at the top fluctuates with the value of their investments. This should temper our anxieties when we see a chart showing the growth of the top 1%'s wealth. It does no harm.

A stock price goes up because demand for that stock rises. The increased demand can generally be accounted for by one of two things or their combination: an increase of available capital with which to invest, or factors related to the performance of the company. If the increased stock price is related to the company's performance, whether real or predicted, then why would we worry? The performance of the company is increasing wealth and job creation, and the capital gains are simply mirroring that increased wealth or are accurately predicting improved performance. More importantly, *the increased value of the stock takes nothing away from anyone; it is new wealth creation.*

At first, it may seem that taxing these gains would be much more justifiable than taxing the gains from directly investing in business expansion. Leftists usually complain that wealthy people "do nothing" to earn the increased value of their stocks. Setting aside the fact that investors actually work very hard to research and study their investments, the truth is that wealthy people worked hard to own the stocks in the first place. Is there an increased justification for taxing the appreciated value of my home because I "did nothing" to earn it? On the contrary, when someone works hard to own *any* asset, only they have the natural right to reap its increased value. Perhaps more importantly, such taxes would certainly discourage the exchange of stock, decreasing prices and affecting everyone in the middle class with a 401(k) or stock options. In the United States, stock ownership is spread broadly across income classes. The exchange of stock increases wealth just as all freely-made exchanges do, often benefiting more than just the rich. Creating new wealth, whether through rising stock prices or by direct investment in labor and equipment simply cannot come about *at the expense of others,*(except as described below) but only has the potential to create *more* jobs and opportunity as more wealth is created.

If, on the other hand, increasing stock prices are due to an increase in available capital, we have nowhere to look other than the central bank for providing that capital out of thin air. In this case, we very much have a reason to complain because government is creating money out of nothing, and the first to receive newly created money are banks, traders, and hedge funds. This means the wealthy who ply these trades enjoy a rise in asset prices as the increased supply of money creates more demand for investments. Meanwhile the poor and middle class are stuck with simply rising prices without correspondingly increasing wages. The Federal Reserve's unprecedented "quantitative easing," fueling a booming stock market, is the primary reason the wealthiest 1% saw their wealth grow particularly fast over the last 5 years while median incomes have fallen and economic growth has been weak.[35]

We have now come across a revealing and embarrassing contradiction in left-wing economics, as well as a perfect example of the bungling nature of government actions. As left-wing economists are calling for "quantitative easing" to help the economy, those actions are, instead, merely spurring the capital gains which they so vehemently deride and wish to tax.

The only possible explanation for how wealthy people limit opportunities for the poor is that they are able to exert more influence over government through lobbying and outright corruption. This will then lead to less opportunities for smaller entrepreneurs to compete and will generally keep prices high, which disproportionately affects the poor. But this is as much a function of government being too big as it is a function of wealth. The more government does, the more incentive wealthy people have to exert influence over those activities in order to protect themselves or to benefit from them.

Some assert that large wealth disparity in developing nations is evidence of its harmful effects. In fact, the wealth disparity in developing nations is nearly always the result of cronyism and government-sanctioned monopolies. This is certainly the case in Mexico where, since colonial times, the wealthy have been able to maintain near-complete control over government.

When Mexico sold its state-owned telephone company Telmex in the early 1990s, rather than break up the company into smaller competing parts, the entire telecommunications market was quite literally handed over to a group led by Carlos Slim. The Mexican Government explicitly granted a monopoly to the privatized company and even allowed payments for the purchase to be made from future profits. To this day, it is "unclear" how or why such a generous deal was given. Slim was wealthy before the deal but the Telmex monopoly allowed him to compete for the title of world's richest person. Of course, Mexico's poor were left with some of the highest phone bills in the world along with some of the worst coverage.[36] Anyone paying attention to the news is well-aware of how similar, though less sinister, crony deals are multiplying in the U.S., distorting prices and limiting opportunity for the rest of us.

The tens of thousands of pages of regulations and the numerous redistributive anti-poverty programs in the United States have done little to stop income inequality. On the contrary, the growth of government only seems to have fueled wealth disparity.[37] Politicians usually ally themselves with wealthy donors and key industries, which, in turn, get special favors, gaining them an advantage over smaller businesses. A good example of this is the Dodd-Frank financial "reform" bill which institutionalizes the concept that big banks should be protected by government. This makes it harder for smaller banks to compete as larger banks will seem like the safer investment given that they have the backing of the full faith and credit of the United States. The bill contains other provisions which make it comparatively more expensive for smaller banks to do business.[38]

A study done for the Small Business Administration found that for companies with more than 500 employees, the cost to comply with *just environmental laws* was $717 per employee annually. Companies with fewer than twenty employees had an *annual compliance cost of $3,228 per employee*.[39] Such government policies burden small businesses and, by extension, their employees, comprised primarily of poor and middle-class workers. Thus, misguided government policy strongly contributes to increasing wealth disparity. Free markets certainly result in wealth disparity for a variety of reasons but big government more often makes it larger.

The same people who have cheered on the growth of government are usually the loudest to denounce the lobbyists and "special interests," employed by the wealthy, that exert so much influence over legislation. But asking for legislation without influence from the wealthy in a democracy is like asking for salt water without the salt; you cannot have one without the other as long as voters decide elections. Pending legislation will prompt the affected industries to hire all the lobbyists they can to shape that legislation to their advantage. Politicians are obliged to listen because if they do not, they lose the support of key donors and industries. Not only that, but regulators are required by law to take public input. Given that most of us are busy with our jobs, the only people with the time and resources to give input, i.e. lobby, are the wealthy. Campaign finance reform will never change this. The surest way to reduce the influence of lobbyists is to reduce the amount of legislation coming from Congress. This is one of the primary reasons the rule of law must restrain government. Politics are ugly and that will never change. To make things better, we must reduce the influence of politics and cronyism by reducing the influence of government.

If people do become wealthy at the expense of others' opportunities, i.e. through bribery, corruption, fraud and other illegal activities, they should be prosecuted with vigor. Income inequality is only bad as far as it is an indicator of corrupt and misguided practices, such as the Fed's quantitative easing (you decide whether it is corrupt or just misguided). If we want to decrease real inequality in America then we should reduce the size and scope of government, thereby decreasing the prospects for wealthy people to manipulate government in their favor.

The redistribution crowd, in its haste to point out inequality statistics, routinely ignores or misinterprets the crucial concept of income mobility. Inequality is often measured by evenly dividing the population into five income quintiles. It is not at all adequate to point out a growing share of income for the top quintile (wealthiest 20% of the population) and a decreasing share for the bottom quintile without discussing the ability of people to move in and out of the quintiles. The same people who were poor ten years ago may not be poor anymore. When we look at the data we find that mobility today is indeed as strong as it was in 1970.[40] That is encouraging, particularly when we understand that once a family moves to a higher level of income their children's opportunities to move higher still are greatly improved.

There does exist what economists call "stickiness at the ends"; people born into wealth and poverty tend to remain there; 43% of people born in the poorest quintile will remain there, and 40% of people born in the wealthiest quintile will remain there.[41] First, there should be no complaint that the wealthy remain wealthy; we should not want people to get poorer. But people do complain about extravagant inheritances and claim that many wealthy people should be heavily taxed because they did not earn their money. However, the data reveal that wealth is very fluid: 80% of America's millionaires are the first in their families to reach that status.[42] And the flip-side of the previous statistic shows that 60% of those born in the top quintile will not stay there.

Looking at the poorest quintile is likewise somewhat of a glass-half-full or half-empty scenario. It is certainly not good news that 43%

remain in the bottom quintile, but it does mean that 57% of people born there will climb their way out as adults. That is great news. There is certainly a wide-ranging discussion that could be had as to why so many remain in poverty but the main point here is to show that it is not *because of* income inequality; and it is certainly not because of a lack of taxes and transfers to the poor ($60,000 per year per poor family of three as reported in Chapter Five).

More importantly, we have to consider more than just mobility among quintiles to understand how well-off people are, such as how the quintiles change over time. For example, progressives like to point out that during the 1950s, we enjoyed much more economic mobility than we do today, implying that things were better back then. According to census data, the upper limit of income for the fourth (where the top quintile begins) and bottom quintiles in 2012 was $119,000 and $27,000 respectively, while in 1955, it was $51,000 and $16,000 respectively, in 2012 dollars.[43]   That reveals we were not better off in the 50s, *everybody* was poorer. Moreover, it is easier to move up to the next quintile when the quintiles are compressed among a smaller range of incomes, but that does not tell us anything about the prospects of poor people to increase their standard of living.

In fact, today's larger wealth disparity, combined with the fact that mobility among quintiles remains the same as in 1970, indicates that mobility is actually *stronger* today than in the past because it takes a greater amount of wealth to move into the next quintile. In 1970, a household had to go from $27,000 to $82,000 (constant 2012 dollars) to make it from the bottom to the top quintile. In 2012, a household had to go from $27,000 to *$119,000* to make the same quintile leap; yet, the probability of making that leap remains the same.[44]   That indicates rather strongly that there are more opportunities for *everyone* to gain wealth today than there were in the past. More pertinently, it indicates that increased inequality has likely had little effect on opportunities for the poor; in fact, it is more likely an indicator that opportunities have expanded.

Some have also tried to point out that income mobility in the U.S. is lower than in Western Europe. But for the same reason we just discussed, of course it is! The United States has 45% of the world's individuals with a net worth over $50 million; while France, Germany, the U.K., Italy and Spain combined have about 20%; indicating that the top quintile in America has more wealth than the top quintile in Western Europe.[45]   North America is actually the least income mobile region in the world in terms of movement among quintiles *including*

Africa! Somehow I don't think we'll find anyone contending that we would be better off living in Mali. Again, this demonstrates simply that a lower mountain is easier to climb than a higher one, but it tells us nothing about people's ability to climb.

Even so, we find that mobility among quintiles in Europe is only slightly better than in America. According to one study, the probability of moving up one quintile over a 30-year period is 19% in Europe and 17% in North America; while the probability of moving up 2 quintiles is 10% in Europe and 10.1% in North America.[46] (Comparable data were not available for the U.S. alone.) Once again, the fact that America has a similar level of mobility but more inequality is a *positive* sign because it means people move up along a larger spread of income with a similar level of probability. That indicates that absolute mobility is likely stronger in America than in Europe.

Income quintiles have limited usefulness because they are a *relative* measure. Essentially, quintiles over time represent nothing more than a changing measuring stick as more wealth is created. If I have a meter stick and painted over the lines to make the centimeters bigger that will not make what I measure any smaller.

When considering income mobility and inequality it is crucial to also look at *absolute* growth in income; for example, a person's ability to go from a $30,000 to $50,000 salary, regardless of which quintiles those incomes fall in. What do these data tell us? According to a Pew Research study, 84% of Americans, and a whopping 93% of those whose parents were born in the bottom quintile, enjoy a higher income than their parents had at the same age.[47]

These numbers are even more significant when we consider standards of living. Lower-income people today are able to afford luxuries our parents could not, such as cell phones, bigger homes, DVD players and much more. Also, older technologies such as washing machines and refrigerators are relatively much cheaper and of higher quality than they were in the past. Finally, the higher incomes we enjoy go much farther because households are smaller today than a generation ago, meaning we have more income per person in each household. When adjusting for household size, the Pew study found that median incomes between our generation and that of our parents' for the bottom three quintiles have risen from $11,000 to $19,000, $20,000 to $36,000, and $27,000 to $51,000 respectively (in 2008 dollars).[48]

There are several other factors which put income inequality in a more accurate light. One of those is the changing composition of the workforce. During the 1980s, and particularly the 1990s, the U.S. saw a flood of immigrants, most of whom occupied low-paying jobs. That substantially lowered the average wages for the bottom quintile. Indeed, because the United States is the only developed nation in the world that shares a border with a developing nation, it makes meaningful comparisons of inequality with other developed nations very difficult. Some say the poor in other developed nations are much better off than in the U.S., but no other developed nation has such a large and steady influx of low-skilled workers. It is also worthy of note that this influx of immigrants indicates that they see something promising in the United States which the detractors of income inequality do not.

Another unique factor in the U.S. is the government's policy toward Native Americans. Many Native Americans live in abject poverty on reservations as a direct result of government's disastrous policies toward them going back hundreds of years. Their poverty certainly weighs on statistics for the bottom quintile and has nothing to do with a failure of capitalism but a failure of government. No other developed nation of which I am aware has a comparable situation.

Another factor is the way we measure inflation, which can have a substantial impact on the way we interpret a variety of monetary factors. There are five legitimate ways which economists use to measure inflation. One of those methods shows a bleak picture for wages in the bottom quintile; the one typically highlighted in news reports. However, using other measures of inflation shows that wages in the bottom quintile actually increased by as much as 18% from 1976 to 2006.[49]

Finally, the changing composition of income is a big factor. Over the last 3 decades, non-cash benefits such as health care, retirement accounts and paid vacation have become bigger shares of many employees' overall compensation. Health care is the big one. One study showed that from 1995 to 2008, incomes for the poorest Americans actually grew faster than incomes for the wealthy when health benefits were included.[50] Other data show that from 1979 to 2010 the after-tax comprehensive incomes of the bottom quintile and middle-three quintiles grew by nearly 50% and 40% respectively.[51] These other factors reveal that increasing inequality is not nearly as disproportionate as many popular reports claim.

The evidence is clear; compared to a generation ago, *all* quintiles are more prosperous, income mobile, wealthy, enjoy higher standards of living, and have higher incomes; indicating that increased income inequality has not harmed poorer American's opportunities for success in any meaningful way. If income inequality causes social unrest it is only because of our attitudes towards it rather than its effects on the economy. It is no argument to say that income inequality should be reduced simply because you don't like it.

The poor and middle class certainly face challenges but growing wealth in the top quintile is not one of them. The increasing cost of health care, not income inequality, is the single largest factor in stagnating median incomes, as the companies that pay for this price inflation simply pass along the cost to employees through lower or slow-growing wages.[52] What has caused this? Government's price distorting programs (Medicare), regulations, and tax distortions are the main culprits.[53]

More broadly, the problem that should most concern us is not income inequality, it is poverty; and we know what causes that: drugs, alcohol, divorce, dropping out of high school, and out-of-wedlock births.[54] It is more than an interesting observation that the wealthy began gaining a greater share of wealth in 1970, precisely at the height of the counterculture movement which glamorized drugs and promiscuity, and when large numbers of Vietnam veterans began returning with mental illnesses to a country that spat on them. Census data show that after a period of sharp decline, poverty rates began leveling off right at this time (again, in spite of LBJ's war on poverty), and have generally continued unchanged since.[55]

No other developed nation has the level of income inequality that we do, partly because no other developed nation consumes as much drugs or raises as many children in single-parent homes;[56] while at the same time our powerful capitalistic system continues to work well for most who avoid these pitfalls. The massive culture shift of the 60s and 70s cannot be dismissed as a source of poverty that reverberates to this day. The correlation between a variety of social ills and income inequality has been irrefutably proven, not only across nations, but even within the 50 states.[57] The causality of these social ills on poverty, and thus, income inequality is immediately obvious; while an explanation for how inequality causes social ills is, at best, unclear. Did Warren Buffet's portfolio cause someone to get hooked on drugs; or did the Kennedy's inheritance cause someone to drop out of school?[58]

Not only was there a massive cultural shift around 1970 which contributed to poverty, but 1971 was the year we officially abandoned the gold standard, opening the door to profligate money creation from the Fed. Since 1971, the dollar has lost 82% of its value. As has been discussed, loose money creation helps the wealthy at the expense of the poor. The combination of culture shift and profligate money creation around the same time offers the most plausible explanation for why income inequality resumed growth in the early 1970s.

There is simply no plausible mechanism which explains how income inequality hurts the poor or the economy in a free market system absent a misguided central bank. The quest to find such a mechanism is usually tainted by emotional anecdotal stories and misguided or dishonest interpretation of data. Moreover, complaints of wealth disparity are fundamentally plagued by a misunderstanding of wealth creation. When we say that the richest 1% own 40% of the country's wealth, the initial reaction is to be aghast that so few have hoarded so much of "the country's" wealth for themselves; but it does not belong to the country, it belongs to the people who create it. If it were not for the 1%'s activities the wealth would not exist at all. Complaining that a greater share of new wealth is not going to people who did not create it is entirely senseless. Worse, those who would confiscate and redistribute the new wealth are oblivious to how it is already contributing to the welfare of others through job creation and the production of products and services we all demand.[59]

Not only do we find that income inequality does not diminish opportunities for the poor, or harm the economy, but we also have strong evidence that high taxes on the wealthy are counterproductive to the very intentions of those who would levy them. We simply cannot tax at a high level without harming economic growth and, by extension, everyone else. No amount of statistics will save progressives' arguments from that indisputable fact. We can certainly tax to decrease inequality, but decreasing inequality offers no benefit other than to make the wealthy poorer if we do not somehow leverage those tax receipts to help the poor, and government has proven to be very bad at doing that.

In the 1980s, two economists, Christophe Chamley and Kenneth Judd, independently discovered the Income Redistribution Impossibility Theorem, which showed that the optimal tax rate on capital gains is *zero*; meaning that *any* tax on capital investment of *any* kind will produce more harm than good. "Under standard, pretty flexible assumptions, it's impossible to tax capitalists, give the money to workers, and raise the total long-run income of workers."[60] Put another way, *any tax* on capital will result in lower wages for workers in the long run. The results of Chamley and Judd have been confirmed and strengthened numerous times by other economists and have never been disproven.[61] These results, of course, get ignored for a variety of reasons but they stand nonetheless.

In addition to this there is an overwhelming amount of evidence, documented at the end of this chapter, which shows that all kinds of taxes harm growth. If the evidence that income inequality has not harmed the poor put arguments against it on life support, the evidence on taxes pulls the plug. Even so, the 30st Amendment would not disallow capital gains or any other taxes; it would simply ensure that they cannot be raised beyond a certain level.

The debate over income inequality reveals how irrational the complaints against it truly are. The value of equality is so powerful that many people would literally rather there be less wealth than more, if it were not distributed equally. This has actually been confirmed in experiments. In one such experiment, recounted in the book "Sway" by Ori and Rom Brafman, German researchers gave $10 to a pair of people. The catch was that only one of the pair could decide how to split the money and could not communicate or negotiate with the other. If the other rejected the offer then neither person received any money. Most of the time, people opted to split the money 50-50. However, in cases where the 'divider' gave herself a greater share, the other person overwhelmingly rejected the offer and neither received any money. This result remained consistent even when the experimenters increased the amount of money to $100. The vast majority of people opted to have no money rather than take $40 for doing nothing simply because they perceived an unfair deal.[62] Clearly, this is completely irrational. Unfortunately, it reveals that complaints about income inequality are based in a deeply rooted, yet misguided, human trait; and are consequently not going to be discarded easily, especially when inequality statistics are easily manipulated to create a scary picture. But our policies must be based on rationality rather than knee jerk and stubborn responses to perceived inequities.

The wealth of the top quintile is not a threat to the rest of us. Much of that wealth becomes available to others to start a business, go to school, or buy a home. Why would we complain that a few wealthy people keep adding to this "account" in disproportionate numbers? The rich are not a group of criminals who set out to enslave the country. They are hard-working and talented people who, perhaps, had a good idea and got a little lucky. What is that to you? How is Mark Cuban, or Leonardo DiCaprio, or T. Boone Pickens, or Warren Buffet, or Mark Zuckerberg a threat to you? Bill Gates' $60 billion net worth does not create less opportunity for others. In fact, just the opposite is true. He has his wealth only because he created value for millions of people in all classes - which has, in turn, allowed millions more to create still more value for others - increasing standards of living across all economic classes.

Stop worrying about how much the rich make, unless they make it through improper influence on government or are benefiting from misguided Federal Reserve policy. We must rid ourselves of the scarcity mentality which says more for you means less for me. We must also purge the irrational stubbornness of punitive tax and redistribution policies. The 30st Amendment is manifestly designed to end divisive, destructive and utterly irrational class warfare so that we might get on with the business of actually helping the poor by growing the economy rather than soaking the rich.

You may not like what the wealthy do with their money while others in the world suffer. That is a noble sentiment which all good people should feel, but it does not justify vigilantism by majority vote, especially when we know the adverse consequences of high taxation. We cannot undermine the central tenets of capitalism without undermining the benefits which every fair-minded person recognizes it creates. Progress is slow and punitive taxation and redistribution will not speed it up. Be patient, save, invest, work, be charitable, stay off drugs, save child-bearing for marriage and capitalism's march to end poverty will continue just as it has over the last 30 years.[63]

Another excuse for raising taxes or keeping them high is the belief that the Federal Government does not have enough money. Of course, this raises the issue of what government should and should not be doing. We discussed that in the previous chapter but one key point is worth repeating here. It has been shown that only modest spending restraint could eliminate deficits in five years or less, with no cuts and *no tax increases*.[64] The President's budget, on the other hand, would not accomplish that feat in 10 years *with tax increases*.[65] Therefore, the need for more tax revenue is simply non-existent from a simple budgetary standpoint, unless you propose to increase spending above the current trend, which is completely absurd given our future fiscal outlook.

Even if we approve of every purpose for which Congress is spending, can it really be said that government doesn't have enough money? If we looked at the current deficit we might conclude that the answer is a simple yes. But a closer look at the budget reveals not only that government does too much, but that it does it with enormous inefficiency and a terrible mismatch between claimed priorities and budgetary realities.

For instance, a claimed priority may be to care for the poor. But the two largest entitlement programs, Social Security and Medicare, give benefits to *every worker* including the wealthy. If the priority of these programs is to care for the poor and vulnerable then we should not be spending trillions subsidizing the middle class. But of course, since most voters are in the middle class, prioritizing resources for where they are truly needed takes a back seat to getting reelected.

Then there's the fact that State and Federal Governments combined already spend about $60,000 a year for every poor family of three in America.[66] Yet a great deal of that money goes to the bureaucracies that deliver it, not to mention fraudsters, rather than the people who need it. Again, if the priority is the poor, why is the massive bureaucracy taking home such a huge portion of the budget? For the entire budget, the government itself estimates that there is about $250 billion of waste each year.[67] What kind of nerve does it take to demand more of somebody else's money when you are mismanaging the money you have so poorly?

Don't tell me you need more revenue when you have three agencies inspecting catfish.[68] Don't tell me you need more revenue when more than 600 renewable energy programs are fragmented across 23 agencies.[69] Don't tell me you need more revenue when the Pentagon operates at least 234 golf courses around the world[70]; or when you spend $27 million on pottery classes... *for people in Morocco*[71]; or when the State Department simply misplaces $6 billion.[72]

It is an insult to call for tax increases with the kind of madness we see in the budget. How would your friends and family respond if you asked for help with the mortgage at the same time you are blowing money on alcohol and gambling? The excuse that the waste in the budget is only a fraction of what is needed to bring it into balance is simply unconvincing. Even if it were merely a symbolic gesture, Congress should clean up this mess before asking for more revenue. The truth is if we had disciplined programs targeting the truly needy, then $3 trillion, which is roughly what the Federal Government will collect in 2014, would be far more than enough to cover all of the essential functions of government.

The key words are prioritize and economize, as anyone who has ever had to deal with a budget knows. But as long as Congress has the Federal Reserve to create money out of thin air and an unrestrained income tax these words will never mean anything to Washington. Politicians have been talking about cutting out fraud, waste and abuse for years yet it never happens. Why not? What's stopping Congress? Cutting waste should be as bipartisan of a legislative effort as anything yet the status quo continues year after year. Decades of inaction should tell us that Constitutional amendments which limit the capacity of Congress to tax and spend are the most plausible way to impose discipline on the federal budget.

The next thing to consider is whether or not tax increases would actually net the government a significant amount of additional revenue. The answer may be that it won't. Part of the reason is because of the principle illustrated by the Laffer curve, which shows that at a certain point, an additional tax increase will not yield a corresponding increase in revenue to the government. In other words, at some point tax increases become counterproductive to raising revenue. People nearly always respond to higher taxes by finding ways to avoid paying them.

The Laffer Curve

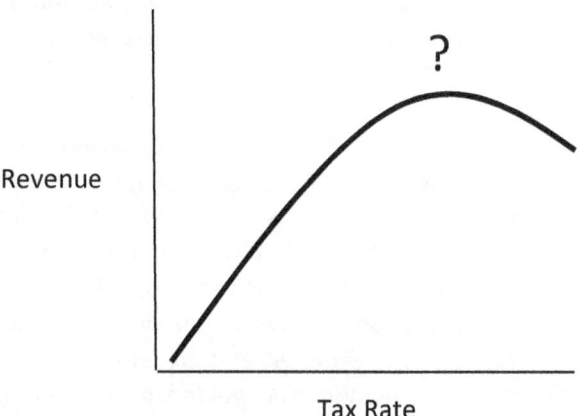

The Laffer curve has generated much controversy because there is no agreement about where the curve begins sloping downward. The reality is that the Laffer curve should not be used to justify any particular tax rate or cut. It is merely conceptual, meant only to show that taxes do not *always* generate more income for government. The point at which this happens is contingent on a variety of factors from psychological, such as tax payer's belief that their money will be put to good use, to economic, such as the need to hold on to more money when times are tough. For example, if we were in the midst of a war, which most citizens believed to be just, then the Laffer curve would certainly bend at a higher tax rate as more citizens would be willing to support the cause. But if citizens were being taxed to pay for catfish inspections or the State Department's ineptitude, the bend would certainly occur at a lower tax rate as more citizens would not want to pay those taxes.

The Laffer curve also works in the opposite direction; meaning that sometimes tax cuts will actually result in more revenue as the base of tax payers grows. Republicans love to point out that this is what happened when the capital gains tax was decreased in the early 2000's. On the other hand, Democrats love to point out that under Clinton's tax increases in the early 90's government revenue, and the economy, went up. These seemingly contradictory results show the fluidity of the Laffer curve and bolster the point that it is merely conceptual. When times are good, as in the 90's, people may be more willing to pay higher taxes if they anticipate being able to make more money in the future, thus pushing the Laffer curve upward. When the capital gains tax was decreased under Bush, more people became willing to report higher capital gains, thus increasing the government's revenues from that source, pushing the curve downward. Another bit of evidence for this effect is the fact that over the last several decades, corporate tax rates have steadily fallen in most developed countries but corporate tax *revenues have gone up.*[73]

Understanding the Laffer curve is important because it provides a conceptual framework for understanding how government can best provide for its revenue needs. The lesson is simple; don't kill the golden goose! If you want the golden eggs then the wisest thing to do is create the most comfortable place possible for the goose, i.e. keep taxes low and a steady stream of revenue for government will be readily available. Continuing with this analogy, we must also signal to the golden goose that we aren't going to squander the golden eggs. People need to believe that government has a basic level of respect for other people's money. Most Americans are perfectly willing to pay their taxes and indeed, actually want to contribute to their government. But as government becomes increasingly reckless and flippant with other people's money, more citizens will resist higher taxes.

It is also essential to understand that government revenues should not be the primary concern. Some Democrats amazingly refuse to believe that there is any Laffer curve at all and thus, essentially argue that taxes should be as high as politically possible. On the other side, some Republicans try to push *every* tax cut as though it would pay for itself. Such thinking misses the mark by accepting the notion that we should actually be *trying* to maximize government revenues. *The goal should not be to maximize government's revenue; it should be to maximize economic growth.* Therefore, whether or not a tax cut or tax hike would increase government revenue is essentially irrelevant. What is relevant is the growth of the economy, the golden goose that provides the revenue.

The lame excuse that tax cuts would undermine social safety nets is totally unfounded. The amount of money we spend on so-called safety nets is enough to care for the vulnerable of half the world if spent wisely and only on the truly needy. In any event, if we want to help people then growing the economy should be the highest priority as the empirical evidence shows.

What's more is that government will continue to command a vast amount of revenue when the 30th Amendment passes. Some simple calculations may show that this amendment would not undermine government revenues. First, a 20% cap would not be as drastic a reduction as it might seem because even though the top marginal rate is currently 39%, most high-income earners pay a far lower effective rate after all adjustments. Congressional Budget Office numbers show that from 1979 to 2009, the total average federal effective tax rate for the top quintile of income earners averaged 25.6%.[74] Assuming the Federal Government's estimate of collecting about $3 trillion in revenue for 2014 is accurate,[75] the top quintile of earners pays about 70% of those taxes or $2.1 trillion.[76] To be conservative, we will calculate the loss in revenue from a rate cut to 20% by assigning an effective rate of 30% for the entire top quintile as opposed to 25.6%. This would result in a roughly 33% reduction in tax revenues from this group, or about $700 billion if no deductions or credits were eliminated. Another $100 billion in excise taxes would also be lost. However, the Tax Policy Center estimates that all tax expenditures (credits, deductions and adjustments) will total about $1.4 trillion for 2014.[77] Essentially, the 30th Amendment would generate an $800 billion tax cut, but would eliminate $1.4 trillion in tax loopholes, implying that the amendment could generate another $600 billion in revenue each year if the wealthy were taxed at the highest allowable rate of 20%.

However, the value of tax expenditures does not take into account the changes in behavior that would occur if they were eliminated. Also, we cannot know what rates Congress would assign to each income bracket under the proposed amendment. Therefore, it is very difficult to estimate the amount of money that could be collected under this Amendment. Nevertheless, the lopsided amount of tax expenditures compared to the revenue loss from the cut in rates and elimination of the excise tax may be solid enough evidence that this amendment would not greatly harm government revenues. This conclusion is further bolstered by the Laffer curve. It is nearly certain that a tax cap and cut of this magnitude would encourage a flood of investment to pour into the country, thereby increasing earnings, growth and taxable income.

We should note the 30th Amendment's elimination of the excise tax. The potential benefits of eliminating excise taxes are enticing. The three main excise taxes levied by the Federal Government are on fuel, air travel and telecommunications. A repeal of these taxes would disproportionately benefit the poor and middle class, as all these things would become cheaper.

It may turn out that the States would replace federal excise taxes but if so, it would at least have the effect of transferring more revenue to the States, thereby enhancing federalism. States levying these excises would be much better because taxpayers would benefit from tax competition among the States, which would keep them low and force State governments to create value for those excises.

The rationale for keeping taxes low could not be stronger, but in case the logic escapes you, take a look at the empirical evidence. In a 2012 special report, the Tax Foundation compiled the results of 26 academic studies relating to taxes and economic growth.[78] The studies overwhelmingly show that higher taxes negatively affect economic growth and/or lower taxes strengthen it. All but three of the studies found this to be true and the three that did not found no relationship. A table from that report has been reproduced here. It references each study and summarizes the findings. One of the most significant of these studies was conducted by David and Christina Romer (number 6 on the list), two of President Obama's former economic advisers. They found that a tax increase of 1% of GDP leads to a 3% fall in economic output after two years.

The case for capping federal taxes is overwhelming. High taxation harms everyone. A call for the rule of law is not only a call for legal limits on government; it also requires us to allow unbiased empirical data to guide the formation of our laws. In this new competitive world we must send a clear message to the talent and wealth at home and abroad that the United States is committed to being the land of opportunity it has traditionally been. The American traditions of freedom and property rights have always been the source of that opportunity, and they ought to be strengthened by Constitutional amendment.

Taxes Harm Economic Growth

	Reference	Method/Data	Economic Effects	Relevant Findings
1	Ergete Ferede & Bev Dahlby, *The Impact of Tax Cuts on Economic Growth: Evidence from the Canadian Provinces*, 65 National Tax Journal 563-594 (2012).	Canadian provinces (1977-2006)	Negative	Reducing corporate income tax 1 percentage point raises annual growth by 0.1 to 0.2 points.
2	Karel Mertens & Morten Ravn, *The dynamic effects of personal and corporate income tax changes in the United States*, American Economic Review (forthcoming) (2012).	U.S. Post-WWII exogenous changes in personal and corporate income taxes	Negative	A 1 percentage point cut in the average personal income tax rate raises real GDP per capita by 1.4 percent in the first quarter and by up to 1.8 percent after three quarters.
3	Norman Gemmell, Richard Kneller, & Ismael Sanz, *The Timing and Persistence of Fiscal Policy Impacts on Growth: Evidence from OECD Countries*, 121 Economic Journal F33-F58 (2011).	17 OECD countries (Early 1970s to 2004)	Negative	Taxes on income and profit are most damaging to economic growth over the long run, followed by deficits, and then consumption taxes.
4	Jens Arnold, Bert Brys, Christopher Heady, Åsa Johansson, Cyrille Schwellnus, & Laura Vartia, *Tax Policy For Economic Recovery and Growth*, 121 Economic Journal F59-F80 (2011).	21 OECD countries (1971 to 2004)	Negative	Corporate taxes, both in terms of the statutory rate and depreciation allowances, reduce investment and productivity growth. Raising the top

				marginal rate on personal income reduces productivity growth.
5	Robert Barro & C.J. Redlick, *Macroeconomic Effects of Government Purchases and Taxes*, 126 Quarterly Journal of Economics 51-102 (2011).	U.S (1912 to 2006)	Negative	Cut in the average marginal tax rate of one percentage point raises next year's per capita GDP by around 0.5%.
6	Christina Romer & David Romer, *The macroeconomic effects of tax changes: estimates based on a new measure of fiscal shocks*, 100 American Economic Review 763-801 (2010).	U.S. Post-WWII (104 tax changes, 65 exogenous)	Negative	Tax (federal revenue) increase of 1% of GDP leads to a fall in output of 3% after about 2 years, mostly through negative effects on investment.
7	Alberto Alesina & Silvia Ardagna, *Large changes in fiscal policy: taxes versus spending, in* Tax Policy and the Economy, Vol. 24 (Univ. of Chicago Press, 2010).	OECD countries (fiscal stimuli and fiscal adjustments, 1970 to 2007)	Negative	Fiscal consolidations based upon spending cuts and no tax increases are more likely to succeed at reducing deficits and debt and less likely to create recessions.
8	International Monetary Fund, *Will it hurt? Macroeconomic effects of fiscal consolidation, in* World Economic Outlook: Recovery, Risk, and Rebalancing (2010).	15 advanced countries (170 fiscal consolidations over the last 30 years)	Negative	1% tax increase reduces GDP by 1.3% after two years.
9	Robert Reed, *The robust relationship between taxes and U.S. state income growth*, 61 National Tax Journal 57-80 (2008).	U.S. States (1970-1999, 5 year panels)	Negative	Robust negative effect of state and local tax burden.
10	N. Bania, J. A. Gray, & J. A. Stone, *Growth, taxes, and government expenditures: growth hills for U.S. States*, 60	U.S. States	Negative	Taxes directed towards public investments first add then subtract from GDP.

	National Tax Journal 193-204 (2007).			
11	Young Lee & Roger Gordon, *Tax Structure and Economic Growth*, 89 Journal of Public Economics 1027-1043 (2005).	70 countries (1980 - 1997, cross-sectional and 5 year panels)	Negative	Reducing corporate income tax 1 percentage point raises annual growth by 0.1 to 0.2 points.
12	Randall Holcombe & Donald Lacombe, *The effect of state income taxation on per capita income growth*, 32 Public Finance Review 292-312 (2004).	Counties separated by state borders (1960 to 1990)	Negative	States that raised income taxes averaged a 3.4% reduction in per capita income.
13	Marc Tomljanovich, *The role of state fiscal policy in state economic growth*, 22 Contemporary Economic Policy 318-330 (2004).	U.S. States (1972 to 1998, multi-year panels)	Negative	Higher tax rates negatively affect short run growth, but not long run growth.
14	Olivier Blanchard & Robert Perotti, *An Empirical Characterization Of The Dynamic Effects Of Changes In Government Spending And Taxes On Output*, 107 Quarterly Journal of Economics 1329-1368 (2002).	U.S. Post-WWII (VAR/event study)	Negative	Positive tax shocks, or unexpected increases in total revenue, negatively affect private investment and GDP.
15	F. Padovano & E. Galli, E., *Tax rates and economic growth in the OECD countries (1950-1990)*, 39 Economic Inquiry 44-57 (2001).	23 OECD countries (1951 to 1990)	Negative	Effective marginal income tax rates negatively correlated with GDP growth.
16	Stefan Folster & Magnus Henrekson, *Growth effects of government expenditure and taxation in rich countries*, 45 European Economic Review 1501-1520 (2001).	Rich countries (1970 to 1995)	Negative	Tax revenue as a share of GDP negatively correlated with GDP growth.
17	M. Bleaney, N. Gemmell	OECD	Negative	Distortionary taxes

	& R. Kneller, *Testing the endogenous growth model: public expenditure, taxation, and growth over the long run*, 34 Canadian Journal of Economics 36-57 (2001).	countries (1970 to 1995)		reduce GDP growth. Consumption taxes are not distortionary.
18	R. Kneller, M. Bleaney & N. Gemmell, *Fiscal Policy and Growth: Evidence from OECD Countries*, 74 Journal of Public Economics 171-190 (1999).	OECD countries (1970 to 1995)	Negative	Distortionary taxes reduce GDP growth.
19	Howard Chernick, *Tax progressivity and state economic performance*, 11 Economic Development Quarterly 249-267 (1997).	U.S. States (1977 to 1993)	Negative	Progressivity of income taxes negatively affects GDP growth.
20	Enrique Mendoza, G. Milesi-Ferretti, & P. Asea, *On the Effectiveness of Tax Policy in Altering Long-Run Growth: Harberger's Superneutrality Conjecture*, 66 Journal of Public Economics 99-126 (1997).	18 OECD countries (1965-1991, 5 year panels)	None	Estimated effective tax rates on labor and capital harm investment, but effect on growth is insignificant. Effective consumption taxes increase investment, but not growth. Overall tax burden levels have no effect on investment or growth.
21	Stephen Miller & Frank Russek, *Fiscal structures and economic growth: international evidence*, 35 Economic Inquiry 603-613 (1997).	Developed and developing countries	Negative	Tax-financed spending reduces growth in developed countries
22	John Mullen & Martin Williams, *Marginal tax rates and state economic growth*, 24 Regional Science and Urban Economics 687-	U.S. States (1969 to 1986)	Negative	Higher marginal tax rates reduce GDP growth.

	705 (1994).			
23	William Easterly & S. Rebelo, *Fiscal Policy and Economic Growth: An Empirical Investigation*, 32 Journal of Monetary Economics 417-458 (1993).	Developed and developing countries	None	Effects of taxation difficult to isolate empirically.
24	Reinhard Koester & Roger Kormendi, *Taxation, Aggregate Activity and Economic Growth: Cross-Country Evidence on Some Supply-Side Hypotheses*, 27 Economic Inquiry 367-86 (1989).	63 countries	Negative	Controlling for average tax rates, increases in marginal tax rates reduce economic activity. Progressivity reduces growth.
25	Jay Helms, *The effect of state and local taxes on economic growth: a time series-cross section approach*, 67 Review of Economics and Statistics 574-582 (1985).	U.S. States (1965 to 1979)	Negative	Revenue used to fund transfer payments retards growth.
26	Claudio J. Katz, Vincent A. Mahler & Michael G. Franz, *The impact of taxes on growth and distribution in developed capitalist countries: a cross-national study*, 77 American Political Science Review 871-886 (1983).	22 developed countries	None	Taxes reduce saving but not growth or investment.

Source: http://taxfoundation.org/article/what-evidence-taxes-and-growth

CHAPTER ELEVEN

SEPARATION OF POWERS

Amendment 31

1. Congress shall not have power to delegate any legislative, rulemaking, or regulatory authority which may have a substantial impact on individuals or businesses; no law, rule or regulation of the United States shall be of any effect unless passed in the manner prescribed by this Constitution. The Executive branch of the United States shall be empowered to make necessary rules for the execution and administration of the laws, rules and regulations passed by Congress, provided that such rules do not alter the intent or function of the laws. This section shall not alter or abolish any regulatory rules in effect at the time of ratification of this amendment.

2. Whenever one third of both houses of Congress shall concur, they shall have standing to bring suit before the Supreme Court against the President or any executive officer for any violation of statute or of this Constitution.

3. Congress shall not have power to appropriate money to any State or local government. Congress shall have 10 years from the time of ratification of this amendment to make necessary provisions for the implementation of this section, after which it shall take full effect.

4. Every act of Congress shall embrace but one subject and matters properly connected therewith, which subject shall be expressed in the title. Each of the several States, individually or collectively, shall have standing to sue Congress for any violation of this section.

Even if we slow down Congress's ability to tax and spend we must still address the fact that they will continue to inundate our economy and legal system with complex rules and regulations. This complexity has led to a considerable erosion of the separation of powers. What are our options? We cannot simply repeal large swaths of the legal and regulatory code at once. Though that might be desirable, it is simply impractical. How could we specify what to keep and what not to keep? Making such a long list would not be a proper or practical thing to insert in the Constitution and relying on Congress to do it by statute is futile. As has been the theme with the other proposed amendments we must find a practical solution that balances meaningful restraints with drastic upheaval. The 31st Amendment is designed to do just that. It will significantly slow down the rate of government regulation and restore the badly needed doctrine of separation of powers while having a minimal impact on current systems.

The Federal Government has become a madhouse of unelected bureaucrats, boards, agencies, overlap, waste, abuse, corruption and unaccountable law makers. It is no wonder that Congress has an approval rating around 10%. Much of this mess is due to the rise of government since Constitutional restraints were abandoned. As government operates with no proper understanding of its purpose or legal constraints politics, money, and power have come to define the way Washington works. This book would be incomplete without addressing how we might more fundamentally change our system so that it works with more transparency, accountability and reasoned deliberation.

Sections 1 and 2: Separation of Powers

The first words of the Constitution following the preamble are these: "All legislative powers herein granted shall be vested in a Congress of the United States..." The intention of these words is straightforward: no other body of government should have the authority to pass laws other than the people's chosen representatives. This Constitutional principle is based on a natural law which was explained by John Locke:

> The power of the legislative, being derived from the people by a positive voluntary grant and institution, can be no other than what that positive grant conveyed, which being only to make laws, and not to make legislators, the legislative can have no power to transfer their authority of making laws, and place it in other hands.[1]

This natural law has been completely ignored by the Federal Government. Today, dozens of federal agencies have law-making and rule-making authority which is not theirs to possess even if they had congressional approval, which, in many cases they do not. The result is the staggering number of laws and regulations recounted in Chapter Five. This large and complex legal system weighs heavily on liberty, stifles economic growth and gives the wealthy and big-businesses an advantage over smaller competitors.

The sheer size and number of federal agencies required to administer this mess creates an impossible scenario for even the best of managers who would be the President tasked with executing Congress's regulatory schemes. With 15 cabinet departments, over 160 different agencies with regulatory authority, and more than two million employees in the executive branch, it would be absurd to assume that any one person could effectively create accountability throughout all that madness. When we have millions of government workers running around with money they did not earn and the ability to create law without a vote from Congress it is inevitable that that power will be abused. Even worse is that few are ever held accountable once the power *is* abused. The recent IRS, Benghazi and NSA scandals clearly demonstrate the danger though it has been demonstrated with equal force by many previous administrations. The President can simply claim ignorance and it is perfectly believable given the size of the executive branch. This pattern has been repeated through numerous administrations in both parties.

Something must be done to slow down the growth of laws and rein in the power of federal agencies. Accountability must be restored by putting the law-making authority exclusively in the hands of elected representatives as the natural law and the Constitution demand. The 31st Amendment will achieve this badly needed fix. Not only is this a modern imperative but it is a restoration of a Constitutional principle which has been abused and neglected to the point where it no longer operates in any meaningful way.

One of the earliest cases dealing with non-delegation was the 1825 case of *Wayman v Southard*. This case involved a statute in which Congress had delegated authority to the courts to "make and establish all necessary rules for the orderly conducting business in the said courts, provided such rules are not repugnant to the laws of the United States."[2] The law was challenged on the grounds that Congress had not the power to delegate legislative authority. Chief Justice Marshall bluntly agreed in principle stating "It will not be contended, that congress can delegate to the courts, or to any other tribunals, powers which are strictly and exclusively legislative."[3] However, he went on to point out that the difficulty in such cases is to determine what is "strictly legislative" and what is not:

> The line has not been exactly drawn which separates those important subjects, which must be entirely regulated by the legislature itself, from those of less interest, in which a general provision may be made, and power given to those who are to act under such general provisions, to fill up the details.[4]

Anyone can see that the executive agencies charged with administering the laws passed by Congress must necessarily establish procedures and rules for carrying out their duties. But at what point do those procedures begin to take on a form more like law rather than mere "details?" A review of a few more court cases will shed some light on what has been the traditional answer to this question. It is evident from the record that we have strayed from the early limitations of Congress's ability to delegate.

Throughout the first 100 years of the republic there were numerous instances when Congress delegated some authority to the President to act in certain matters. From time to time complaints arose that these delegations were unauthorized by the Constitution. In 1892 the Supreme Court decided the case of *Field v. Clark* concerning the McKinley Act. That law delegated to the President the authority to suspend duties on particular goods from some countries if certain conditions were met. Marshall Field & Co., an importer of the goods in question challenged the Constitutionality of the act as an improper delegation of legislative authority. In its ruling, the Court rehearsed nearly a dozen acts of Congress in which the President was delegated some authority. In nearly every one of these acts, Congress gave the President *specific instructions and conditions which narrowly set the parameters of his discretion*. For example, in 1809 Congress passed the Non-Intercourse Act which gave the President the authority to enact an embargo on France or Britain if either should violate the United States' neutrality in the war between the European powers. The embargo was authorized by Congress to take effect when certain conditions, which they specified, were met. The President's only discretion was to ascertain whether or not those conditions were present. Even with this narrow delegation there were strong enough opinions to bring suit against the government for violating the Constitutional separation of powers.

These opinions were correct. There is no reason to assume that Congress cannot ascertain on its own whether certain conditions are necessary for a law to take effect. Indeed, this is the very essence of legislating; ascertaining national and international conditions and making appropriate legislation to meet the exigencies of those conditions. Given the sacred importance of the separation of powers and its prominent place in the Constitution, caution should have been exercised and extreme care taken to guard it. Unfortunately, the early Court did not see it that way and ruled that this narrow delegation of authority by Congress was valid.[5]

However, their ruling made it clear that Congress could not delegate legislative authority. We have not even scratched the surface of the present government's complete disregard for the separation of powers doctrine. In the 1892 case concerning the McKinley Act, the Court reaffirmed the principle:

> That congress cannot delegate legislative power to the president is a principle universally recognized as vital to the integrity and maintenance of the system of government ordained by the Constitution.[6]

Though they did not find that the McKinley Act was inconsistent with this principle, the Court's subsequent commentary gives us some more insight about the distinction for which we are seeking clarification.

> Legislative power was exercised when congress declared that the suspension [of tariffs] should take effect upon a *named contingency*. What the president was required to do was simply in execution of the act of congress. It was not the making of law.

He was the mere agent of the law-making department to ascertain and declare the event upon which its *expressed will* was to take effect.[7] (emphasis added)

In 1928, nearly 40 years after the McKinley Act, Congress went a step further, as democratic bodies always do, and delegated authority to the President to actually *set the rates* for duties at *his discretion*. Unsurprisingly, the law was challenged and the result was perhaps the most famous of non-delegation court cases: *J.W. Hampton Jr. v United States*. Until this case, Congress had never delegated authority to set rates of any kind, which was one of the main reasons the plaintiffs filed suit. Unfortunately, the Courts upheld the act, but it did issue more warnings about improper delegation:

The field of Congress involves ...many varieties of legislative action, and Congress has found it frequently necessary to use officers of the executive branch within *defined limits*, to secure the *exact effect intended by its acts of legislation*, by vesting discretion in such officers to make public regulations interpreting a statute and directing the details of its execution. ...If Congress shall lay down by legislative act *an intelligible principle* to which the person or body authorized to fix such rates is directed to conform, such legislative action is not a forbidden delegation of legislative power.[8] (emphasis added)

The last sentence, namely the phrase "intelligible principle," has received the most attention in non-delegation cases ever since and has become the standard test used by the courts to determine the propriety of congressional delegation. But what is an intelligible principle? It is hard to say, but acting on an intelligible principle certainly sounds broader than merely "filling up the details" as Justice Marshall put it. Adjusting the rates of duties, which have a substantial impact on economic activity, can hardly be called "details." Moreover, the task of setting duties is explicitly given to Congress in the Constitution. Certainly it would not be conceded that Congress could authorize the President to set tax rates, even within "defined limits" or if given an "intelligible principle." It is therefore evident that the Court erred by repeatedly moving the line back; each case allowing Congress to take a larger step toward delegation of "strictly legislative" authority. But even now we *still* have not approached the level of abuse that Congress and the President has undertaken in our day.

Though the intelligible principle requirement is somewhat vague, the Court offered some clarification when it struck down the National Industrial Recovery Act in 1935. This was the first time the Court voided an act of Congress based on the non-delegation doctrine so it will be instructive to learn the Court's reasoning. NIRA gave broad powers to the President to regulate the economy. We need not focus on the particulars of the legislation but only on the language of the Court which might tell us upon what grounds we can distinguish between "strictly legislative" actions and actions with a clear enough intelligible principle. Here is a sampling of the Court's scrutiny:

> ...we look to the statute to see whether the Congress has *declared a policy* ...whether the Congress has set up a *standard for the President's action*; whether the Congress has required any finding by the President in the exercise of the authority... [NIRA] does not state whether or in *what circumstances or under what conditions* the President is to [act] ...It *establishes no criterion* to govern the President's course. It does not require any finding by the President as a *condition of his action.* ...it gives to the President an unlimited authority to determine the policy ...And disobedience to his order is made a crime punishable by fine and imprisonment. ...The Congress left the matter to the President *without standard or rule*, to be dealt with as he pleased.[9] (emphasis added)

At last, the Court enforced *some limit* for congressional delegation of authority. But the good news was short-lived. NIRA was so broad and so sweeping in what it allowed the President to do that plenty of room remained for Congress to continue delegating more legislative discretion, and for the Courts to play along. In truth, the damage had already been done by the *Hampton* ruling. Subsequent acts of Congress delegated such broad authority as the following: to the Federal Communications Commission to make regulations for the "public interest"[10] (1943); to a 'Price Administrator' to fix commodity prices which "in his judgment will be generally fair and equitable"[11] (1944); to allow the Federal Power Commission to determine "just and reasonable rates"[12] (1944); to allow federal agencies to reclaim what they deemed to be "excessive profits" from defense contractors[13] (1948); to the Occupational Health and Safety Administration to set a standard which "adequately assures... that no employee will suffer any impairment of health"[14] (1980); to the Attorney General to designate a drug as a "controlled substance" if it is "necessary to avoid an imminent hazard to the public safety"[15] (1991).

It is no coincidence that delegation began running wild in the 1940s, with people paying little attention to anything other than the war and willing to cede power to the government, as always happens in wars. This also shows the consequences of Roosevelt's unprecedented third and fourth terms as he was able to stack the Supreme Court with his government-loving appointees. Apparently, enough people saw this as a bad thing as they passed the 22nd Amendment nearly as soon as FDR died. It is also no coincidence that an explosion of delegations occurred soon after the Court's rulings in *Helvering* and *Wickard*.

Once these rulings vastly expanded the scope of congressional legislation, the need for delegating authority became much more urgent as Congress did not have the ability to keep up with all the complex managing that supposedly had to be done. In the 1989 case of *Mistretta v. United States* the Court made this point and also revealed how far the concept of delegation has been stretched since the days of 'filling up the details':

> ...our jurisprudence has been driven by a practical understanding that in our increasingly complex society, replete with ever changing and more technical problems, Congress simply cannot do its job absent an ability to delegate power under *broad general directives*. Accordingly, this Court has deemed it "Constitutionally sufficient" if Congress clearly delineates the *general policy*, the public agency which is to apply it, and the boundaries of this delegated authority.[16] (emphasis added)

Of course, this is true only if you believe that it is the "job" of Congress to regulate all of society's "technical problems." Not only is it improper and largely unnecessary for Congress to have this job, but a proper reading of the Commerce and General Welfare Clauses reveals that it is constitutionally prohibited. That is why it is offensive to see the Supreme Court declare that a "complex society" should dictate what Congress can do rather than the Constitution. Interestingly enough, the *Mistretta* Court wasn't the first to give this excuse for allowing government more power than what the law allows. Benito Mussolini declared: "We were the first to assert that the more complicated the forms assumed by civilization, the more restricted the freedom of the individual must become."[17]

The truth is that the more complex society becomes the *less* justification there is for more state control. As things become more complex they become less understandable and by extension, less manageable from the top down. The whole world, particularly in the private sector, is adapting to this reality as the traditional top-down corporate structure is being replaced by more autonomous groups empowered to make decisions on their own. The specialization of the sciences is also a good example. A few hundred years ago, all science was one subject. Today there are thousands of scientific specializations, each with a lifetime of study required to reach the pinnacle of that field.

It may be tempting to believe that this is precisely the specialization that Congress should attempt to achieve by creating more autonomous regulatory bodies to oversee different fields. However, a government agency overseeing millions of people and organizations in a complex industry is far different than an executive team delegating authority to a highly specialized group of individuals within a private organization. More importantly, the specialization and autonomy of bureaucratic agencies makes government increasingly detached from accountability to the people and increasingly despotic. As Adam Smith told us in the Wealth of Nations more than two centuries ago:

> The statesman who should attempt to direct private people ...would ...assume an authority which could safely be trusted, not only to no single person, but to no council or senate whatever, and which would nowhere be so dangerous as in the hands of a man who had folly and presumption enough to fancy himself fit to exercise it.[18]

In fact, the very type of person we find in these positions of authority tend to be just the sort that is dangerous; those who like to be obeyed and to direct, control and plan. Society's complexities therefore do not reveal a need for more government agencies; they reveal a need for more freedom.

While it is true that some advances in technology and complexity will require new laws, such as the regulation of stem cell research, it does not necessarily follow that the number of laws must advance hand in hand with technology. Unlike the sciences, the law is incapable of linear progression.   Natural and fundamental law will remain so regardless of society's complexities. Fraud remains fraud whether it is committed over the internet or on a paper contract. Assault with a light saber is the same as assault with a Bronze Age sword.   Privacy is violated whether by spying from a tree or from a drone. The complicated rules and regulations propagated by government are therefore largely unjustified by the claims that "technical problems" require them.

The Court's excuse to allow Congress to delegate broad authority illustrates another real danger of abandoning Constitutional restraints. As Congress deems that more complexity gives them more power, it must delegate more of it to keep up. The more they delegate, the more Americans are overseen by unelected agencies with legislative and even judicial power. In turn, the further removed from the people our government becomes. This lack of accountability is part of the reason why so much abuse and scandal permeates Washington. What's worse is that delegations of authority gradually take on a broader scope over time. We have seen how the Court went from "filling up the details" to "intelligible principle" and finally to the *Mistretta* Court's "broad general directive" as a guide for congressional delegation. Such a test is not likely to invalidate hardly *any* congressional delegation of authority. At least the Court did make mention of the long-standing requirement that Congress must delineate the "boundaries" of the delegated authority. But in the next case we examine, the Court erased *even that minimal standard.*

In the 2001 case of *Whitman v. American Trucking Associations Inc.*, the Clean Air Act was under review. In this law, Congress had delegated to the Environmental Protection Agency the authority to set clean air "standards at a level that is requisite to protect public health" with an "adequate margin of safety."[19] This broad delegation technically meant that the EPA could ban *any* pollutant if it deemed it necessary for the public health. If the EPA ever did institute a ban, it might have an enormous impact on the lives and fortunes of millions of Americans. To any fair-minded person, *that is law-making authority.* The Constitution never intended for such a power to be wielded by anyone other than the people's elected representatives. But the Supreme Court, blinded by the numerous precedents before them, refused to recognize that plain truth and overturned a lower court's decision which struck down the law. The majority flatly stated: "Statutes need not provide a determinate criterion for saying how much of a regulated harm is too much to avoid delegating legislative power."[20]

In other words, Congress need not provide the boundaries of the delegated authority as the *Mistretta* Court said was necessary. It may be true that in the past Congress did not set boundaries on such things as how high or low the President could set duties. But they did at least specify the particular products for which the President could determine the duties. To grant an agency the power to regulate *any* pollutant at *any* level is a mockery of the requirement that boundaries must be set in a delegation of authority. A father could technically say he was giving his teenage son "boundaries" when going out with his friends by requiring only that the son not leave the country, but those boundaries would bear little resemblance to responsible parenting.

Contrast these last two rulings with some of the Court's earlier rulings. The Court declared in *Whitman* and *Mistretta* that Congress can give "broad general directives" with no "determinate criterion" for how much discretion is too much. Yet the previous Court rulings in *Hampton*, *Field* and *Panama Refining* demanded that when Congress delegates they must give "defined limits," a "named contingency" on which to act, "an expressed will" and the circumstances and conditions in which the party receiving the authority is to act. Going back even further to the *Wayman* case, it is clear that Congress has gone well beyond allowing agencies to simply "fill up the details." This stems from the Court's curiously intense focus on the vague "intelligible principle" test, at the expense of the equally important phrases just named, and worse, at the expense of the text of the Constitution itself.

In some respects it is difficult to be too critical of the Court's decisions. We are working with the hindsight of two centuries of legal experience and congressional overreach. The issue of delegation is inherently ambiguous to begin with. Clearly Congress must delegate at least *some* discretion to other agencies to carry out their duties. But part of the problem with the intelligible principle doctrine is that it does not distinguish between broad and narrow delegations. The result is that the Courts focus on whether or not there is an intelligible principle rather than on the scope of the authority being delegated.

Once the Courts allow a narrow delegation to take place, from a legal perspective, it is only a small step further to allow delegations to take place under very broad confines. It is nearly impossible to draw a line once the delegation of power is given. If one small step of delegating authority justifies another then it becomes very easy for the next small step to be close enough to the previous in order to pass Constitutional muster. By the time we arrive ten steps down the line however, we are faced with something so completely different from the first step that it can hardly be judged the same way. The *Whitman* Court's mistake, as is often the case in our time, was to lean too heavily on recent precedent. Our government has strayed so far from

Constitutional moorings that such precedent has little relevance to what is actually authorized by the Constitution itself.

The Courts made a commendable attempt to rein in delegation with the language of their rulings. But they actually struck down only two acts of Congress in more than two centuries of lawmaking under the non-delegation doctrine. And all that legislation has led to one of the largest governments in the history of mankind with numerous agencies wielding law-making authority. Every Court decision in non-delegation cases affirmed that Congress cannot delegate legislative authority. Yet volumes of federal regulations have been written independent of Congress. If we put all of the laws, rules and regulations of the Federal Government into bound volumes, the laws passed by Congress and signed by the President would be about *one sixth* of the volumes required to contain the regulations written by federal agencies.[21] There is simply no way the Court could continue to say that delegation was not authorized by the Constitution, while approving every post-New Deal delegation passed by Congress and still remain on intellectually solid ground. Either the Court did not understand what the word "legislation" meant or it did not understand what the Constitution meant. Intelligible principles, to say nothing of "broad general directives," actually do allow federal agencies to exercise "strictly legislative" authority.

A few of the Justices in the *Whitman* case chose to accept the reality that the EPA had indeed been given legislative authority. In his separate opinion, Justice Clarence Thomas agreed with the majority that the "directive to the [EPA] is no less an "intelligible principle" than a host of other directives that we have approved." However, he went on to point out the shortcoming of relying on precedent rather than the Constitution:

> The parties to this case who briefed the Constitutional issue wrangled over Constitutional doctrine with barely a nod to the text of the Constitution. ...I am not convinced that the intelligible principle doctrine serves to prevent all cessions of legislative power. I believe that there are cases in which the principle is intelligible and yet the significance of the delegated decision is simply too great for the decision to be called anything other than "legislative."[22]

Justice John Paul Stevens came to the same conclusion that "the power delegated to the EPA is legislative" by sensibly arguing:

> If the [air quality standards] that the EPA promulgated had been prescribed by Congress, everyone would agree that those rules would be the product of an exercise of legislative power. The same characterization is appropriate when an agency exercises rulemaking authority...[23]

He went on to bluntly state "that agency rulemaking authority is "legislative power."" While Justice Stevens was faithful to this reality, his faithfulness to the Constitution was much less stringent. Somehow, he actually believes that it is constitutionally permissible for Congress to delegate legislative authority. Setting that aside, his opinion on the previous point is intellectually honest.

At least a few Justices recognized that the Court's rulings have effectively allowed Congress to delegate legislative authority. In spite of what Justice Stevens would have you believe, this has turned the Constitution on its head. "All legislative powers herein granted shall be vested in a Congress of the United States;" simple and unmistakable. A law is anything which legally compels or prohibits a person or business to act or behave in a certain manner under threat of punishment. *When an agency puts forth a rule, with or without an intelligible principle from Congress, which compels a person or business to substantially alter their methods or behavior, under threat of fine or imprisonment, it is, by any sensible definition, a law, and therefore inconsistent with the separation of powers doctrine which demands that only Congress exercise legislative powers.*

If we are to be faithful to both reality *and* the Constitution then we cannot escape the facts: 1) federal agencies today are legislating, and 2) such legislation is constitutionally prohibited. Constitutional scholar Robert Levy proclaimed that the *Whitman* decision drove "what may have been the final nail in the coffin of non-delegation doctrine..." The courts have proven they will not enforce the Constitution on this issue. Given that reality, we have no choice but to resolve the issue in the same way we resolved previous problems associated with errant judicial review; that is, we must amend the Constitution in order to expressly contain legislative power in its rightful place.

Having set out the legal foundation, it now becomes our task to explain why Section 1 of the 31st Amendment would be good policy. We begin with some examples of the impact government agencies are having on the American people beginning with the EPA.

Small businesses have an annual compliance cost of more than $3,000 per employee, just for environmental rules.[24] The former head of California's state pollution control agency Joel Schwartz summed up the situation best:

[air] pollution reductions are expensive, costing Americans at least tens of billions of dollars each year. It would be nice if we didn't have to give up anything in order to achieve additional reductions in air pollution. But in the real world, the costs of air pollution control mean higher prices, lower wages and lower returns on investment, reducing the resources we have available for everything else that affects our health, safety and quality of life.[25]

Schwartz went on to point out a problem which affects nearly all federal agencies:

As a powerful, highly specialized agency with a staff that is passionate about air quality, the EPA unavoidably suffers from tunnel vision: the pursuit of a single-minded goal to the point where it does more harm than good. Environmental regulators will pursue the next increment of air pollution reduction, and the next, regardless of whether the increasingly marginal benefits are worth having or the costs worth bearing.[26]

Every agency must justify its existence. There are many more agencies aside from the EPA which are highly specialized and passionate about their particular field of regulation. In order to make themselves useful they have to keep coming up with the next idea or the next rule or the next increment. Multiply this by hundreds of federal agencies over decades of rule-making and we begin to see the urgency of putting a stop to this out-of-control system.

The Food and Drug Administration is one of the most powerful and least-accountable federal agencies. It regulates more than $1 trillion of food, drugs, cosmetics and other products; 25 cents of every consumer dollar spent in the U.S.[27] The FDA wields tremendous power over the process of taking medical drugs to market, a process which has a substantial and direct impact on investments and the health of millions of Americans.

The FDA was first created in 1906 with the simple mission of increasing the safety of food and drugs. In 1938, true to form, the New

Deal Congress greatly expanded the agency's powers with the Food, Drug and Cosmetic Act. Then in 1962, Congress delegated to the FDA the power to ensure the efficacy of drugs, not just safety, in addition to extensive powers over clinical testing procedures. It was these changes that gave the FDA its current character as an agency with too much power and too little accountability.

In 1973, economist Sam Peltzman conducted an analysis on the effects of the 1962 changes. His study revealed that the FDA's new powers caused a significant decrease in the number of new drugs introduced into the market.[28] A proponent of the FDA might have replied that the decrease was because fewer ineffective drugs were being introduced, but in a 1983 analysis from Grabowski and Vernon it was concluded that such an argument is "not generally supported by empirical analysis."[29] From 1962 to 1967 the average approval time for getting a drug to market jumped from 7 months to 30 months. Total drug development jumped from 3 years to 10 years between 1960 and 1970.[30] No one can know how many lives may have been saved or prolonged had more drugs been brought to market during this time.

You might expect that given this effect, some changes would have been made to ensure that less impact was had on the number of drugs being introduced. But in fact, it has only become more expensive and time consuming for drugs to get to market. Recent estimates put the total average time to develop a drug at about 15 years and the cost at over $1 billion.[31] But the real impact of this is the human cost. Access to drugs is lessened not only because FDA rules make them more expensive, but because they deny them to people in desperate need. In 2001, a cancer patient named Abigail Burroughs was denied access to an investigational drug which had showed promising signs in early trials. Abigail died waiting for the drug which later went on to full production and is being used today to treat cancer patients.[32]

This episode prompted the founding of the Abigail Alliance which advocates for relaxed FDA rules for terminally ill patients. In 2007, representatives of the Abigail Alliance published an article in the Wall Street Journal chronicling the 12 drugs for which they had sought to expand early access. They estimated that more than 1 million lives could have been saved or prolonged had early access to *just these drugs* been permitted.[33] All 12 drugs went on to gain approval and constituted standard care at the time the article was written. Of course, many more life-saving drugs have been held back by the FDA while they could have been saving lives. We may never know how many lives might have been saved or prolonged had it not been for the FDA's rules.

The retort to this is that the FDA has probably saved many lives by preventing bad drugs from getting to market. The problem is that there is no reason to believe that drug companies, doctors and informed patients could not do an adequate job of ensuring the safety and efficacy of drugs because of the natural incentive to do so. But regardless of the FDA's effectiveness in preventing the introduction of bad drugs, the fundamental question is whether the government, to say nothing of an unelected bureaucracy, should have its thumb on the scale of life and death. It is grotesquely improper for government to decide that the lives of people who might have been saved with experimental drugs are less of a priority than the lives of people who might have been saved because they didn't get access to a bad drug. Such issues are best left to doctors and patients exercising their fundamental right to decide what level of risk they wish to take in their individual circumstances.

The FDA has allowed for "compassionate use" of some drugs in the early stages of development for terminally ill patients. Consider the perverseness of this scenario: if you want to try a drug that might save your life, you first need the government's permission.

Fair-minded people can debate how we can ensure the effectiveness and safety of medical drugs. But if government is to play a significant role in these decisions then, at the very least, such regulation should be handled directly by the people's representatives so that if mistakes are made the people responsible can be fired at election time. As things stand now, bureaucrats are as likely to get promoted after a mistake as they are to get fired.

It is important to note here that the 31st Amendment is not designed nor intended to undo the current regulatory structure. I am not advocating for Congress to review and vote on each new drug. I am advocating for an amendment that would make it possible to get rid of a ridiculous system that involves government, in the first place, in the process of deciding which drugs should go to market. The examples given here are simply intended to demonstrate the problems associated with delegation of legislative authority. When the amendment is ratified, the FDA, EPA and other agencies will continue to operate as they do now under present law with the exception that they cannot make new rules without the explicit approval of Congress. That may be disappointing to some, but there is simply no proper way to specify in the Constitution which regulations should be set aside and which should stay in place unless we want to add a few thousand pages to it. Constitutions should only specify general rules. It is simply impractical to immediately abolish all regulatory agencies. The 31st Amendment will simply prevent any further delegations from taking place. The political process will still be available to reduce the numbers of regulations on the books. Once a roll back does take place, the 31st Amendment will ensure that delegated authority cannot grow back.

Some have suggested a sunset rule in which regulations would automatically expire unless expressly renewed by Congress. Such a provision might greatly improve the 31st Amendment but there are some difficulties with it. For example, if Congress has to renew each provision individually, (which they would have to do given the one subject one vote rule of section 4) then they might be at it until the sun runs out of fuel. If Congress were allowed to renew everything at once then it would not change the current system in any meaningful way as Congress would reauthorize the bureaucracy without skipping a beat. And if the sunset only applies to new rules, it has the same effect I have already created in the 31st Amendment which requires Congress to approve of any new rule. With that let's continue making the case for ending the practice of delegation.

Unlike the FDA and EPA, the next example of improper delegation, the Affordable Care Act, is explicitly intended to be dismantled by Constitutional amendment, though by the 30th not the 31st. The ACA created a downright scary example of delegation run wild: the Independent Payment Advisory Board (IPAB). The infamous "death panel" has been the subject of much hyperbole but here we will stick to the facts. In spite of assurances from IPAB's supporters, this 15 member board has been given an unprecedented amount of power to create law, inconsistent not only with the Constitution, but even with the Supreme Court's broad interpretations of delegation cases.

The Affordable Care Act initiates a tremendous amount of new entitlement spending. Much of that spending will come from cuts to Medicare. To that end, IPAB was created primarily to control the growth of per-enrollee Medicare spending. Other than a few specific prohibitions, virtually no direction is given to IPAB as to the measures they can implement to keep Medicare spending down. IPAB can even initiate appropriations, which is explicitly reserved for the House of Representatives under the Constitution.[34] It can also impose taxes, price controls, regulations and can even ration care in spite of claims to the contrary. While the ACA States that IPAB "shall not include any recommendation to ration health care", the law allows the board, together with the secretary of HHS, to define what 'rationing' means.[35] The board could therefore, narrowly define rationing so that their proposals might fall outside a technical definition of the term but could still have the same effect as rationing care. This is lawyering at its worst. Allowing IPAB these broad powers is enough to be unconstitutional. But from there, things only get worse.

Much of the fear and inflammatory rhetoric about IPAB is generated because nobody knows what the board will actually do. Former Obama administration official and supporter of IPAB Peter Orszag admitted that ACA vests the board with "an enormous amount of potential power."[36] Not only does IPAB have broad powers, but the ACA deliberately restricts Congress from having the same oversight and authority over the board which it has over other agencies such as the EPA. Without this accountability, it appears that IPAB could exercise broad powers without any real mechanism for stopping it. For example, at any time, Congress could block any EPA rule with a simple majority vote and replace, or not replace it, with a rule of their own. In the case of IPAB however, if Congress fails to act within a certain time period, the IPAB proposal automatically becomes an irrevocable law, meaning Congress is prohibited from repealing it, ever. Even if Congress acts in time, they can only substitute IPAB's rule with one which will have the same effect *and,* the Senate is effectively required to achieve a three-fifths super-majority in order to make changes to IPAB's proposals.[37] Worse, if Congress fails to repeal IPAB within a narrow six month window in 2017, then Congress will lose the power altogether to replace or challenge *any* IPAB rule after 2020. The ACA also prohibits IPAB proposals from judicial and administrative review. That means that IPAB does not have to hold hearings or review evidence from the public as other agencies are required to do when proposing new rules. It also means that no one can challenge an IPAB rule in court.

If you thought it couldn't get worse, you're wrong. The authors of the ACA originally named IPAB the Independent *Medicare* Advisory Board.[38] The fact that they changed "Medicare" to "Payment" in the name is an indication that the ACA's authors meant for IPAB to regulate more than just Medicare spending. The ACA gives power to IPAB to make proposals designed to reduce the growth rate of national health care expenditures if that growth rate exceeds the growth of per-enrollee Medicare spending.[39] What those proposals might be is anyone's guess, but they will become law if Congress does not act to stop them as discussed above. The ACA also grants IPAB the authority to regulate private health care and insurance markets if the actions are "related to the Medicare program."[40] It has already been demonstrated what a large effect Medicare has on private markets and vice-versa. We also know that governments will interpret their powers as broadly as possible. Combine these factors and it becomes clear that IPAB will have little difficulty finding ways to regulate private health markets in a way that easily satisfies the ambiguous language "related to the Medicare program." When we consider also the characteristics of IPAB discussed above, we are faced with a scenario of unaccountable power which cannot be described as anything other than frightening.

For an unelected body to wield such power over our health care is patently offensive to the Constitutional separation of powers. To call IPAB's edicts "proposals" is misleading in the extreme. If Congress fails to act, IPAB's "proposals" automatically become law and if IPAB is not abolished in 2017 with a super-majority vote from both houses then Congress loses its Constitutional authority to rewrite the laws passed by IPAB.[41] That puts IPAB's law-making authority on par with that of Congress, effectively altering the Constitutional system of passing legislation. As Cato scholars Diane Cohen and Michael Cannon put it, "The Constitution is not a hostage that one Congress can threaten to shoot in order to control the behavior of future Congresses."[42]

Congress has created many laws offensive to the Constitution, but many of them have had at least a loose connection to some part of it. IPAB, on the other hand, attempts to effectively rewrite the Constitution. It is so blatantly and defiantly unconstitutional that it likely will not survive long. In fact, the Obama administration has admitted that Congress can technically override IPAB in spite of the clear meaning and intent of the ACA.[43] But this cannot excuse us from the eternal vigilance which liberty demands. We must fight hard to ensure that Congress cannot delegate its authority to legislate, particularly to the extremes of IPAB.

The trend of delegating more power to unelected bodies of "experts" is growing. There is an increasing frustration with democracy's seeming inability to "get things done." The more responsibilities government attempts to take on, the clearer its inability to manage them becomes. The inevitable result is that representative bodies are chided as inept and incapable of meeting the country's needs. None other than President Obama came to this conclusion while trying to explain why he hasn't been able to change things the way he planned:

> ...we have these big agencies, some of which are outdated, some of which are not designed properly. We've got, for example, 16 different agencies that have some responsibility to help businesses, large and small, in all kinds of ways, whether

it's helping to finance them, helping them to export. ...So, we've proposed, let's consolidate a bunch of that stuff. The challenge we've got is that that requires a law to pass. And, frankly, there are a lot of members of Congress who are chairmen of a particular committee. And they don't want necessarily consolidations where they would lose jurisdiction over certain aspects of certain policies.[44]

This apparent epiphany on the part of the President is very revealing. It shows that everyone is aware of government's inefficiencies; but the question becomes what to do about it. The only solution, it is contended by some, is to diminish democracy by delegating rule-making authority. Many progressives have admitted that they want less democracy. Peter Orszag wrote that "part of the response to polarization and gridlock must involve creating more independent institutions." He continued:

In other words, radical as it sounds, we need to counter the gridlock of our political institutions by making them a bit less democratic. ...I believe that we need to jettison the Civics 101 fairy tale about pure representative democracy and instead begin to build a new set of rules and institutions that would make legislative inertia less detrimental to our nation's long-term health. ...What we need... are ways around our politicians.[45]

Governor Bev Perdue (D-NC) made an equally radical proposal during a discussion of how Congress might better manage the economy:

You have to have more ability from Congress, I think, to work together and to get over the partisan bickering and focus on fixing things. *I think we ought to suspend, perhaps, elections for Congress for two years* and just tell them we won't hold it against them, whatever decisions they make, to just let them help this country recover.[46] (emphasis added)

This is the inevitable mindset that eventually takes hold in democracies. It was predicted by the great economist Fredrick Hayek as he described how societies evolve to accept totalitarian governments:

The inability of democratic assemblies to carry out what seems to be a clear mandate of the people will inevitably cause dissatisfaction with democratic institutions. Parliaments come to be regarded as ineffective "talking shops," unable or incompetent to carry out the tasks for which they have been chosen. The conviction grows that if efficient planning is to be done, the direction must be "taken out of politics" and placed in the hands of experts—permanent officials or independent autonomous bodies... [democracy] is an obstacle to the suppression of freedom which the direction of economic activity requires.[47]

Orszag and Perdue are correct; democracy is incapable of producing a government which can efficiently manage an economy. But what is also true is that *no system* can produce a government which can efficiently "manage" an economy. This is the fundamental reason why we have capitalism; markets work better when no central planners attempt to manage them. Democracy is incapable because it invariably becomes dominated by politics, special interests and gridlock, especially when we have abandoned Constitutional restraints. Orszag and Perdue are simply realizing what the Founders already understood in the 18th century; that democracies do not work well, particularly in large countries like ours. That is why they did not create a democracy. They created a federalist republic. Unfortunately, the solution Orszag and Perdue would have us adopt is to give up *more* power to the Federal Government by giving a free pass to unelected bodies to regulate as they see fit.

I have also spoken negatively of democracy and politics for the same reasons the Founders did. That does not mean we should replace politics with tyranny. It means we should replace politics with liberty and limited government. If we can come to the point where we agree with the left that democracy isn't working then we can begin an honest debate about what direction we should take. Should we move more toward the rule of law, limited government and greater liberty; or should we move more toward totalitarian government complete with communist-style boards empowered to regulate and redistribute as they see fit? If we continue with the mindset that government should be responsible for managing our lives and businesses then the latter is the clear choice. But if we instead choose liberty then limiting government with a strengthened and clarified Constitution becomes the clear choice. Of course, there is a large sliding scale between liberty and tyranny, but at some point a threshold exists where state control becomes so great that economic growth and individual liberty are too seriously threatened. We are at that threshold.

In this sense, cliché as it sounds, America truly is at a crossroad. We can go the direction of tyranny and top-down control or we can go the direction of liberty. There is something deeply embedded in our souls that yearns to go down the right path. Do you want to run your business and life the way you choose or the way a bureaucrat chooses? While that sounds simplistic, it is none-the-less an accurate construct of the basic decision before us. While the statists will zealously insist that we need managers who understand society's complexities, the liberty path works. This is more than an abstruse and distant theory concocted in the 18th century. Social science has virtually proven that when people are autonomous and self-directed they are more productive, happy, and virtuous.[48] This is true in the work-place, in family life, and certainly in societies.

When understood from this point of view, we get a better understanding of why it is important to remove the power of delegation from Congress. Rather than going down the road of more power and less accountability in the hands of unelected boards, what we need is for government to stop, deliberate, and think. We don't need government to speed up; we need it to slow down. The Constitution created checks and balances precisely for that purpose. If we cannot come to a majority consensus on a particular issue then we should not turn it over to unelected boards to decide for us; it should be left in the hands of free, self-governing adults. Government's ultimate responsibility is to protect that freedom, not to "fix" society's problems. That responsibility falls on a free and moral people.

Another argument in favor of more delegation is that Congress lacks the technical expertise necessary to enact the right policies and we therefore need boards of "experts" to do the job. The truth is that Congress is perfectly capable of finding the information it needs. All Congress needs to do, as it does already, is create a board or commission to make recommendations on which they will debate and vote. This is the intended method for the creation of new rules under the 31st Amendment. If this slows down the process, that is the point!

In any event, most agency heads are not technical experts but are political appointees. Also, bodies of technical experts are incentivized to make themselves seem as important as possible so that they might hold on to and expand their power. This makes them just as politically motivated as members of Congress. As Robert Levy put it:

"Administrative rule making is no less a struggle for political power than is congressional legislation."[49]   When the President chooses agency leaders he nearly always chooses political allies as opposed to technical experts.

If the decision is minute enough to require technical expertise which Congress is incapable of discerning then the issue should not be regulated by government. It is a natural rule that governments should only act in cases where a given law or policy is clearly needed and the reasoning behind it is easily discernable to voters. Complicated decisions are best handled by technical experts who advise private citizens to freely choose for themselves. Only individuals are apprised of the knowledge required to make informed decisions respecting each unique circumstance.

The more Congress delegates to executive agencies the more political power is given to the President, who is responsible for managing those agencies. Many in Congress complain about executive power but it is they who have given it up. The thousands of agencies and millions of executive employees creates an impossible management scenario for even the best of leaders and makes accountability and oversight difficult at best.

Ideally, the rule of law in a republic should severely limit what government can regulate.   But if government is to exercise broad legislative authority, as it does today, it should be reserved to the people's representatives. Only then can we ensure better accountability for bad laws while also ensuring that the rules which govern our behavior are subject to open debate and open votes rather than being passed by an obscure board. Ultimately, there is no perfect way to ensure liberty. The struggle with government usurpation and expansion of power will always be with us. But the 31st Amendment is certainly a step in the direction of more freedom and accountability as opposed to going further in the direction of more unelected boards with more power.

It is impossible to ignore the dangers of an ever-growing regulatory state. It has been estimated that the cost to businesses of all federal regulations is a staggering $1.8 trillion.[50] Resentment and disrespect for government are growing with each new rule. With each new law, regulation and rule Americans become more compressed, enervated and restrained; more like sheep and government the shepherd. Either we can choose to accept that humans fundamentally desire to be free or we can continue to pile rules upon rules until government loses nearly all credibility. When that happens, a more acute break-down in the rule of law will be close behind. That dangerous path must be avoided.

When ancient Solomon's son Rehoboam took over the kingdom of Israel, the people asked him for relief: "ease thou somewhat the grievous servitude of thy father, and his heavy yoke that he put upon us, and we will serve thee." The people showed their willingness to be loyal if they could have but a little more freedom. But Rehoboam didn't listen and he continued to burden the people. The result was that Israel rebelled and the kingdom was split in two never to recover.[51]

Fortunately, the Founders gave us Article V of the Constitution; a method that doesn't require an appeal to the better nature of kings, but one which allows the state legislatures to force change upon our national leaders through the amendment process. This is another instance in which we cannot hope that Congress will act. The advantages of delegation for members of Congress are too great. They get to reap the political rewards of any good effects of delegating while being able to distance themselves from agencies which make bad decisions. They hold their hearings which result in no substantive action but merely serve as a campaign platform for them to appear like they are doing something. The best hope we have is for the States to pass this amendment and force Congress to be accountable for the laws, rules and regulations of the United States. That was the vision of the Constitution and it is a natural rule of good government.

"What more can an enlightened and reasonable people desire?" This was the question Alexander Hamilton asked after explaining the necessity of subjecting the President to the control of Congress in cases where he abused his authority.[52] Over recent decades, we have seen an alarming increase in the authority of the executive and in the abuses of that authority. Section 2 of the 31st Amendment would provide an additional check on executive power that is badly needed to restore the separation of powers so central to the design of our Constitution.

There are many cases in which the executive violates a statute or the Constitution but no person holds sufficient standing to sue in court. Under the current system, the Courts have been unwilling to grant standing to members of Congress who sue the President. It is therefore necessary to add to the Constitution a means of checking executive authority which, in many instances, currently gives the President virtually free reign.

Here is the legal background. During the 1787 Convention the Framers grappled with how to hold the President and his officers accountable for misconduct. Some thought that the electoral process was sufficient by itself and that giving the power of impeachment to Congress would cripple the President's ability to do his job. Others believed that impeachment and elections were not nearly enough to hold the President accountable. In the end, there was not enough of a consensus to withhold the power of impeachment from Congress on the one hand, or to insulate the President from other forms of accountability, on the other hand. The Convention did not produce any clear understanding of exactly how, or if, the President would be held accountable outside the electoral and impeachment processes. Over the years, differing opinions on the matter have been put forth but none with any definitive authority. For a long period the President was restrained and law-making authority mostly kept within the sphere of congressional power.

But with the vast constitutional changes of the New Deal it was only inevitable that Presidents would expand and abuse their authority. Enter President Richard Nixon. Earnest Fitzgerald, an analyst with the Air Force, testified to Congress about a transport plane which had experienced huge cost overruns and many technical difficulties. The testimony was damaging and embarrassing to his superiors. A short time later, Fitzgerald was removed from his position for what he alleged was retaliation for his testimony to Congress. He sued President Nixon and what followed was a lengthy legal battle which culminated in the 1982 Supreme Court case *Nixon v Fitzgerald*.

The implications of the case for which we are concerned are whether or not the President's actions are subject to judicial scrutiny. Should the President be free to exercise his official duties without any constraint from the possibility of a law suit? In a sad day for liberty and limited government, the Court concluded in a sharply contrasted 5-4 decision that the President of the United States "is entitled to *absolute immunity* from damages liability predicated on his official acts."[53]

The Court based its decision on two points. First, they argued that a "diversion of [the President's] energies by concern with private lawsuits would raise unique risks to the effective functioning of government."[54] So, according to the Court, federal agencies, under the direction of the President, can scrutinize the decisions of private citizens and businesses through an endless maze of regulations, even if it grinds the economy and the advance of liberty to a morbidly slow pace, but the President of the United States, in his duties, must not be slowed or inconvenienced by accusations of abuse of power. Such a construction of law replaces the concept of a limited government and free people with a philosophy of a limited people and a free government.

Secondly, and even more incredibly, the Justices argued for presidential immunity based on the separation of powers doctrine, asserting "the dangers of intrusion on the authority and functions of the Executive Branch."[55] What the justices failed to understand is that the separation of powers doctrine does not imply the creation of three branches of government operating in a mutually exclusive fashion with an unchecked authority to carry out their functions without interference. Rather, the separation of powers in the Constitution created an interplay of various checks and balances designed to allow each branch to constrain the other if they exceeded their authority. It is no violation of the separation of powers to demand judicial review of the President's acts when those acts are unlawful. On the contrary, it is a confirmation that the separation of powers is functioning.

Consider this short list of Constitutional provisions which allow one branch to "intrude" on the functions of the other. The President can veto acts of Congress. The courts can declare an act of Congress unconstitutional. The President can choose the members of the Court with the confirmation of the Senate. The House can begin impeachment proceedings on the President which shall be tried in the Senate, and so forth. This structure does not admit, as the Court held, that the President can act independently without review or constraint. The exact opposite is true. The President must be checked by the separation of powers if he begins to exercise legislative authority by violating the language and intent of the acts of Congress or if he clearly violates other Constitutional limits. As Congress is empowered to write the laws, they must also be empowered to ensure that the President "shall take care that the laws be faithfully executed."

Some sympathy can be had for the Court's decision in this case. It would potentially be a hampering force against the President if he were subject to lawsuits from every side. The President should have at least some protection from lawsuits while discharging the duties of his office. But under Section 2, one third of the members of each house are required to sign on to a law suit before proper standing is reached. This eliminates the complaint that the President will be too frequently subjected to lawsuits to effectively perform his duties. The real problem is that the Court granted *complete immunity* rather than a partial immunity limited to specific cases. As the minority in the *Nixon* decision said: "Attaching absolute immunity to the Office of the President, rather than to particular activities that the President might perform, places the President above the law."[56]   This has made it too tempting for the President to abuse his power. He can fire or hire anyone in the executive branch for any reason. He can use his office to award political allies, punish political enemies or to silence whistleblowers.

Should not the President of the United States be held accountable *at all* in at least a portion of his official duties? We need whistleblowers in government more so than anywhere else. A lengthy review could be given of news reports recounting the many abuses of Presidents past and present which are increasing in frequency and intensity; but I trust the reader will be informed enough of these reports.[57]

The 31st Amendment is designed to balance the dangers of completely exposing the President to a myriad of lawsuits against the dangers of absolute immunity which places the President above the law. In the case of Constitutional violations it will be admitted that Congress holds no higher ground than the President.   But as the people's representatives they are the clear choice to be endowed with the power to bring suit against the President. It may be safely relied on that there will always be at least a third of the members of Congress who would be willing to challenge the President for Constitutional and/or statutory violations; while it would not be easy to find a third of both Houses to bring arbitrary or frivolous suits.

The *Nixon* Court attempted to assuage any fears that the nation is without protection against presidential misconduct by assuring that Congress could still impeach the President or that scrutiny from the press and congressional oversight were disincentives to misconduct. They also threw in the paltry reassurance that presidents care about their legacy.[58]   Others have put forth that Congress always has the power of the purse to stop executive overreach. What have these protections yielded other than a constant stream of congressional hearings and "60 Minutes" reports with no resolution? Perhaps an underling or two is fired and there is always an "internal investigation" but business inevitably continues as usual. The idea that Congress controls the purse is Constitutional fact but if the executive has ignored the Constitutional separation of powers there is no reason to believe that a President will be inconvenienced by congressional requirements on how to use federal money. Indeed, Presidents have already found ways to spend money for purposes not intended by Congress.[59]   These protections are helpless in the increasing advance of executive overreach.

Shall we trust that Congress will get the situation under control on its own? No. Congress enjoys any situation that allows it to shift blame. Indeed, that is one of the central creeds of politics. If the President has the power then Congress is not responsible. If blame can be shifted then politicians can make themselves look good while criticizing the people who are supposed to be responsible while not having to solve the problem. In fact, not solving the problem is in their best interest; else how could they make themselves look good if they aren't busy holding a hearing or investigating those who *should* be responsible. No; the States must force responsibility on Congress by Constitutional amendment and give them a meaningful method of reining in presidential misconduct. There must be some means to hold the President accountable beyond public scrutiny and the President's concern for his legacy. The dissenting Justices in the *Nixon* case painted a scary picture which has too often come to life.

> A President ...may, without liability, deliberately cause serious injury to any number of citizens even though he knows his conduct violates a statute or tramples on the Constitutional rights of those who are injured. ...He would be immune regardless of the damage he inflicts, regardless of how violative of the statute and of the Constitution he knew his conduct to be, and regardless of his purpose.

> The Court intimates that its decision is grounded in the Constitution. If that is the case, Congress cannot provide a remedy against Presidential misconduct and the criminal laws of the United States are wholly inapplicable to the President.[60]

This being the case, we should not be surprised when a scandal happens and the President is untouchable. He declares himself "unaware" and promises a full investigation. This includes nearly every President in modern history going at least as far back as Watergate, to which the minority referred directly when laying down the consequences of the majority's decision.

> By the same token, if a President, without following the statutory procedures which he knows apply to himself as well as to other federal officials, orders his subordinates to wiretap or

break into a home for the purpose of installing a listening device, and the officers comply with his request, the President would be absolutely immune from suit.[61]

And the President *was* immune from suit as history has shown, as have been other Presidents in a variety of cases. For example, let's examine the War Powers Act of 1973. Toward the end of the Vietnam War, Congress sought to limit the war-making powers of the President. They did so with this act, which allows the President to use military force for sixty days without congressional approval. After that, Congress must either approve the use of military force or declare war. But what if the President uses military force beyond the sixty days or otherwise violates the War Powers Act? Who has standing to sue in these cases? If the President violates his war powers the offended party is Congress. But when one branch of the Federal Government sues another, the typical response from the courts has been to not get involved, claiming that the matter is purely political and should be decided by elections. But elections do not dictate what is, and what is not, Constitutional.

There have been at least two clear violations of the War Powers Act in which members of Congress have sued the President. The first was concerning the U.S. bombing campaign in the Balkans in the late 1990s under President Clinton. On March 24, 1999, President Clinton announced the commencement of a U.S.-led bombing campaign against Yugoslavia. In compliance with the War Powers Act President Clinton notified Congress within the required 48 hours. However, the bombing campaign lasted for 79 days without congressional approval, 19 longer than is allowed under the War Powers Act, a clear violation of the law. Any citizen found violating an act of Congress would be prosecuted and punished. But when 31 members of Congress sued the President, the Court held that Congress did not have standing to sue and that it would "...dismiss the complaint to avoid meddling in the internal affairs of the legislative branch."[62] This is a puzzling conclusion. By this standard nearly any declaration of the Constitutionality of a law could be deemed "meddling in the internal affairs" of Congress.

The second instance of a violation of the War Powers Act occurred when President Obama involved the U.S military in the bombing of Libya. From March 31, 2011 to October 31, NATO forces, including U.S. aircraft conducted thousands of missions over Libya, clearly violating the U.S. War Powers resolution which requires the President to seek congressional approval within 60 days. Once again, 10 members of

Congress sued the President and once again, the Court dismissed the lawsuit on the same grounds as the previously cited War Powers dispute. Georgetown Law professor Jonathan Turley, who represented the 10 members of Congress in this case, said:

> Notably, the court did not rule on the Constitutional questions. Instead, the decision holds that a critical part of the Constitution cannot be effectively enforced in the courts. It is a position that runs contrary to the views of the Framers and certainly these members.[63]

How can it possibly be that a critical part of the Constitution is not reviewable by the Court? The very purpose of the Court is to enforce Constitutional restraints on the other branches of government. Article III of the Constitution states: "The judicial power shall extend to *all Cases*, in Law and Equity, arising under this Constitution [or] the Laws of the United States." (emphasis added) Once again, the courts have failed to do their duty. It is therefore necessary to change the Constitution to make it unmistakable that *someone* can challenge the President when he violates the law. This is much more likely to effect change than waiting either for the Courts to come around or hoping that the President will restrain himself.

In the famous case of *Marbury v Madison*, the Supreme Court considered the constitutionality of the actions of the Secretary of State, an officer in the executive branch of government. The opinion of the Court affirmed its right to review the Constitutionality of executive actions. Quoting Blackstone, they stated:

> "...it is a general and indisputable rule that where there is a legal right, there is also a legal remedy by suit or action at law whenever that right is invaded." ...The Government of the United States has been emphatically termed a government of laws, and not of men. It will certainly cease to deserve this high appellation, if the laws furnish no remedy for the violation of a vested legal right.[64]

The Court went on to ask whether entire confidence "is placed by our Constitution in the Supreme Executive ...for any misconduct respecting which the injured individual has no remedy?"[65] They answered their own question by asserting that such a situation "is not to be admitted." While the Court went on to claim that there are some political powers for which the President is not accountable, they unmistakably affirmed that he is not completely immune from suit.

It is curious that the case which established the Court's ability to strike down unconstitutional acts of the other branches of government was ignored in modern decisions dismissing lawsuits against the President, once again showing the evolution of the Courts away from original Constitutional doctrine.   The Court's assertion that the President should enjoy complete immunity but not his underlings is a distinction unwarranted by anything in the Constitution. The President should be held to as much accountability as any of his appointees in the executive branch. As the Supreme Court said in an unrelated case: "Accountability of each individual for individual conduct lies at the core of all law - indeed, of all organized societies."[66]

Jonathan Turley recently testified before Congress on the urgency of reigning in executive authority. In that testimony he very nearly summed up the thesis of this book:

> We are in the midst of a Constitutional crisis with sweeping implications for our system of government. There has been a massive gravitational shift of authority to the Executive Branch that threatens the stability and functionality of our tripartite system. ...Many have embraced the notion that all is fair in love and politics.   However ...in our system it is often more important *how* we do something than *what* we do. ...It is not enough to refer to the value of a program to justify its extraconstitutional means. Such Constitutional relativism cuts the entire system free of its moorings; leaving the system adrift in a sea of politics where the ability to act is treated as synonymous with the authority to act. There is no license in our system to act, as President Obama promised, "with or without Congress"[67]

Turley went on to implore Congress to fix the separation of powers problem by urging them to gain standing in court in order to sue the President. The problem is that Congress has no way to get the courts to recognize member standing.   The only solution is to amend the Constitution. Indeed, Turley recognized that "Absent a Constitutional amendment, a change in the interpretation of Article III [the part in the Constitution which describes the extent of judicial review] can only come from the Court itself."[68] Only a convention can bring back into balance the separation of powers which the courts have allowed to warp.

Section 3: Federalism

Not only does the Federal Government rely on delegation to executive agencies to run its programs, but it also relies on the States to administer a great deal of federal spending. The Federal Government spent roughly $560 billion in 2013 on what is called the grants-in-aid system.[69] Through a variety of complex programs, the feds dole out money to the States for everything from health care and education to a $125 million grant for healthy marriages.[70] Of course, if the feds are paying for it you can be sure they exercise a great deal of control over how it is spent. This spending nearly always comes with strings attached, which greatly diminishes the State's role in setting policy for their constituents. This blunts policy innovation across States and consolidates power in Washington. It also produces unnecessary overlap and waste in government spending at both levels and further undermines accountability. The third section of the 31st Amendment will help to correct these issues.

In the 19th century, federal aid to the States was virtually non-existent as most understood the proper separation of powers between the two governments.   But of course, following the permanent installment of the federal income tax in 1913 and the New Deal of the 1930s, grants-in-aid began to multiply. The number of grants-in-aid programs grew from 15 in 1930 to 132 by 1960. From there, Johnson's "Great Society" programs, including Medicaid, the largest state-aid program, caused the number to rise to 530 by 1970. In spite of efforts by Presidents Nixon, Carter and Reagan to consolidate or reform the system, the number of state-aid programs continued to grow. Today, there are more than *1,100 state-aid programs* operated by the Federal Government.[71]

These programs cause massive amounts of waste and inefficiency. One reason is that over the years, there has been no consistent or coherent strategy on grants-in-aid spending. There has never been a Congress which has formulated a plan or overall purpose for state aid. As Congress began to accumulate more power in the 20th century, special interest groups began to multiply and focus their efforts on convincing Washington to fund their particular agendas. Rather than starting with a coherent plan, congressional committees simply responded to this lobbying by adding one program at a time with little consideration for redundancy or even need. That ad hoc development has created a tangled mess of complexity and waste. In 1940, when state-aid programs could still be measured in the dozens, an article in Congressional Quarterly lamented:

> The grants-in-aid system in the United States has developed in a haphazard fashion. Particular services have been singled out for subsidy at the behest of pressure groups, and little attention has been given to national and state interests as a whole.[72]

Nothing has changed the way state-aid programs develop today. They have simply been piled on top of each other as each committee in Congress seeks to makes itself seem more useful by pandering to a variety of special interest groups.

The lack of a consistent strategy has led to federal programs which do not address issues that can only be addressed by the Federal Government. It was the Founders' wish that Congress would "legislate in all cases, to which the separate States are incompetent."[73] That element of Constitutional design cuts against the current policy of having the Federal Government fund and direct domestic policy through the administration of the States. Cases to which the States are incompetent do not necessarily include issues which are common among them. There are many issues faced by a plurality of States which are not necessarily problems that are national in scope. For example, many States have natural wonders that should be protected, but it does not follow that it must be the federal, rather than the state governments who are charged with protecting them. Likewise, the mere fact that education is important to all Americans does not make it an issue which requires federal action. The same could be said of most domestic policy issues.

If nobody has planned or organized the grants-in-aid system then no one is accountable for it. Congress can give money to the States and claim the political benefits for spending on a given program while pointing the finger at the States if something goes wrong. By the same token, state politicians can claim credit for bringing in more money to the State while blaming Washington for not giving them enough control over the funds. As Cato scholar Chris Edwards put it: "When every government is responsible for an activity, no government is responsible."[74] The pass-the-buck mantra of politics is very much alive in the grants-in-aid system; and by "system" I mean a tangled heap of overlapping, redundant, confusing and wasteful programs.

The Founder's vision was to have as clear a line as possible between state and national responsibilities. That vision was described by Edmund Pendleton in the Virginia ratifying debates when he said that the State and Federal Governments "Being for two different purposes, as long as they are limited to the different objects, they can no more clash than two parallel lines can meet."[75] The grants-in-aid system has helped make the parallel lines as indiscernible as possible. It is difficult enough to use politics and elections to form better public policy, but when voters cannot clearly understand who is responsible for what, beyond a vague mandate to "make things better", then it becomes nearly impossible.

Another reason the grants-in-aid system is so wasteful is that for most programs States must spend a certain amount of money in order to trigger a corresponding increase in federal funding. That arrangement entices States to spend more money on programs than they otherwise might. The States tend to believe that federal money is free and that *not* taking the money is for suckers. After all, they don't have to raise taxes for it. But in the long run, the States will be the losers. The Federal Government can run up more debt than the States by borrowing from other countries, or they can simply print more money. When States take federal money they become complicit in creating huge federal deficits and increasing the burden of government spending.

Money comes from somewhere and it is never free. Whether paid by current or future taxpayers, or by inflation, the bills must be paid. Legislatures also tend to adopt the attitude that since their State pays federal taxes, they should fight to get back as much as they can. But this mentality creates a race to the bottom as competing States enter a frenzy for federal money. That frenzy, in turn, leads the Federal Government to believe that money for state-aid programs is in "high demand," and induces even more spending. When States participate in the gluttony of the grants-in-aid system they are every bit as guilty as Congress for finding ways to spend money without accountability. Such a scene shows blatant disregard for the vital Constitutional link between taxation and representation.

Another reason grants-in-aid are inefficient is because of the unnecessary filtration of money through the Washington bureaucracy. It simply makes no sense to tax money from the people in the States then give it to the States to administer. That unnecessary step only skims money off the top to fund a middle man which adds no value to the equation. The States are perfectly capable of taxing their constituents and spending on their behalf in ways agreeable to them, just as Congress can. Those who claim that there is a "lack of resources" at the State level seem to be oblivious to the fact that it is the Federal Government which undermines the States' ability to raise revenue when they tax at much higher rates. The Federal Government's revenue-raising advantage exists partly because it can print money or borrow from other countries. Those are arguments *against* relying on Washington to raise revenue, not for it. Some might lament that relying more on the States to raise revenue for and administer domestic policy would cause a shortage of public services because of tax competition. But once again, as we saw in the last chapter, tax competition is an argument *for* federalism not against it. We actually *want* discipline in government spending, which is more likely when governments with much more limited credit cards are primarily responsible for the bills. That will create domestic programs which will be more sustainable and less subject to fraud, abuse and mismanagement.

What these arguments are really getting at is that Washington needs more control. Progressives seem to fear that too many people won't want to be taxed enough to fund government programs (imagine that!). Therefore, only the Federal Government can tax, borrow and print at a high enough level to fund "essential" programs. But centralized power runs counter to the Constitutional design and makes government even more inefficient and less accountable than it already is naturally.

Once the States are hooked on federal money, they become more willing to give up their power to Washington. With each new deal and each new program more power is consolidated in the Federal Government. While some claim that state-aid programs create harmless incentives for States, there is often a fine line between coercion and incentive when it comes to grants-in-aid. In 1984, Congress passed an act which directed the Secretary of Transportation to withhold a percentage of federal highway funds from States who did not enforce a minimum drinking age of at least 21. South Dakota, whose drinking age was 19, sued and lost in a case that went to the Supreme Court. Unfortunately, that case confirmed that Congress has broad discretion in determining the strings it attaches to the money given to States.[76] As a result, Congress has repeatedly coerced the States into compliance with its will, greatly undermining federalism and centralizing power.

Rather than a top-down hierarchy of authority from the national government to the States, the Constitution created a system of mutually exclusive authority over separate issues. It is true that the Federal Constitution is the supreme law of the land, but it is not true that every extraconstitutional federal program overrides State authority. Unfortunately, unless the Constitution is amended, this vision is little more than forgotten history.

The following figure contrasts the view most Americans have of the relationship between federal and state governments with that which the Constitution created. The States are not the subordinates of the Federal Government; they are co-equal partners endowed with distinct yet broad powers.

Scope of Federal and State Powers

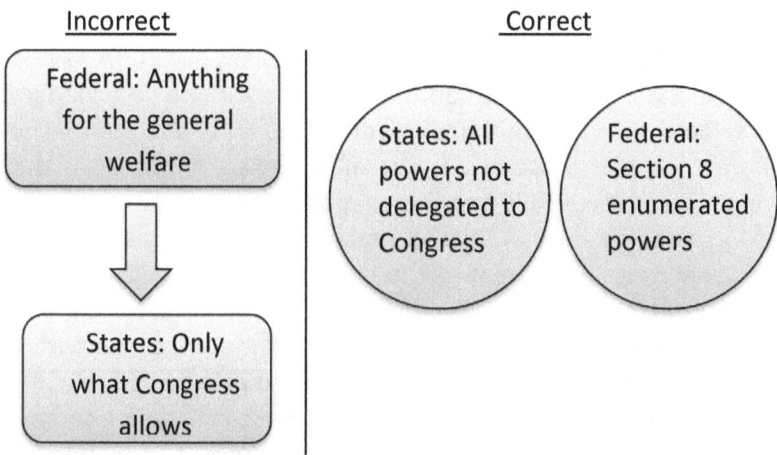

Just as centralized power within one branch of the Federal Government is dangerous, so it is with centralized power consolidated from the States. It corrupts those who wield it and leads to waste and inefficiency. The framers understood this well and were careful to craft a Constitution that not only dispersed power among federal branches, but retained significant power for the States. The time is long past due to rearrange the Constitutional system so that it more closely reflects this original intention.

It may be unlikely that the States will voluntarily give up receiving money from the Federal Government. But the only sure way to restore federalism is to completely deny the ability of the national government to give money to the States. This would be the most effective way to re-create the Constitutional line between federal and state power.

Because so much dependency on the State-aid system has been created, Congress is given a full ten years to phase out its programs.

This section of the 31st Amendment would essentially abolish Medicaid as we know it. This would certainly garner great opposition so it is necessary to address this head-on. The argument is simple. If a State wants to have a Medicaid program then they should pay for it. Any argument that is made about the necessity of helping the poor with medical expenses is moot. We can help the poor with medical expenses. We just need to pay for it ourselves. But the retort is that the burden would be too great for the States to bear! The burden is the same whether paid by current generations or paid by our children and grandchildren. Money is not free. It has to come from somewhere and that somewhere is the taxpayers who live in the States.

The reason States should bear the cost is so that those costs are transparent and discernable to voters. When money pours in from the Feds the States get the illusion that it comes with no cost. In fact, it is the same cost as though the taxpayers in the State paid for it. The only difference is that politicians can credibly make the claim that they are being fiscally responsible because they don't have to raise the taxes for the increased spending. What federalism accomplishes is to remove the veil which conceals the real cost of these programs. Shifting the cost to Washington does not *decrease* the cost, it only hides it.

This system is nothing short of a scam on future citizens who have no voice. In the long run there is nothing to gain by selfishly mugging future generations. It may be argued that we can sustain a certain level of debt and thereby increase our purchasing power to help people. But this argument ignores how politicians actually operate. Do you really believe that with nearly unlimited credit and a money-making machine, (the Federal Reserve) politicians will not continue to expand programs? Where is the end of government's "charity?" When the debt burden gets to be unsustainable what happens? Do they cut back? No. They say "raise taxes!" This pattern reveals that governments don't tax and spend; they spend first and tax later. And it is the later taxpayers who pay the price for earlier generation's benefits.

We can help the poor; just don't ask our kids to pay for it! If a small amount of debt is sustainable then let the States take it on. The advantage of that system is that power is dispersed among 50 States, each with unique ideas some of which may work and others that may not. In this system the bad ideas can be easily jettisoned and the good ideas emulated. Such is the genius of the federalist system. In a centralized system, such as the one we have now, we are all stuck with the bad ideas and with the debt.

Interestingly, we can look to Canada, in many ways a bastion of progressive government philosophy, as an example of a successful federalist system. In that country, 38% of total government spending is federal while 62% is provincial (state) or local. In the United States, by contrast, federal spending is 71% of total government spending compared to 29% state and local.[77] Federalism is not just a sound theory; it is proven as an effective and wise way to govern. At a minimum, Canada's experience shows that we can shift a greater burden of spending to the States without the sky falling.

Section 3 of the 31st Amendment will restore to the States the responsibility which the Constitution originally gave them: to decide for themselves how best to provide for the well-being of their citizens, if government is needed at all. Let the debate rage on what government's role should be. Just let it take place at the State level so that we can avoid the dangers of consolidated power the Constitution was meant to prevent; and so that voters can plainly see the costs of government involvement.

Section 4: One Issue, One Vote

In October of 2009 Congress passed and the President signed a $680 billion defense spending bill into law. There was nothing unusual about it except that part of the bill expanded hate crimes to include assaults on people because of their sexual orientation. Another defense bill, passed by Congress in 2005, had a curious attachment to it: the REAL ID act, which set federal standards for state issued drivers licenses. In 2006, Congress was deliberating the Security and Accountability for Every Port Act, designed to improve security at the nation's ports. *Hours before the Senate voted on the bill*, an amendment was added which outlawed online gambling, a law which had been unable to gain support on its own. These earmarks or riders, as they are called, have been a big contributor to Congress's laughing stock status. They add a level of complexity that allows measures to be sneaked into legislation with little or no debate, grossly undermining a transparent legislative process. Worse, they have become the favored tools of bribery and corruption in Congress.

Earmarks to defense bills began to multiply rapidly after Congress passed the Budget Enforcement Act of 1990 which set limits on non-defense "discretionary" spending, and required spending increases to be offset by cuts in other areas. Did Congress's self-imposed spending restraint work? About as well as their self-imposed debt limit has worked. Rather than comply with the requirements, Congress simply began attaching unrelated spending measures to defense appropriations which were not subject to the new controls. Senator Tom Harkin led the way when he earmarked $210 million of funding for breast cancer research to the Department of Defense budget.[78] This prompted the creation of an entirely new bureaucracy within the DOD to manage this type of spending. Advocacy groups and lobbyists saw an opportunity to get easy funding for their projects as resistance to defense appropriations is usually light; and the earmark requests from Congress began piling up. Today, the DOD spends billions on medical research unrelated to battlefield injuries.[79] This highlights how earmarks and riders bloat federal budgets and contribute to puzzling organizational structures which undermine accountability and oversight, to say nothing of common sense.

It also shows the futility of using statutory limits to control spending and debt. Congress simply comes up with creative and dishonest ways to bypass the limits or change them with new legislation. For fiscal year 2011, Congress passed more than 6,700 earmarks totaling $8.3 billion.[80]

Public outcries over earmarks had been growing steadily louder and in a rare move of meaningful reform, Congress adopted a moratorium on earmarks in 2011 which is still in effect today. But out-of-place appendages to bills still find their way into legislation as we saw in the emergency relief package for Hurricane Sandy, which allocated $118 million to Amtrak[81]; and in the more recent budget deal which ended the government shutdown, which contained $2.8 billion for a dam project on the Ohio River.[82] One is left to wonder why these gems were not nixed because of the moratorium on earmarks. Whether it was because of some technicality in congressional rules or lack of a clear definition of an earmark is irrelevant because the end result is the same: spending and legislation which has no place in the original bill. When Congress tries to limit itself, those limits will eventually be eroded as voters shift their attention elsewhere. It is only a matter of time before the moratorium is completely ended or otherwise bypassed.

Earmarks, however you define them, lead to the passage of measures which do not receive adequate debate or vetting from our elected representatives. Everything which Congress passes ought to stand on its own merits. If a measure cannot be passed on its own after vigorous debate then it should not be passed. The ugly practice of earmarking, or otherwise attaching senseless amendments unrelated to a bill's original purpose, undermines a transparent legislative process. If it is the law, it should have been approved by elected representatives after open debate, on its own. Few principles are more essential to a properly functioning legislative body.

Earmarks also lead to difficult choices for lawmakers which exacerbate the ugliness of politics. Most congressmen are afraid of voting against more popular bills, such as defense appropriations, because they know they could be hammered at election time. The requesters of earmarks know that a popular bill will not get held up because of a less important attachment. What should a congressman do; vote against a popular and important bill because it has an unrelated amendment worth a few million dollars, or vote for the bill anyway? We have seen how most politicians answer this question. In popular debates representatives can be skewered for voting for measures which they do not truly support. For example, in September of 2013, the Senate was debating an "energy efficiency" bill with numerous senators proposing unrelated amendments, including one from Senator David Vitter which would weaken the Affordable Care Act.[83] How does a Democrat, acting in good faith, vote on legislation containing important environmental concerns while also weakening what they see as a good health care law? Either way they vote, they could be punished at the polls and in the media. Elected representatives should not be subject to these dilemmas. They should be free to vote their conscience, one issue at a time. Without that principle in place, the effectiveness of legislative bodies is greatly diminished. When people vote for a representative, they should have a right to expect that that person will be able to vote according to their views, free from the coercion, distortion and manipulation of back-room trade-offs and special carve-outs.

The worst part about these types of amendments is the corruption which they breed. All too often, bills are passed by swapping earmarks or other unrelated attachments intended to benefit a particular member in exchange for their vote. Some cynics contend that this is simply a good way to gain the support for important bills and to "get things done." One of the most infamous of these dirty deals was the "Cornhusker Kickback" which helped assure the passage of the Affordable Care Act. Senator Bill Nelson of Nebraska was reluctant to vote for the legislation, but his vote was secured when Nebraska was given a much higher rate of federal funding than other States for expanding Medicaid. The fact that the special deal for Nebraska was later repealed doesn't make the situation any better. The deal was given, the law passed, and the damage was done. Legislation should be passed only when a majority of members genuinely support the measure, not because a few of those members get special deals which may help their re-election campaigns. Will Congress fix this corrupt scene on its own? We all know the answer.

One example will serve to illustrate a range of problems which the 31st Amendment is meant to solve. To set the stage, when someone is accused of a crime they are guaranteed certain protections. The Fourth and Fifth Amendments imply a presumption of innocence and ensure a right to due process. It has long been a grey area as to how non-government organizations should apply the presumption of innocence doctrine in their dealings with the accused. Should a college or employer also extend the presumption of innocence in their disciplinary actions? For many years, most colleges and universities relied on a standard which required "clear and convincing" evidence that the accused was guilty before disciplinary action was given.[84] That standard is not unlike the "beyond a reasonable doubt" standard used in criminal court cases. Most people would agree that even schools should generally follow a strict presumption of innocence standard. But in April 2011, the federal Education Department's Office for Civil Rights (OCR) issued a letter ordering colleges and universities to begin using the "preponderance of evidence" standard in sexual harassment and assault cases. This meant that schools only had to show that the accused was *more likely* to have committed the crime than not. In other words, if there is a 51% chance of guilt then the accused should be disciplined. That greatly weakened the burden of proof required to punish the accused and is thus a serious threat to a person's right to presumption of innocence.

The first problem illustrated by this example is that an unelected body of bureaucrats effectively passed a law dealing with a fundamental right and protection for accused criminals. Worse, in this case the Education Department did not take advice and comments from the public as most agencies do when considering a policy change. Any arguments about the merits of the policy in question are moot. The issue is that such serious policy decisions should be reserved for elected representatives.

Patrick Witt knows very well the implications of the policy. As a student at Yale, Witt was being considered for a Rhodes Scholarship. When it came to light that he was being accused of sexual harassment, the Rhodes Trust withdrew their consideration unless the University would still recommend him. Fearful of the Education Department's directive, Yale declined.[85] The loss of a scholarship or expulsion from college can be a permanent black eye on a person's reputation and could be detrimental to them for years after their time in college. Such issues should not be influenced by an unelected government board.

The 31st Amendment would remove the ability of executive agencies to issue rules governing the lives of individuals and businesses, and would give Congress the ability to sue the executive branch for such abuses of power. Constitutional scholar Richard Epstein noted that the department never considered that their authority over the issue "was anything less than absolute."[86] If the Education Department can do this to schools then there is no reason to believe that the Securities and Exchange Commission could not find a way to do something similar to financial institutions; or the FDA to drug makers; or the EPA to manufacturers etc. Under executive agency fiat, we have created a legal system with far too much arbitrary power.

The second problem illustrated is the erosion of federalism. We must not allow Congress to give money to the States because when it controls the money its control over policy becomes nearly absolute. The extent of that control is well-illustrated by this example. The vast majority of colleges went along with the Education Department's directive because they do not want their funding threatened. Richard Epstein explained:

> Central to understanding this case is the enormous power of the United States government through the conditions that it attaches to the grants that it gives to universities for scientific research. ...It is important not to underestimate the iron fist that comes attached to these grants.[87]

Rule-making authority is much more likely to be abused by federal agencies because they control the money States receive. This case illustrates well how the consolidation of power has developed as Congress has multiplied state-aid programs.

The third problem illustrated by this example is the tendency of government actions to jumble a variety of issues into a confusing mess of overlapping and contradictory policies. A reasonable person would conclude that the Department of Education should be dealing with education, while the Justice Department would be dealing with sexual assault and legal issues such as the presumption of innocence. This further underscores the importance of not only restoring rule-making authority to Congress but in forcing it to consider these issues one at a time so that we might have more transparency, consistency and reason in the process. A society that reveres the rule of law should demand nothing less.

This example shows an agency of unelected bureaucrats, writing a law which had a significant impact on a fundamental legal right, without input from the public and which constrained the authority of the State's public institutions. The 31st Amendment would ensure that if presumption of innocence, or any other meaningful issue, were to be considered, it would be considered by elected representatives as a stand-alone issue without the threat of coercion through the withholding of money. Such a system would be very preferable to passing laws through obscure agencies of so-called experts scattered across dozens of departments and affecting an unlimited number of issues. A hundred volumes of space could be filled with examples similar to the directive issued by the Department of Education. Such is the urgency of passing the 31st Amendment which will restore separation of powers, slow down federal rule-making, and increase transparency.

CHAPTER TWELVE

CLOSING ARGUMENTS

Several other amendments are worthy of consideration in the new convention. I wish to mention two. One would be an amendment to strengthen civil liberties. The recent IRS and NSA scandals are not new; they have been going on for years through multiple presidencies. Scandals such as this happen because, as with the problems associated with amendments 29-31, the courts have refused to enforce the plain meaning of the Constitution. A new civil liberties amendment should be designed to strengthen at least two pillars of individual rights:

First: privacy. The right to privacy should be explicitly extended to electronic devices and communications. We should also strike down by amendment the court's so called "balancing test" which allows government to provide a "compelling interest" for violating Fourth Amendment rights. This has led directly to constitutionally prohibited, but court-sanctioned, searches and seizures without warrant or probable cause.

Second: due process and burden of proof. The IRS is particularly culpable in denying citizens the right to due process and trial by jury. Many federal agencies routinely deny citizens the right to a presumption of innocence. This should be explicitly granted in a new amendment and it should apply to *all cases*. The accused, whether for tax evasion, work safety violations, or murder, should enjoy a speedy jury trial. If a federal agency suspects a violation of law, they should get a warrant, do an investigation and bring the case before an impartial judge and jury. The burden of proof should always be placed on government. Without these protections, numerous federal agencies can continue to harass and intimidate citizens.

The Bill of Rights does not have asterisks or footnotes of exceptions. Where exceptions were intended they were explicitly provided, as in the case of grand jury appointments during armed conflicts.[1] The Framers never claimed that government would not have a compelling interest that would necessitate violating individual rights. *It is precisely because government is good at making a compelling case for violating rights that we put explicit protections in place.* Government can always fall back on the reliable claim that their actions are necessary for public safety or health. Individual rights should not have to be balanced against "state interests." Individual rights should be supreme.

If government wants to act in violation of natural rights, it must apply due process; get a warrant, make an investigation, and convince an impartial jury that the accused has willfully violated the law, *in all cases*. If that puts too much of a burden on government then that is the point! The Bill of Rights was intended to place the burden on government and keep it off of the people. In truth, the problem is not a compelling state interest; the problem is the proliferation of laws, spurred by the Constitutional revolution of the 1930s, which has required that government make end runs around the Bill of Rights in order to enforce a gargantuan number of rules. That is why the interdiction of drugs, for example, has created such a horrible scene of violations of individual rights. Only a massive and intrusive police state can attempt to stop it. But if government would mind its own Constitutional business, the necessity of having an army of officers and regulators which intrude on individual rights would go away. Nonetheless, compromise can be achieved. If the government wants to enforce all these laws (most of which are unconstitutional) then they must do it within the confines of the Bill of Rights. Such should be clearly spelled out by Constitutional amendment in order to correct the Court's misguided acquiescence to a "compelling state interest."

The next amendment which must be discussed at the new convention is one which would check or abolish the Federal Reserve. The Constitutional fight over a central bank has been going on literally since the first Congress established it. The Federal Reserve exerts an enormous amount of power over the economy yet our elected officials have little to do with its operations and in fact, don't even know much about what it does. At a minimum, a new amendment should demand that 1) Congress audit the Fed annually and publish the results; 2) The Fed should be explicitly barred from giving money to foreign banks or any foreign government; 3) The Fed should be given some sort of oversight with regard to setting interest rates. The Federal Reserve System is an illustration of the separation of powers problem. It is Congress which the Constitution specifically tasks with regulating the value of money, yet that dangerous and powerful function has been delegated to a quasi-private bank which operates in secrecy and whose revolving door is a direct conduit to Wall Street.

The Federal Reserve is directly responsible for the two worst economic catastrophes of this country's history (1929 and 2007-08).[2] Its express purpose was to prevent a great depression, yet, that is precisely what we had less than 20 years after its establishment. We have seen time and again how great societies have been destroyed because they debased their currencies. The Fed continues to create money out of thin air, driving stock market inflation and lining the pockets of the wealthy. This banking cartel system has drawn the ire of both the political left and right, and for good reason. A substantive and effective financial reform, in other words one based on free-market principles and accountability, is long overdue.

When Gutenberg's printing press began churning out books in the middle of the 15th century it revolutionized the world with the spread of ideas. That revolution culminated in the liberalization and democratization of governments around the world beginning with our own. Over the decades however, those governments have grown large and slow, encrusted with the barnacles of corruption, special interests and a presumption of unwarranted power. Now there is a new revolution underway. It is being spurred by the internet and communications technology. The printing press allowed the credentialed and well-placed to spread their ideas rapidly. The internet allows *everyone* to spread ideas. Of course, that means we are all bombarded with a mass of information. But I believe that humans will gravitate toward the truth in an open market of ideas. That is part of the reason libertarianism is gaining ground rapidly. And this revolution is not just working in political thought. All around the world barriers to entry in all kinds of endeavors are being broken down. People are being lifted out of poverty by the millions. But the old guard in Europe and North America is moving in the opposite direction. The United States, on the rise for most of the previous two centuries, is now on the decline. The question before us is this: Will we turn it around in time to stay on the right side of history or will we join the junk yard heap of societies who abandoned their founding principles and became content to let government take care of them?

There are good reasons to hope that we can change things. For starters, most Americans understand that big government is the problem. Polls show that large majorities cite big government as the biggest threat to our country.[3] There is a natural law which says that those who abuse power are destined to lose it. Government can only go so far before a backlash puts them back in their place. At our very core, we long for freedom. Most of us want to be left alone and to live our lives in peace, free from coercion and interference.

The challenge for us now is to channel our longing for freedom in the right direction. For the better part of a century, lovers of liberty have struggled to limit government to little avail. It should be painfully obvious now that politics and elections are incapable of delivering the necessary changes. We will have to use elections to some extent to begin the amendment process and to achieve ultimate success; but straight elections will never produce candidates at the federal level who can overcome the corruption in Washington.

We need a grass-roots push at the State level to begin the process of calling for an Article V convention. In December of 2013 nearly a hundred state legislators from States all over the country met at Mount Vernon, George Washington's home, to begin laying the groundwork for the convention. Movements are underway in many State Legislatures to call a convention. We must do all we can to urge our representatives in the States to fulfill their important role as a check on federal power.

No doubt, powerful forces will join against us. They will make every claim in the book starting with labeling the convention movement "radical" and "extreme." But those labels only have a chance of applicability if our history is ignored. An understanding of that history reveals that the progressive vision of the early twentieth century has been fully realized. We have everything they sought for: labor protections, minimum wage, environmental protections, progressive income tax, welfare, strict regulation, Social Security, health care for the poor and elderly, and public education. Indeed we can say that in many respects the 20th century was the progressive century. They won.

However, it now seems that government is grasping for more to do with its vast powers; for some way to apply early 20th century notions of progressivism to a 21st century world where government power has already extended as far as possible without undermining common sense. That is why we see the National Labor Relations Board declare that college student-athletes can unionize[4] and the EPA claim regulatory authority over dry washes under the Clean Water Act.[5] We have gone far past the point of reasonable government action. It is time to put a stop to a leviathan state with nothing better to do than to look for more ways to apply worn-out theories of government's ability to manage our lives. A solid case could be made that employers should be legally obligated (by the States) to limit work hours and ensure a safe working environment; but now to hear the contention that employers should be forced to provide contraception for workers is part of a tragic comedy. That government should provide some sort of security in old age may also be fairly contended; but should we bankrupt the country to do it? There must be some point beyond which government cannot go. The projections of government spending in the near future tell us that that point will be leaped over without a blink unless meaningful reforms are enacted.

Our history also shows that the struggle to limit government through elections or Court decisions is hopeless, especially when so many depend on government. But the States have a real incentive to rein in Washington by invoking an Article V convention. Not only do they stand to enhance their own power, but their survival depends on it. If the Federal Government defaults they will suffer as well.

An objective mind could not help but conclude that the amendments proposed in this book are moderate and fair. The amendments proposed are designed more to rescue the country from disaster than they are to promote any particular political ideology. Most of the progressive apparatus can still remain in full force after their ratification and the debate over the proper role of government will continue. When presented with the correct history and the empirical evidence on government's ineptitudes, fair-minded people can agree that something must be done to place meaningful restraints on federal powers.

There is nothing extreme or radical about limiting government. The exact opposite is true. The extremist position is to suppose that government should not be limited but that liberty should; and that we can ignore future unfunded liabilities as easily fixable by taxing the rich. The view that the political process is capable of producing the necessary changes only strengthens this head-in-the-sand mindset. The surest way to achieve limited government is to change the structural framework in which government operates.

Amending the Constitution will require a paradigm shift in the minds of many Americans. We have to come to the realization that we have been fooled. We have grown up in a world where it has been taken for granted that government should play an activist role in managing the economy. We have deceived ourselves into believing that governments can progress or come up with new and innovative policies that no one has ever thought of. We coin terms like "public-private partnership" to conceal these ideas from what they really are: more power for government and more cronyism which benefits the wealthy and limits opportunity and liberty for the rest of us.

There is no scale of legal progress which demands an ever growing role for government. Everything government does moves us in one direction or another along the sliding scale between liberty and tyranny. Government can only operate by force or it can leave people free to choose. There are no creative ways around that simple fact. We must rid ourselves of the fear and superstition which suggests that free people operating in a capitalist system will result in chaos, dilapidated neighborhoods, and an enslaved class of destitute laborers. Every ounce of logic and historical evidence reveals the exact opposite; it is bad government policy that creates those outcomes. We must have the courage to let go; let go of our lust for power, our desire to be taken care of, and our unjustified belief that government must control our lives and manage the economy.

Let us move forward in reestablishing the principles of limited government so crucial to freedom and prosperity. Let us set aside fear and apprehension. Whatever obstacles arise, whether from the political left or right, they cannot defeat the cause if we focus on the objective. Let us have the courage and faith necessary to believe that free people will find a way to succeed and cooperate without government coercion. Liberty is not an unknown or mysterious force which exposes the vulnerable to the exploitation of others; it is a sacred right and an essential prerequisite for progress and opportunity – a right which can only flourish if we restore limited government ...by Constitutional amendment.

NOTES

CHAPTER ONE

[1] David Gaub McCullough Quotes, http://www.qotd.org/search/search.html?aid=1469

[2] U.S. Constitution, Article 1 Section 8

[3] The following discussion on the ratification of the Constitution and the Bill of Rights is largely based on: Kevin R. Gutzman, *James Madison and the Making of America*, (St. Martin's Press, 2012) Chapters 4-6

[4] Ibid., 188

[5] In reality the Anti-Federalists were a much more assorted bunch than what is presented here. Some wanted a new convention while others wanted to remain under the Articles of Confederation. In the end, however, they were all forced to accept that only amendment after ratification would appease their demands.

[6] James Madison, Alexander Hamilton and John Jay, "The Federalist Papers", (Signet Classic, 2003), pages 258-259

[7] Hamilton, *The Federalist Papers*, 513

[8] Gutzman, *James Madison*, 256

[9] Alexander Hamilton, Constitutional Convention Debates, June 18, 1787, in Ralph Ketcham ed., *The Anti-Federalist Papers and the Constitutional Convention Debates*, (Signet Classics, 2003) 70-77

[10] Jeffrey T. Renz, "What Spending Clause? (Or the President's Paramour): An Examination of the Views of Hamilton, Madison, and Story on Article I, Section 8, Clause 1 of the United States Constitution", *John Marshall Law Review*, Vol. 33, 1999. Available at SSRN: http://ssrn.com/abstract=223735

[11] *Anti-Federalist Papers*, 78-79

[12] Ibid., 77

[13] Annals of Congress, 3rd Cong., 1st sess., 169, January, 1794

[14] Alexander Hamilton, *Report on Manufacturers*, 5 December 1791, in Philip B. Kurland and Ralph Lerner, eds., *The Founder's Constitution*, vol. 2, (Chicago: University of Chicago Press, 1987), 446

[15] James Madison, *The Bank Bill*, 2 February 1791, in Ibid.

[16] The Real George Washington, (National Center for Constitutional Studies; 2009), 544

[17] Annals of Congress, 4th Cong., 2nd sess., 1723-1726

[18] Ibid., 2nd Cong., 2nd sess. 363

[19] *The Real Thomas Jefferson*, National Center for Constitutional Studies, 2009, 202-203

[20] John C. Eastman, *Restoring the General to the General Welfare Clause*, Chapman Law Review, Vol. 4, No. 63, 2001

[21] Thomas Jefferson to Albert Gallatin, 16 June 1817, in Kurland and Lerner, eds., *The Founder's Constitution,* vol. 2, 452

[22] James Monroe, "Views of the President of the United States on the Subject of Internal Improvements", May 4, 1822, in Gerhard Peters and John T. Woolley eds., The American Presidency Project, http://www.presidency.ucsb.edu/ws/index.php?pid=66323&st=James+Monroe &st1=

[23] Ivan Eland, *Recarving Rushmore: Ranking the Presidents on Peace, Prosperity and Liberty*, The Independent Institute, 2009, chapter 6

[24] Kurland and Lerner eds., *Founder's Constitution*, vol.2, 446

CHAPTER TWO

[1] Joseph Story, *Commentaries on the Constitution of the United States*, vol. 2, (Hilliard, Gray and Company, 1833), 369

[2] Ibid., 382

[3] Ibid., vol. 1, 417

[4] Ibid., vol. 2, 371

[5] Ibid., 377

[6] Ibid., 394

[7] Ibid., 368

[8] Elliot's Debates, vol. 1 p. 254, August 21, 1787; see also *Founder's Constitution*, 411-12

[9] 4 Cong. Deb., 1634, (1828)

[10] Story, *Commentaries on the Constitution*, vol. 2, 394

[11] James Madison to Mr. Stevenson, 27 November 1830, in Story, *Commentaries on the Constitution*, 395-400

[12] Story, *Commentaries on the Constitution*, 379-80

[13] Ibid., 390

[14] Madison to Stevenson, in Story, *Commentaries on the Constitution*, 395-400

[15] U.S. Constitution, Amendment 10

[16] It is true that Washington also took a relatively expansive view of the Constitution but he could have declared himself king with little protest from the country. My objective here is to show the predominant understanding of the Constitution at the time as reflected in presidential elections. Washington was so revered that he could have advocated nearly anything and still would have had the support of the people. At any rate, Washington's views were strongly influenced by his experiences with an angry and underpaid army which made him a proponent of a central bank to allow for better funding. It may also be argued that James Monroe took an expansive view of the General Welfare Clause. However, at the time of his first election he was a strong proponent of the Madison view. He was re-elected based on his adherence to Madisonian principles. It was only during his second term that he inexplicably reversed course. In any event his reversal was mild has he vetoed an internal

improvements bill as being unconstitutional. Again, as far as *elections* go, only the Adams presidents were elected by a country that knew they were proponents of big government.

[17] Andrew Jackson, "State of the Union Address", 1 December 1834, in The American Presidency Project, http://www.presidency.ucsb.edu/ws/index.php?pid=29476

[18] U.S. House Journal, vol. 43, 97-98, (1847)

[19] U.S. Senate Journal, vol. 45, 363, (1854)

[20] Quoted in Eastman, "Restoring the General Welfare Clause"

[21] Morrill Act of 1862, 37th Cong., (1862)

[22] Grover Cleveland, Veto Message; February 16, 1887, online by Gerhard Peters and John T. Wooley, *The American Presidency Project*, www.presidency.ucsb.edu/ws/index. php?p id = 71489&st=Grover+Cleveland &st1=, accessed 4/8/14

[23] For example, Thomas Jefferson made the Louisiana Purchase without prior congressional approval; something he himself admitted was unConstitutional.

[24] 4 Cong. Deb., 1634, (1828)

[25] Kansas v. Colorado, 206 U.S. 46 (1907)

CHAPTER THREE

[1] Steven Horwitz, "Herbert Hoover Father of the New Deal", Cato Briefing Paper No. 122, 29 September 2011

[2] Railroad Retirement Board v. Alton Railroad Co. 295 U.S. 330 (1935)

[3] Ibid.

[4] United States v. Butler, 297 U.S. 1 (1936)

[5] Ibid.

[6] Ibid.

[7] Ibid.

[8] For more on this see William E. Leuchtenburg, *The Supreme Court Reborn: The Constitutional Revolution in the Age of Roosevelt*, (Oxford University Press, 1995), chapter 5

[9] Franklin D Roosevelt, "46 – Fireside Chat", March 9, 1937   The American Presidency Project, http://www.presidency.ucsb.edu/ws/index.php?pid=15381

[10] Ibid.

[11] U.S. v Butler

[12] Ibid.

[13] Helvering v Davis, 301 U.S. 619 (1937)

[14] While the Court has announced some limits for other reasons, the General Welfare Clause has never been used to strike down any legislation.

[15] William E. Leuchtenburg, *The Supreme Court Reborn: The Constitutional Revolution in the Age of Roosevelt*, (Oxford University Press, 1995), 142

[16] Quoted in Ibid., 155

[17] Ibid

[18] Ironically today, progressives invoke stare decisis to defend against Constitutional objections to the current government system, claiming it would be improper to overturn the past 80 years of precedent; apparently oblivious to the fact that new dealers overturned the previous 150 years of precedent.

[19] Quoted in Leuchtenburg, *Supreme Court Reborn*, 176

[20] Ibid. These statements referred particularly to the minimum wage case of *West Coast Hotel Co. v Parrish* decided around the same time but are representative of the change in Court opinion which resonated through to the Social Security decision given only weeks later.

[21] Railroad Retirement Board v Alton Railroad Co.

[22] West Coast Hotel Co. v Parish, 300 U.S. 379 (1937)

[23] Hamilton, *The Federalist Papers*, 468-469

[24] Railroad Retirement Board v Alton Railroad Co.

[25] Steward Machine Company v Davis, 301 U.S. 548 (1937)

[26] Franklin D. Roosevelt to Samuel B. Hill, 6 July 1935, in The American Presidency Project, http://www.presidency.ucsb.edu/ws/? Accessed 3/13/14

[27] Leuchtenburg, *Supreme Court Reborn*, 219

[28] Rexford G. Tugwell , *Model For a New Constitution,* (James E. Freel & Associates, 1970) 19-20

[29] Quoted in Pilon, *Constitutional Corruption*

[30] Bailey v Drexel Furniture Co., 259 U.S. 20, 1922

CHAPTER FOUR

[1] Wickard v. Filburn, 317 U.S. 111 (1942)

[2] Randy E. Barnett, "The Original Meaning of the Commerce Clause", *Georgetown University Law Center*, 2001

[3] Story, *Commentaries on the Constitution,* vol. 1, 372

[4] Robert A. Levy and William Mellor, *The Dirty Dozen: How Twelve Supreme Court Cases Radically Expanded Government and Eroded Freedom,* (Cato Institute, 2009), Kindle version, chap. 2

[5] Jeff Rowes, quoted in John Stossel, "War On The Little Guy", November 20, 2013, Real Clear Politics, http://www.realclearpolitics.com/articles/2013/11/20/war_on_the_little_guy_120715.html

[6] National Federation of Independent Businesses v Sebelius U.S. 11-393 (2012)

[7] Ibid.

[8] Ibid.

CHAPTER FIVE

[1] *U.S.GovernmentSpending.com*, customized government spending chart, http://www.usgovernmentspending.com/spending_chart_1792_2017USp_13s 1li111mcn_F0t, accessed 12/13/2012

[2] Ibid.

[3] John S. Baker and Dale E. Bennett, "Measuring the Explosive Growth of Federal Crime Legislation", (no date given) The Federalist Society for Law and Public Policy Studies

[4] Ibid.

[5] *In Custodia Legis*, Library of Congress Blog, "Frequent Reference Question: How Many Federal Laws Are There", entry by Jeanine Cali, March 12, 2013, http://blogs.loc.gov/law/2013/03/frequent-reference-question-how-many-federal-laws-are-there/, accessed 3/20/13

[6] Baker and Bennett, "Explosive Growth"

[7] Ibid.

[8] *AmericanActionForum.org*, "The Affordable Care Act at 3: Big Cost Burden Big Consumer Impact", March 25, 2013, http://americanactionforum.org/topic/affordable-care-act-3-big-cost-burden-big-consumer-impact accessed March 26, 2013

[9] Baker and Bennett, "Explosive Growth"

[10] Bryan Walsh and Tiffany Joslyn, "Without Intent, How Congress is Eroding The Criminal Intent Requirement in Federal Law", The Heritage Foundation and National Association of Criminal Defense Lawyers, 2010

[11] Ibid.

[12] For more on this see John Taylor, *Getting off Track: How Government Actions and Interventions Caused, Prolonged, and Worsened the Financial Crisis*, (Board of Trustees of the Leland Stanford Junior University, 2009)

[13] FederalReserve.gov, Beige Book, March 6, 2013, http://www.federalreserve.gov/monetarypolicy/beigebook/beigebook201303.htm#top, accessed April 8, 2013

[14] Clyde Wayne Crews, "$1.8 trillion Shock: Obama Regs Cost 20 Times Estimate", Competitive Enterprise Institute, September 20, 2012, http://cei.org/citations/18-trillion-shock-obama-regs-cost-20-times-estimate, accessed 12/1/13,

[15] Whitehouse.gov, Historical Tables, "Summary of Receipts, Outlays, and Surpluses or Deficits 1789 – 2019" http://www.whitehouse.gov/omb/budget/Historicals/

[16] DownsizingGovernment.org, home page chart, "Shares of Total Federal Spending", accessed 4/19/14

[17] Michael D. Tanner, "Bankrupt: Entitlements and the Federal Budget", March 28, 2011, Cato Institute Policy Analysis #673

[18] DownsizingGovernment.org, home page chart 5 of 6, accessed 3/25/14

[19] Manmohan S. Kumar and Jaejoon Woo, "Public Debt and Growth", IMF Working Paper, July, 2010

[20] *DownsizingGovernment.org*, "Refocusing U.S. Defense Strategy", http://www.downsizinggovernment.org/defense/refocusing-us-defense-strategy, accessed April 4, 2013

[21] *Catalog of Federal Domestic Assistance*, "CFDA Statistics: Programs at a Glance", https://www.cfda.gov/, Accessed April 8, 2013

[22] Chris Edwards, "Agricultural Regulations and Trade Barriers", June 2009 http://www.downsizinggovernment.org/agriculture/regulations-and-trade-barriers, Accessed April 8, 2013

[23] Ibid

[24] Ibid

[25] Tad DeHaven, "Corporate Welfare in the Federal Budget", Cato Policy Analysis #703, July 25, 2012

[26] Ibid

[27] Joseph Story, Commentaries vol. 1 373

[28] Andrew Coulson, "The Impact of Federal Involvement in America's Classrooms", Testimony to Committee on Education & the Workforce; United States House of Representatives February 10, 2011, http://www.cato.org/publications/congressional-testimony/impact-federal-involvement-americas-classrooms, accessed 4/18/14

[29] Michael D. Tanner, "The American Welfare State: How We Spend Nearly $1 trillion a Year Fighting Poverty – And Fail", Cato Institute Policy Analysis #694, April 11, 2012

[30] Ibid

[31] *U.S. Census Bureau*, "Number in Poverty and Poverty Rate 1959-2010", http://www.census.gov/hhes/www/poverty/data/incpovhlth/2010/figure4.pdf

[32] While no credible source could be found for this quote, its truthfulness is manifest regardless of its author or context.

[33] Susan Epstein and Alan Kronstadt, "Pakistan: U.S. Foreign Assistance", Congressional Research Service, http://www.fas.org/sgp/crs/row/R41856.pdf, October 4, 2012

[34] *Taxpayers for Common Sense*, "Analysis of Selected Provisions in Hurricane Sandy Emergency Spending Proposals", last updated 10 January 2013, http://www.taxpayer.net/library/article/brief-analysis-of-selected-provisions-in-proposed-senate-supplemental-appro, accessed April 8, 2013

[35] Alexis de Tocqueville, *Democracy in America,* vol. 2, translated by Henry Reeve, (Thomas Copperthwaite & Co. 1840; Alfred A. Knopf Inc. 1945) 318-19 from the 1945 version

CHAPTER SIX

[1] Michael Cannon, "The President's Duty to Execute Faithfully The Patient Protection and Affordable Care Act", testimony to Committee on the Judiciary United States House of Representatives, , December 3, 2013, http://judiciary.house.gov/_cache/files/2e560cd7-a90d-4694-a097-f1284b491e03/120313-cannon-testimony.pdf

[2] Edward L. Glaeser and Jesse M. Shapiro, "The Benefits of the Home Mortgage Interest Deduction", National Bureau of Economic Research, Working Paper 9284, October 2002

[3] Mark Calabria, "Federal Homeownership Policy: Money for Nothing", Blog Post downsizinggovernment.org, August 28, 2013,http://www.downsizinggovernment.org /federal-homeownership-policy-money-nothing, accessed 4/22/14

[4] Of course, some contend that this growth was due to federal involvement such as federal loans to veterans. But these programs had little to do with the increase. One study found that veteran's housing benefits accounted for a mere 10% of the overall increase in home ownership. See: Daniel K. Fetter, "Housing Finance and the mid-century transformation in US home ownership: the VA home loan program", October 2010, http://economics.rutgers.edu/dmdocuments/DanielFetter.pdf, accessed 4/22/14

[5] U.S. Census Bureau, News Release, January 31, 2014,http://www.census.gov/housing/hvs/files/qtr413/q413press.pdf, accessed 4/22/14

[6] See Gary Becker, *The Economics of Discrimination*, (University of Chicago Press, 1971)

[7] Abe Bortz, "A Brief History of Old Age Pensions", http://www.socialwelfarehistory.com/programs/old-age-pensions-a-brief-history/ (no date given)

[8] Abe Bortz, "Historical Development of the Social Security Act", lecture, http://www.ssa.gov/history/bortz.html (no date given)

[9] Hammer v. Dagenhart, 247 U.S. 251, 1918

[10] U.S. Department of Labor, "Child Labor Facts and Figures", Bureau Publication No. 197, October 1933, 56-57

[11] Census Bureau, "Comparative Occupation Statistics 1870-1930 Part II", p 92 and 97

[12] This committee did receive an endowment from Congress a few years after it was founded but the point is that private citizens started the movement independent of government.

[13] Bortz, "Social Security Act"

[14] Census Bureau, "Historical Statistics of the United States 1789-1945", 1949, p. 67

[15] Ibid

[16] Center for Disease Control, "Achievements in Public Health: 1900 – 1999", Morbidity and Mortality Weekly Report Vol. 48 No. 22, June 11, 1999. http://www.cdc.gov/mmwr/preview/mmwrhtml/mm4822a1.htm, The number given in 1913 was estimated by the Bureau of Labor Statistics while the 1933 number was estimated by the National Safety Council using a different reporting method. However, even if the different reporting methods showed significantly different numbers it would not likely undermine the generally agreed on fact that work-place fatalities dramatically declined during this time period.

[17] Jim Powell, "FDR's New Deal, Obama's New New Deal and High Unemployment", Cato Commentary, 18 August 2011, http://www.cato.org/publications /commentary/fdrs-new-deal-obamas-new-new-deal-high-unemployment, accessed 7/12/13

[18] "Recession of 1937-38", Wikipedia, last modified 5 March 2014, http://en.wikipedia.org/wiki/Recession_of_1937%E2%80%931938

[19] Quoted in Powell, "FDR's New Deal".

[20] James Madison, *The Federalist Papers*, 72

[21] Farrand, Records of the Federal Convention, vol. 1: 432

[22] For more on this see Gary and Carolyn Alder, *The Evolution and Destruction of the Original Electoral College*, 2010

[23] Kurland and Lerner, *Founder's Constitution*, vol. 2, 187

[24] Ibid., 189

[25] See the work of George Mason University Law Professor Todd Zywicki, for example, "Repeal the 17th Amendment" National Review online article, November 15, 2010, http://www.nationalreview.com/articles/252825/repeal-seventeenth-amendment-todd-zywicki

[26] F.A. Hayek, *The Road to Serfdom*, (University of Chicago Press 1944; the Estate of F.A. Hayek 2007), 111, page refers to the 2007 edition

[27] "Democracy and Capitalism.wmv", You Tube video, 13:32, posted by Ajawbolon November 17, 2011, https://www.youtube.com/watch?v=K-o2rgDycVo

[28] James Madison, *The Federalist Papers*, 72

[29] Quoted in E.G. West, "The Political Economy of American Public School Legislation", *Journal of Law and Economics,* October 1967, vol. 10, 106

[30] For more on the development of government education see Ibid.

[31] John Stossel, "Government Gone Bad", Real Clear Politics online article, December 12, 2012, http://www.realclearpolitics.com/articles/2012/12/12/government _gone_bad_1 1639 8.html, accessed 4/2/14

[32] Quoted in Thomas Sowell, *Applied Economics*, (Basic Books 2009) 1

[33] Connecticut Senator Chris Murphy on The Rachel Madow Show, aired, January 24, 2013, "do you want to pass a law that's going to keep more 6 and 7 year-olds alive or do you want to add more convenience for... people who want to pretend like they're soldiers?"

[34] Madison, *Federalist Papers*, 377

[35] Ibid, 379

[36] "Obama Delivers Commencement Speech at The Ohio State University", MSNBC online article, May 5, 2013, http://www.msnbc.com/msnbc/obama-delivers-commencement-speech-the-ohi, accessed 4/13/14

[37] "Jefferson's Draft", The Papers of Thomas Jefferson; Princeton University, before October 2, 1798, https://jeffersonpapers.princeton.edu/selected-documents/jefferson%E2%80%99s-draft, accessed 4/13/14

[38] James Madison, Speech in the Virginia Ratifying Convention on Control of the Military, June 16, 1788 in: *History of the Virginia Federal Convention of 1788*, vol. 1, p. 130 (H.B. Grigsby ed. 1890)

[39] See J. Haavard Maridal, "The Good Samaritan Effect: The Virtuous Cycle of Private Charity", Huffington Post Blog, January 24, 2013, http://www.huffingtonpost.com/j-haavard-maridal/the-good-samaritan-effect_b_2545630.html, accessed 5/15/14

[40] Tocqueville, *Democracy in America*, vol. 2 318

[41] The prosperity-promoting tendency of free markets with minimal government transfers is too complex to admit a full discussion here. My only point is to show the proper legal interpretation of the founding documents and the natural rights they are meant to protect. A further discussion of government's economically destructive tendencies will be given in chapters 9 and 10.

[42] The empirical data prove that people who work for big companies are much better compensated than their counterparts at smaller companies. So even if it could be shown the big corporations have more "bargaining power" they apparently are too dumb to use it. See Bureau of Labor Statistics, Employee Benefits Survey, National Compensation Survey: Employee Benefits in the United States; Financial Benefits Access, March 2013

[43] Gordon S. Wood, *The Radicalism of the American Revolution*, (Alfred A. Knopf Inc. 1992) 206

CHAPTER SEVEN

[1] Thomas Jefferson to Edward Carrington, May 27, 1788, National Archives "Founders Online", http://Founders.archives.gov/documents/Jefferson/01-13-02-0120, accessed 3/29/14

[2] Brown v. Board of Education, 347 U.S. 483 (1954)

[3] James Monroe, "The Views of The President on Internal Improvements" Supra note 21 from chapter 1; U.S. House Journal, 3 March 1817, p. 537

[4] *The Real George Washington*, Farewell Address 1796, (National Center for Constitutional Studies 2009), 665

[5] *The Real Thomas Jefferson*, (National Center for Constitutional Studies 2008), 385

[6] Rexford G. Tugwell, *Model for a New Constitution*, (Center for the Study of Democratic Institutions 1970), 22-23

[7] Barack Obama, Chicago Public Radio Interview, 2001, Youtube video by Joshua Carter, uploaded on October 27, 2008, www.youtube.com/watch?v=2EcmpUHCkk, accessed 4/23/14

[8] Richard Stengel, "Does it Still Matter?", Time Magazine, July, 2011

[9] Jordan Eizenga, "U.S. Debt Limit 101", Center for American Progress, April 28, 2011, http://www.americanprogress.org/issues/budget/report/2011/04/28/9533/u-s-debt-limit-101/, accessed 3/20/14

[10] Rob Bluey, "Pelosi's PAYGO Ploy: Budgetary Gimmick Provides Cover for Liberals", Heritage.org blog post, October 15, 2010, http://blog.heritage.org/2010/10/15/pelosis-paygo-ploy-budgetary-gimmick-provides-cover-for-liberals/, accessed 3/20/14

[11] Alexander Hamilton, *The Federalist Papers*, 526

[12] In a campaign speech on October 31, 1936, Roosevelt defended Social Security against predictions that future Congresses would in fact steel its excess tax receipts: "When they imply that the reserves thus created against both these policies will be stolen by some future Congress, diverted to some wholly foreign purpose, they attack the integrity and honor of American Government itself. Those who suggest that are already aliens to the spirit of American democracy. Let them emigrate and try their lot under some foreign flag in which they have more confidence."

CHAPTER EIGHT

[1] Robert G. Natelson, "Proposing Constitutional Amendments by Convention: Rules Governing the Process", *Tennessee Law Review* 78, (2011) 718

[2] Dred Scott v Sanford 60 U.S. 393 (1857)

[3] Robert G. Natelson, "A Modern Quasi-Convention of States", Blog post on Independence Institute, March 1, 2014, http://constitution.i2i.org/category/article-v-convention/, accessed 3/28/14

[4] Ibid

[5] His scholarly papers can be found at constitution.i21.org; http://constitution.i2i.org/articles-books-on-the-constitution-by-rob-natelson/

[6] Robert G. Natelson "Amending the Constitution by Convention: Practical Guidance for Citizens and Policymakers", Independence Institute, May 2012

[7] John Dewitt [pseud.], Boston American Herald essay, October 27, 1787, in *The Anti-Federalist Papers*, edited by Ralph Ketcham (Signet Classics, 2003), 194

[8] Patrick Henry, Virginia Ratifying Convention speech, June 5, 1788, in Ibid. 203-05

[9] In *Coleman v Miller* 307 U.S. 433 (1939) the Court declared that proposed amendments could be ratified over any time period as long as Congress did not specify a time limit, which they didn't do in the case of the child labor amendment. The 27th amendment was first proposed in 1789 and was ratified in 1992.

CHAPTER NINE

[1] Whitehouse.gov, Historical Tables, table 1.1, http://www.whitehouse.gov/omb/budget /Historicals/, accessed 6/24/13

[2] Ibid

[3] Ibid

[4] Ibid

[5] Downsizinggovernment.org, Home Page, Chart 5: Federal Spending Under Current Policies as a Share of Gross Domestic Product.

[6] Office of Management and Budget, Historical Table, "Summary of Receipts, Outlays and Surpluses or Deficits as Percentages of GDP: 1930 – 2018", authors calculations from selected years

[7] Whitehouse.gov, Historical Tables, table 1.1

[8] OECD (2012), *OECD Economic Surveys: Spain 2012,* OECD Publishing, http://dx.doi.org/10.1787/eco_survey-esp-2012-en

[9] Juan Ramon Rallo, Angel Martin Oro and Adria Perez Marti, "Spain Becomes one of Europe's Highest Taxed Countries", Cato Institute Economic Development Bulletin No. 15, February 29, 2012

[10] OECD, *Economic Survey: Spain 2012*

[11] OECD (2013), OECD *Economic Surveys: Italy 2013*, OECD Publishing, http://dx.doi.org/ 10.1787/eco.surveys-ita-2013-en

[12] CIA World Factbook, Italy, https://www.cia.gov/library/publications/the-world-factbook/geos/it.html accessed 4/1/14

[13] Prakash Kannan, Alasdair Scott and Marco E. Torrones, "From Recession to Recovery: How Soon and How Strong", International Monetary Fund, April 2009

[14] See Andrew T. Young, "Why in the World Are We All Keynesians Again? The Flimsy Case for Stimulus Spending", Cato Policy Analysis No. 721, February 14, 2013

[15] Alberto Alesina and Silvia Ardagna, Copyright "Large Changes in Fiscal Policy: Taxes Versus Spending", National Bureau of Economic Research working paper No. 15438, October 2009

[16] Alberto Alessina, "Tax Cuts Versus 'Stimulus': The Evidence Is In", Wall Street Journal September 15, 2010.

[17] Antonio Afonso and João Tovar Jalles, "Economic Performance and Government Size", European Central Bank Working Paper Series, November 2011

[18] Indermit Gill and Martin Raiser, *Golden Growth: Restoring the Lustre of the European Economic Model*, (World Bank, 2012), 362-63

[19] Ibid., 372

[20] David R. Ranson, "Government Spending Crowds the Private Sector Out and In", National Center for Policy Analysis, Brief Analysis No. 784, June 26, 2013

[21] Ibid

[22] Whitehouse.gov, Historical Tables, Table 1.2, http://www.whitehouse.gov/omb/ budget/Historicals/, accessed 6/24/13

[23] The Independent Institute, "Under Bush, Federal Spending Increases at Fastest Rate in 30 Years", http://www.independent.org/newsroom/news_detail.asp?newsid=31, accessed 6/24/13

[24] Mitchel, Daniel J., "If Spending Is Capped So It Grows at the Rate of Inflation, the Budget Is Balanced in 2018", Blog Post at danieljmitchell.wordpress.com, September 17, 2013, http://danieljmitchell.wordpress.com/2013/09/17/its-amazingly-simple-to-balance-the-budget/, accessed 4/2/14

[25] Chris Edwards, "We Can Cut Government: Canada Did", Cato Policy Report May/June 2012

[26] Ibid.

[27] Ibid.

[28] See Manmohan S. Kumar, Daniel Leigh and Alexander Plekhanov, "Fiscal Adjustments: Determinants and Macroeconomic Consequences", International Monetary Fund working paper, July 2007

[29] Daniel J. Mitchell, "Switzerland's Debt Brake is a Role Model for Spending Control and Fiscal Restraint", Blog post on danieljmitchel.wordpress.com, April 26, 2012, http://danieljmitchell.wordpress.com/2012/04/26/switzerlands-debt-brake-is-a-role-model-for-spending-control-and-fiscal-restraint/, accessed 7/26/13

[30] Ibid.

[31] Ibid

[32] OECD (2013), *OECD Economic Surveys: Switzerland 2013*, OECD Publishing, http://dx.doi.org/10.1787/eco_surveys-che-2013-en, accessed 4/2/14

[33] See Greg Jaffe and Jim Tankersley, "Capital Gains: Spending on Contracts and Lobbying Propels a Wave of New Wealth in D.C.", Washington Post online article, November 17, 2013, http://www.washingtonpost.com/national/capital-gains-spending-on-contracts-and-lobbying-propels-a-wave-of-new-wealth-in-d-c/2013/11/17/6bd938aa-3c25-11e3-a94f-b58017bfee6c_story.html, accessed 2/12/14

[34] Milton and Rose Friedman, *Free to Choose: A Personal Statement*, (Harcourt 1980), 116-118

[35] Downsizinggovernment.org, chart 5 from homepage, "Federal Spending Under Current Policies as a Share of Gross Domestic Product", accessed 7/25/13

[36] Author's calculations based on CBO updated budget projections fiscal years 2013 to 2023

[37] Gill and Raiser, *Golden Growth*, 368

[38] Michael D. Tanner, "Bankrupt: Entitlements and the Federal Budget", Cato Institute Policy Analysis #673, March 28, 2011

[39] Ibid

[40] 2013 Social Security Trustees Report, 2

[41] Eugene Kiely, "Durbin Denies Social Security's Red Ink", factcheck.org, http://www.factcheck.org/2012/11/durbin-again-denies-social-securitys-red-ink/, accessed 11/28/12

[42] Ibid.

[43] Social Security Trustees Report 2013, 58

[44] Ibid.

[45] Ibid., 4

[46] Procon.org, "Did You Know", http://socialsecurity.procon.org/ accessed 2/22/14

[47] Social Security official website, "Contribution and Benefit Base", http://www.ssa.gov/OACT/COLA/cbb.html, accessed 4/2/14

[48] Janemarie Mulvey, "Social Security: Raising or Eliminating the Taxable Earnings Base", Congressional Research Service, September 24, 2010

[49] Michael D. Tanner, "Keep the Cap: Why a Tax Increase Will Not Save Social Security", Cato Institute Briefing Paper No. 93, June 8, 2005

[50] Matt Moore, "Eliminating the Social Security Payroll Tax Cap: A Bad Idea", National Center for Policy Analysis brief No. 470, March 23, 2004

[51] Martin Feldstein, "Rethinking Social Insurance," National Bureau of Economic Research Working Paper no. 11250, March 2005, p. 19

[52] Michael Tanner and Chris Edwards, "Reforming Social Security Retirement", downsizinggovernment.org, August, 2013, http://www.downsizinggovernment.org /ssa/social-security-retirement#_edn50, accessed 4/2/14

[53] Michael D. Tanner, "Still a Better Deal: Private Investment vs. Social Security", Cato Policy Analysis #692, February 13, 2012

[54] William Shipman, "Facts and Fantasies About Transition Costs", Cato Social Security Choice Paper No. 13, October 13, 1998

[55] Social Security Memorandum, "Estimated Financial Effects of a Proposal for Individual Social Security Investment", February, 15, 2005

[56] Michael D. Tanner, "Clinton Wanted Social Security Privatized", Cato Institute Online Commentary, July 13, 2001, http://www.cato.org/publications/commentary/clinton-wanted-social-security-privatized, accessed 4/7/14

[57] Steven Gillon, "The Pact Between Bill Clinton and Newt Gingrich", Reprinted online by U.S. News and World Report, May 29, 2008, http://www.usnews.com/news/articles /2008/05/29/the-pact-between-bill-clinton-and-newt-gingrich?page=4, accessed 4/7/14

[58] This shows that the personal conduct of politicians does matter. More broadly, the fact that Clinton and many Democrats supported privatization undermines the theory that it is Republicans who have radicalized over recent years. The exact opposite is true. It is Democrats that have moved farther to the left than at any time since the New Deal.

[59] Martin Feldstein, "Privatizing Social Security: The $10 Trillion Opportunity", Cato Institute Social Security Choice Paper No. 7, January 31, 1997.

[60] Robert E. Moffit, "Saving the American Dream: Comparing Medicare Reform Plans", The Heritage Foundation; Backgrounder on Health Care, April 4, 2012, http://www.heritage.org/research/reports/2012/04/saving-the-american-dream-comparing-medicare-reform-plans, accessed 2/28/14

[61] Author's calculations based on 2010 census data

[62] CBO, "Monthly Budget Review – Summary For Fiscal 2013", November, 2013

[63] 2013 Medicare Trustee's Report, pages 8-9

[64] Author's calculations based on Census Bureau, "The Next Four Decades; The Older Population in the United States 2010-2050", May, 2010

[65] Department of Health and Human Services, Fiscal Year 2013 Financial Report, page 15

[66] Edwards and Cannon, "Medicare Reforms", downsizinggovernt.org, September, 2010

[67] Jonathon Skinner and Elliot Fisher, "Reflections on Geographic Variations in U.S. Health Care", The Dartmouth Institute for Health Policy and Clinical Practice, May 2010, page 13

[68] Government Accountability Office, Report to Congressional Requesters, October, 2012, page 2

[69] Edwards and Cannon, "Medicare Reforms"

[70] Stopmedicarefraud.gov, About Fraud, www.stopmedicarfraud.gov/aboutfraud/, accessed 4/4/14

[71] Edwards and Cannon, "Medicare Reforms"

[72] Marsha Mercer, "How to Beat the Doctor Shortage", AARP Bulletin, March, 2013, http://www.aarp.org/health/medicare-insurance/info-03-2013/how-to-beat-doctor-shortage.html, accessed 8/9/13

[73] Andrew, Biggs, Kevin Hassett and Mathew Jensen, "A Guide For Deficit Reduction in the United States Based on Historical Consolidations That Worked", American Enterprise for Public Policy Research working paper, December, 2010

[74] Department of Health and Human Services Office of the Actuary, Memorandum, John D. Shatto and M. Kent Clemens, August 5, 2010, pages 5-6

[75] Ibid.

[76] Edwards and Cannon, "Medicare Reforms"

[77] Downsizinggovernment.com, home page chart; Shares of Total Federal Spending 2013", accessed 4/4/14

[78] 2012 Medicaid Actuarial Report, executive summary

[79] Ibid

[80] Chris Edwards, Medicaid Reforms, downsizinggovernment.org, September 2010, www.downsizinggovernment.org/hhs/medicaid-reforms, accessed 4/4/14

[81] Veronique de Rugy, "A Comprehensive Look at U.S. Debt", Mercatus Center George Mason University

[82] Laurence J. Kotlikoff and John C. Goodman, "Medicare by the Scary Numbers", WSJ online article, June 24, 2013, http://online.wsj.com/news/articles/SB10001424127887323393804578555461 959256572, accessed 2/17/14

[83] Veronique de Rugy, "Yes, We Do Have a Debt Problem", Reason.com online article, August/September 2013, http://reason.com/archives/2013/07/16/yes-we-do-have-a-debt-problem, accessed 3/3/14

[84] Ibid

[85] "Restoring North America's Wild Bison to Their Home on the Range", Environmental News Service online article, March 3, 2010, http://www.ens-newswire.com/ens/ mar 2010/2010-03-03-01.html, accessed 2/16/14

[86] S. 245, the "CAP Act"

CHATPER TEN

[1] Ronald Reagan, Interview with Johnny Carson, 3 March 1975, Fox News Insider video; "Hannity: 1975 Warning From Reagan Could Have Been Said Last Night, December 18, 2013, foxnewsinsider.com/2013/12/18/Hannity-looks-back-1975-warnings-reagan-tonight-show-johnny-carson, accessed 4/4/14

[2] Larry DeWitt, SSA Historians Office, Research Note #23, July 21, 2005, http://www.ssa.gov/history/Gulick.html, accessed 10/7/13

[3] Alexander Hamilton, *Federalist Papers*, 87

[4] Brutus [pseud.], Kurland and learner, *Founder's Constitution*, vol. 2; 417

[5] Kurland and Lerner, "The Founder's Constitution" vol. 2 439

[6] An Old Whig [pseud.], Kurland and Lerner eds., *The Founder's Constitution*, vol. 2, 414

[7] Federal Farmer [pseud.], Ibid., 412

[8] Alexander Hamilton, *Federalist Papers*, 193

[9] Edmund Pendleton, Ibid., 440

[10] James Wilson, Ibid., 415

[11] An Old Whig [pseud.], *The Founder's Constitution*, vol. 2, 414

[12] Pacific Insurance Company v Soule, 74 U.S. 433 (1868)

[13] Wikipedia, "Wilson-Gorman Tariff Act", http://en.wikipedia.org/wiki/Wilson-Gorman_Tariff_Act, accessed 4/5/14

[14] Pollack v. Farmers' Loan & Trust Co., 157 U.S. 429 (1895)

[15] Brutus [pseud], *The Founder's Constitution*, vol. 2, 417

[16] Ibid, 413

[17] Ibid, 419

[18] The Founder's Constitution online, "Federal v. Consolidated Government", Chapter 8 Document 13, http://press-pubs.uchicago.edu/Founders/documents/v1ch8s13.html, accessed 4/5/14

[19] Jackie Calmes, "$300 Million in Detroit Aid, But No Bailout", New York Times Online Article, September 26, 2013,

http://www.nytimes.com/2013/09/27/us/300-million-in-detroit-aid-but-no-
bailout.html?pagewanted%3Dall&_r=0, accessed 4/5/14

[20] It is not understood by many that the employer passes along his share of
payroll taxes to the employee through a lower salary or wage. Thus, the full
12.4% of Social Security contributions is mostly borne by the worker.

[21] Larry DeWitt, SSA Historians Office, Research Note #23, July 21, 2005,
http://www.ssa.gov/history/Gulick.html, accessed 10/7/13

[22] Chris Edwards, "Federal Tax Rules: 72,536 Pages", Blog Post, Cato at Liberty,
April 18, 2011, http://www.cato.org/blog/federal-tax-rules-72536-pages,
accessed 4/5/14

[23] Jonathan H. Adler and Michael F. Cannon, "Taxation Without Representation:
The Illegal IRS Rule to Expand Tax Credits Under the PPACA", *Health Matrix:
Journal of Law-Medicine*, Research Paper No. 2012-27, July 16, 2012

[24] Ibid.

[25] Taxpayer Advocate Service, "National Taxpayer Advocate Annual Report to
Congress", January 9, 2013, http://www.taxpayeradvocate.irs.gov/2012-
Annual-Report/FY-2012-Annual-Report-To-Congress-Full-Report, accessed
10/30/13

[26] David Dollar, Tatjana Kleinberg and Aart Kraay, "Growth Still Is Good for the
Poor", World Bank Policy Research Working Paper, August 2013

[27] See: Thushyanthan Baskaranand and Mariana Lopes de Fonseca, "The
Economics and Empirics of Tax Competition: A Survey" Center for European
Governance and Economic Development Research Discussion Paper No. 163,
July 7, 2013, from SSRN: http://ssrn.com/abstract=2290689, accessed
10/10/13; and:
Hansjorg Blöchliger and Jose Pinero Campos, "Tax Competition Between Sub-
Central Governments", *OECD Economics Department Working Papers*, No. 872,
2011

[28] Andres Fuentes, "Making the Tax System Less Distortive in Switzerland",
OECD Economics Department Working Papers, No. 1044, 2013

[29] Foreign Account Tax Compliance Act of 2010, S. 1934, 111 Congress (2010)

[30] Richard Rahn, "IRS Troubles Go Global", The Washington Times, June 11,
2013; and Doug Bandow, "Eduardo Saverin, Not the U.S. Government, Is
Entitled to the Wealth He Earned", Forbes, May 14, 2012

[31] See Richard Cebula and Edgar L. Feige, "America's Underground Economy:
Measuring the Size, Growth, and Determinants of Income Tax Evasion in the
U.S.", http://www.ssc.wisc.edu/econ/archive/wp2011-1.pdf, accessed
10/16/13

[32] Lawrence Wright, "Slim's Time", The New Yorker online article, June 1, 2009,
http://www.newyorker.com/reporting/2009/06/01/090601fa_fact_wright?cur
rentPage=all, accessed 5/7/14

[33] Hunter Lewis, "Thomas Piketty's Improbable Data", Ludwig Von Mises
Institute Mises Daily online article, May 2, 2014, http://www.mises.org/daily/
6741/Thomas-Pikettys-Improbable-Data, accessed 5/3/14

[34] David Rohde, "The Swelling Middle", Reuters infographic, 2012 http://www.reuters.com/middle-class-infographic, accessed 5/14/14

[35] Danielle Kurtzleben, "Why the Fed's QE3 is Great for the Rich", U.S. News and World Report online article, May 1, 2013, http://www.usnews.com/news/articles/2013/05/01/ why-the-fedsqe3-is-great-for-the-rich, accessed 4/5/14

[36] OECD Review of Telecommunication Policy and Regulation in Mexico, January 30, 2012

[37] For more on this see David A. Stockman, *The Great Deformation: The Corruption of Capitalism in Ameri*ca, (Public Affairs, April 2013)

[38] Louise Bennetts, "Thanks to Dodd-Frank, Community Banks Are Too Small to Survive", American Banker, November 9, 2012

[39] Bob Levy and William Mellor, "The Dirty Dozen", chap. 4

[40] Raj Chetty, Nathaniel Hendren, Patrick Kline, Emmanuel Saez and Nicholas Turner, "Is the United States Still A Land of Opportunity: Recent Trends in Intergenerational Mobility", National Bureau of Economic Research; working paper 19844, January 2014

[41] Ibid.

[42] Michael D. Tanner, "Inequality Myths", Cato online commentary, May 14, 2014, http://www.cato.org/publications/commentary/inequality-myths, accessed 5/14/14

[43] Census.gov, "Table F-1. Income Limits for Each Fifth and Top 5 Percent of Families", census.gov/hhes/www/income/data/historical/families/, accessed 5/1/14

[44] Ibid.

[45] Credit Suisse Research Institute, Global Wealth Report 2013, October 2013, 23-24, https://publications.credit-suisse.com/tasks/render/file /?fileID=BCDB1364-A105-0560-1332EC9100FF5C83, accessed 5/1/14

[46] Credit Suisse Research Institute, Global Wealth Databook 2013, October 2013, 119, https://publications.credit-suisse.com/tasks/render/file /?fileID=1949208D-E59A-F2D9-6D0361266E44A2F8, accessed 5/1/14;

[47] Pew Charitable Trusts, "Pursuing the American Dream: Income Mobility Across Generations", July, 2012, http://www.pewtrusts.org/uploadedFiles/ww wpewtrustsorg/Reports/Economic_Mobility/Pursuing_American_Dream.pdf, accessed 5/2/14

[48] Ibid.

[49] Donald Boudreaux, "The Real Truth About the Economy: Have Wages Stagnated", Learnliberty.org video, January 31, 2012, http://www.learnliberty. org/videos/real-truth-about-economy-have-wages-stagnated/, accessed 5/5/14

[50] Richard V. Burkhauser and Kosali I. Simon, "Measuring the Impact of Health Insurance on Levels and Trends in Inequality", National Bureau of Economic Research Working Paper15811, March 2010

[51] Chad Stone, Danilo Trisi, Arloc Sherman, and William Chen, "A Guide to Statistics on Historical Trends in Income Inequality", Center on Budget and Policy Priorities, April 17, 2014, www.cbpp.org/cms/?fa=view&id=3629, accessed 5/5/14;

[52] No, this isn't justification for the misnamed Affordable Care Act or any other price distorting government intrusion into the market place. It is justification for ending government's futile battle against the price system. See Michael Tanner and Michael Cannon, *Healthy Competition: What' Holding Back Healthcare and How to Free it*, (Cato Institute, 2005)

[53] This is certainly a much more complex issue but I don't want to get sidetracked here. Essentially, government has created a system in which third parties (government or big-business) pay the vast majority of costs. The price system simply does not work properly when consumers are spending other people's money or otherwise don't feel the pain of the cost.

[54] Of course, this opens up a range of policy discussions. It is hard for me to avoid that discussion here but I want to stay focused on the main point of this section. Someday I will write a book that addresses this issue more fully. Suffice it to say here that people aren't poor because of a lack of redistribution, funding for education or child support requirements. We can't end poverty by simply supporting people in their poverty, without considering how they got there in the first place and how they can get out; which inevitably includes personal decisions to work, save, and stay off drugs. I am certainly sympathetic to some progressive arguments, such as focusing more on treatment of drug abuse as opposed to punishment, but by and large our current government programs, driven by progressive tenets, have been ineffective at poverty reduction. We cannot simply double down on the policies we have been trying for 40 years without success by expanding government education (to early childhood) and entitlements (Obamacare).

[55] Supra note 31 from Chapter 5

[56] OECD (2014), OECD Family Database; SF1.2, OECD, Paris www.oecd.org/social/family/database, accessed 5/10/14; The United States raises 25% of its children in single-parent homes while the OECD average is 15%. By contrast, Africa, the poster continent of poverty, raises more than 70% of its children in single-parent homes.

[57] Richard Wilkinson, "How Economic Inequality Harms Societies", Ted Talk, July 2011, http://www.ted.com/talks/richard_wilkinson, accessed 5/8/14;

[58] Wilkinson's extraordinarily week causality claims from the research in note 55 include: people are more stressed because of social comparisons in more unequal societies, therefore they are less healthy; and there is more crime in unequal societies because people commit crime when they are looked down on. We are to believe from this that if I live in Europe and observe wealthy people with $10 million it is OK, but if I go to the U.S. and observe someone with $100 million it is simply too much for me to bear and I must commit crime.

Please. And this in spite of the fact that crime rates have fallen dramatically in the U.S. over the last 30 years as income inequality has risen.

[59] I am not unaware of the tendency of many wealthy people to be indolent, selfish and greedy. I am an equal opportunity critic of poor choices. We must do more to encourage genuine charity and selflessness on the one hand, and hard work and self-reliance on the other; forced redistribution undermines both.

[60] Quoted by Garrett Jones, "Redistributing from Capitalists to Workers: An Impossibility Theorem", Library of Economics and Liberty, March 9, 2013, econlog.econlib.org/archives/2013/03/redistributing.html, accessed 5/1/14

[61] Andrew Atkeson, V. V. Chari, Patrick J. Kehoe, "Taxing Capital Income: A Bad Idea", *Federal Reserve Bank of Minneapolis Quarterly Review,* 1999, http://www.minneapolisfed.org/research/QR/QR2331.pdf, accessed 4/30/14

[62] Ori Brafman and Rom Brafman, *Sway: The Irresistible Pull of Irrational Behavior,* (Doubleday, 2008), 116-117

[63] Barna Group, "Global Poverty is on the Decline but Almost No One Believes It", April 29, 2014, https://www.barna.org/barna-update/culture/668-global-poverty-is-on-the-decline-but-almost-no-one-believes-it#.U2gkcV5OXIV, accessed 5/5/14

[64] Dan Mitchell, "If Spending is Capped the Budget is Balanced", Supra Note 25 from Chapter 9

[65] Whitehouse.gov, "The President's Budget for Fiscal Year 2015", http://www.white house.gov/omb/budget, accessed 4/5/14

[66] Michael Tanner, "The American Welfare State", Supra note 29 from Chapter Five

[67] Government Accountability Office, "Annual Report: Actions Needed to Reduce Fragmentation, Overlap, and Duplication and Achieve Other Financial Benefits", April 9, 2013

[68] Ibid.

[69] Ibid.

[70] Laura Gottesdiener, "7 Absurd Ways the Military Wastes Taxpayer Dollars", Salon.com, December 12, 2012, http://www.salon.com/2012/12/12/7_absurd_ways_ the_military_wastes_taxpayer_dollars/, accessed 10/22/13

[71] Tom Coburn, "Wastebook 2012", October 2012

[72] Brianna Ehley, "$6 Billion Goes Missing at the State Department", Yahoo Finance online article, April 4, 2014, http://finance.yahoo.com/news/6-billion-goes-missing-state-163100124.html, accessed 4/5/14

[73] Daniel J. Mitchell, "OECD Launches New Effort to Undermine Tax Competition" Cato Institute Tax & Budget Bulletin No. 68, March 13, 2013

[74] Author's calculations based on Congressional Budget Office Table, "Average Federal Tax Rates For All Households by Comprehensive Household Income Quintile, 1979-2009", October 24, 2012,

http://www.cbo.gov/sites/default/files/cbofiles/attachments
/Average_rates_3.pdf, accessed 4/7/14
[75] Tax Policy Center, "Historical Amount of Revenue by Source", Tax Facts, May 9, 2013, http://taxpolicycenter.org/taxfacts/displayafact.cfm?Docid=203, accessed 10/28/13
[76] Tax Policy Center, "Federal Tax Burden by Income Percentile, Baseline: Current Law 2012", The Numbers, September 13, 2012, http://taxpolicycenter.org/numbers/display atab.cfm?DocID=3505, accessed 10/28/13
[77] Donald Marron, "How Large Are Tax Expenditures? A 2012 Update", Tax Policy Center Tax Notes, April 9, 2012
[78] William McBride, "What is the Evidence on Taxes and Growth?", Tax Foundation Special Report #207, December 18, 2012, http://taxfoundation.org/article/what-evidence-taxes-and-growth, accessed 11/5/13

CHAPTER ELEVEN

[1] John Locke, "Of Property and Government", libertarianism.org, http://www.liber tarianism.org/publications/essays/property-government, accessed 3/12/14
[2] Kurland and Lerner, The Founder's Constitution, vol 2, 37
[3] Ibid.
[4] Ibid.
[5] The Aurora v. United States - 11 U.S. 382 (1813)
[6] FIELD v. CLARK, 143 U.S. 649 (1892)
[7] Ibid.
[8] J. W. Hampton, Jr., & CO. v. U. S., 276 U.S. 394 (1928)
[9] Panama Refining Co. v. Ryan, 293 U.S. 388 (1935)
[10] National Broadcasting Co. v. United States, 319 U. S. 190 (1943)
[11] Yakus v. United States, 321 U. S. 414 (1944)
[12] FPC v. Hope Natural Gas Co., 320 U. S. 591 (1944)
[13] Lichter v. United States, 334 U. S. 742
[14] AFL-CIO v. American Petroleum Institute, 448 U. S. 607, 646 (1980)
[15] Touby v. United States, 500 U. S. 160 (1991)
[16] Mistretta v. United States - 488 U.S. 361 (1989)
[17] Quoted in Road to Serfdom, 91
[18] Adam Smith, The Wealth of Nations, (Barnes and Noble Inc. 2004; original published in 1776), 300
[19] Whitman v. American Trucking Associations Inc. 99-1257 (2001)
[20] Ibid.
[21] Bob Levy and William Mellor, "The Dirty Dozen", chap. 4
[22] Whitman v American Trucking
[23] Ibid.

[24] Levy and Mellor, "The Dirty Dozen", chap. 4

[25] Quoted in Ibid.

[26] Ibid.

[27] Gardiner Harris, "The Safety Gap", New York Times online article, October 31, 2008, http://www.nytimes.com/2008/11/02/magazine/02fda-t.html?_r=0, accessed 11/23/13

[28] Daniel B. Klein and Alexander Tabarrok, "Theory, Evidence and Examples of FDA Harm", FDAreview.org, http://www.fdareview.org/harm.shtml, accessed 11/22/13

[29] Ibid.

[30] Doug Bandow, "End the FDA Drug Monopoly; Let Patients Choose Their Medicines", Cato Institute Commentary, June 11, 2012, http://www.cato.org/publications/comm entary/end-fda-drug-monopoly-let-patients-choose-their-medicines, accessed 4/8/14

[31] Ibid.

[32] Ronald Trowbridge and Steven Walker, "The FDA's Deadly Track Record", The Wall Street Journal Online, August 14, 2007, http://online.wsj.com/news/articles/SB118705 547735996773, accessed 4/8/14

[33] Ibid

[34] Diane Cohen and Michael F. Cannon, "The Independent Payment Advisory Board; PPASA's Anti-Constitutional and Authoritarian Super-Legislature", Cato policy analysis 700, June 14, 2012

[35] Ibid.

[36] Ibid.

[37] Ibid, The ACA changes the Senate's rules when considering IPAB proposals in order to make it more difficult to alter those proposals. If the Senate wants to change the rules back, a three fifths majority is required.

[38] Ibid.

[39] Ibid.

[40] Ibid.

[41] Ibid.

[42] Ibid.

[43] Ibid.

[44] Barack Obama, Interview with Chris Mathews on "Hardball", December 5, 2013, http://www.nbcnews.com/id/53755285/ns/msnbc-hardball_with_chris_matthews /#.Urxhh16A3IU, accessed 12/26/13

[45] Peter Orszag, "Too Much of a Good Thing", New Republic online article, September 14, 2011, www.newrepublic.com/article/politics/magazine/94940/peter-orszag-democracy, accessed 4/8/14

[46] Bev Purdue, "Perdue Jokes About Suspending Elections for Two Years", Under the Dome blog post Newsobserver.com, September 27, 2011, http://projects.newsobserver.com/under_the_dome/perdue_suggests_suspen

ding_ congressional_elections_for_two_years_was_she_serious, accessed 4/8/14

[47] F.A. Hayek, *The Road to Serfdom*, 104 and 110

[48] For an excellent primer on this issue see Daniel Pink, "The Puzzle of Motivation", Ted Talk, July, 2009, http://www.ted.com/talks/dan_pink_on_ motivation, accessed 5/15/14

[49] Levy and Mellor, *The Dirty Dozen,* chap. 4

[50] Paul Bedard, "$1.8 Trillion Shock: Obama Regs Cost 20 Times Estimate", Washington Examiner online article, September 20, 2012, http://washingtonexaminer.com/1.8-trillion-shock-obama-regs-cost-20-times-estimate/article/2508466, accessed 4/14/14

[51] King James Bible, 2 Chronicles 10

[52] Alexander Hamilton, *The Federalist Papers*, 463

[53] Nixon v. Fitzgerald 457 U.S. 731 (1982) emphasis added

[54] Ibid

[55] Ibid

[56] Ibid

[57] If you are interested in a serious review of our current President's abuses see Aaron Klein and Brenda Elliot, *Impeachable Offenses: The Case for Removing Barack Obama From Office* (WND Books 2013)

[58] Ibid.

[59] Jonathan Turley, "Enforcing the President's Constitutional Duty to Faithfully Execute the Laws", Written Statement before the House Committee on the Judiciary, February, 26, 2014, 5

[60] Nixon v Fitzgerald

[61] Nixon v Fitzgerald

[62] Campbell v Clinton, U.S. Court of Appeals, No. 99-5215

[63] Jonathan Turley, "Federal judge dismisses war powers challenged by members of congress", Jonathanturley.org, October 20, 2011, http://jonathanturley.org/2011/10/20 /federal-judge-dismisses-war-powers-challenge-by-members-of-congress/, accessed 4/8/14

[64] Marbury v Madison, 5 U.S. 137, 1803

[65] Ibid.

[66] Complete Auto Transit, Inc. v. Reis, 451 U.S. 401, 1981

[67] Jonathan Turley, "Enforcing the President's Duty", Supra note 56

[68] Ibid.

[69] Chris Edwards, "Fiscal Federalism", downsizinggovernment.org, http://www.downsizinggovernment.org/fiscal-federalism#_edn13, accessed 11/23/13

[70] Ibid.

[71] Ibid.

[72] B. Putney, "Federal-State Relations Under Grants-In-Aid," Congressional Quarterly, July 30, 1940, quoted in Ibid.

[73] "The Virginia Plan", *Founder's Constitution*, 25; while that vague mandate did not survive to the final draft of the Constitution it was repeated enough times in the convention to justify the contention that it was the general sentiment of the framers.

[74] Chris Edwards, "Fiscal Federalism"

[75] Federal Farmer [pseud.], *Founder's Constitution*, 412

[76] South Dakota v. Dole 483 U.S. 203 (1987)

[77] Chris Edwards, "Did Canada Steal Our 10th Amendment?" *Cato at Liberty* blog post, October 18, 2011, http://www.cato.org/blog/did-canada-steal-our-tenth-amendment, accessed 4/12/14

[78] Tom Harkin, "Protecting Women From Breast Cancer", October 4, 2002, http://www. harkin.senate.gov/press/column.cfm?i=187592, accessed 4/12/14

[79] Tom Coburn, "The Department of Everything", Oversight Report, November 2012

[80] Tom Coburn, Working database of all earmarks included in the omnibus spending bill, http://www.coburn.senate.gov/public/index.cfm/rightnow?ContentRecord_id=e07a0af9-c677-4b5a-814f-a40c8ac13f74, accessed 11/8/13

[81] Raymond Hernandez and Jonathan Weisman, "House to Take Up Storm Relief Bill Amid Battle Over Spending", New York Times online article, January 13, 2013, http://www.nytimes.com/2013/01/14/nyregion/house-to-take-up-sandy-relief-bill-amid-battle-over-spending.html?_r=0, accessed 5/5/14

[82] Foxnews.com, "Senate Budget Deal Nearly Quadruples Funding for Ohio Dam Project", October 17, 2013, http://www.foxnews.com/politics/2013/10/17/senate-bill-to-end-partial-shutdown-includes-millions-to-fund-dam-project/, accessed 5/5/14

[83] Alex Brown, "Senate's Energy-Efficiency Bill Bogged Down in Unrelated Amendments", National Journal online, September 15, 2013, http://www.nationaljour nal.com/daily/senate-s-energy-efficiency-bill-bogged-down-in-unrelated-amendments-20130915, accessed 4/12/14

[84] Hans Bader, "Education Department Illegally Ordered Colleges to Reduce Due-Process Safeguards", examiner.com online article, September 21, 2012, http://www.examiner.com/article/education-department-illegally-ordered-colleges-to-reduce-due-process-safeguards, accessed 12/5/13

[85] Richard Epstein, "Title IX or Bust", Hoover Institute Defining Ideas, February 7, 2012, http://www.hoover.org/publications/defining-ideas/article/107626, accessed 12/8/13

[86] Ibid.

[87] Ibid.

CHAPTER TWELVE

[1] U.S. Constitution, Fifth Amendment

[2] See Murray Rothbard, *America's Great Depression*, (Ludwig von Mises Institute, 2000); and John Taylor, *Getting off Track: How Government Actions*

and Interventions Caused, Prolonged, and Worsened the Financial Crisis, (Board of Trustees of the Leland Stanford Junior University, 2009)

[3] Gallup Poll, "Record High in U.S. Say Big Government Greatest Threat", December 18, 2013, http://www.gallup.com/poll/166535/record-high-say-big-government-greatest-threat.aspx, accessed 1/4/14

[4] I'm not opposed to any group which wishes to organize for any rightful purpose it wants, but how this ever became the business of the Federal Government is the issue.

[5] *FoxNews.com,* "EPA Land Grab? Agency Claims Authority Over More Streams Wetlands", 25 March 2014, http://www.foxnews.com/politics/2014/03/25/epa-land-grab-agency-claims-authority-over-more-streams-wetlands/, accessed 4/11/14

www.ingramcontent.com/pod-product-compliance
Lightning Source LLC
Chambersburg PA
CBHW021210290526
45796CB00005B/21